THIS COPY OF

THE TRACTORS
IN MY LIFE

IS SIGNED BY THE AUTHOR

Mike Thorne

MICHAEL THORNE

H&S

THE TRACTORS IN MY LIFE

by Michael Thorne

Founder of the Coldridge Collection of vintage tractors

H&S
Herridge & Sons

Published in 2022 by Herridge & Sons Ltd
Lower Forda, Shebbear
Beaworthy, Devon EX21 5SY

ISBN 978-1-914929-04-5

Printed in Great Britain
by Short Run Press, Exeter, Devon

Contents

Introduction   6

The Autobiographical Bit   8

The Coldridge Collection   32

Biographies   145

Introduction

Once again I would like to thank Herridge and Sons for suggesting that I write a book about the evolution of the Coldridge Collection, always a scary commitment!

I hope that what is set out in the ensuing pages gives readers a fair insight into the items that form the Collection as well as the ethos I have endeavoured to achieve in laying out the display. As one who for a long time has enjoyed and appreciated good design in all its manifestations, the designing and building of these three sheds over a 14-year time span provided me with the opportunity to indulge in some fresh ideas and, with the help of others, actually construct and fit out the sheds. Great fun as well as bringing a quiet sense of achievement.

Following on from our annual Open Days, visitors can now, by appointment, share in what is on display, which for me is enormously satisfying. We have supported North Devon Hospice for many years with donations made by visitors. I have included a section dedicated to people who have helped me with my book writing over the years, all have worked for either Harry Ferguson and/or Massey Ferguson in senior capacities. I hope this is of interest to you all.

I hope the autobiographical aspect gives a bit of insight into my own personal evolution over the past 84 years. I have left out the sex and violence because I don't think that that would be of interest to readers; suffice to say I lost my virginity at 33.

It's nice to put them to work. Here I am ploughing on a Case Model L.

Acknowledgements

Perhaps I should first shine the spotlight on the work that the late Ernie Luxton contributed to so many of the tractors on display within the Collection. I feel that they represent a monument to his dedication and skill in that area.

Also a big thank you to Peter Clarke for the high standard of paintwork achieved on all of the tractors he dealt with.

Following on, I would like to express my sincere thanks for the help I had from two ex-Massey Ferguson employees – David Parnell and Jeremy Burgess. David, having been heavily involved with the building of the Nipper and the last hand-built prototype at Banner Lane, was kind enough to fill me in on numerous technical details of those two projects. He also took the trouble to read and correct my draft as well as adding several details I had overlooked.

Jeremy, while in his role as Licensee Director with Massey Ferguson, was instrumental in arranging the loan by the AGCO Company of six of their tractors to the Coldridge Collection. He also helped significantly by reading my draft about the last hand-built prototype and by making some positive additions and corrections.

To Julie Browning and Peter Smith, my thanks for sharing their knowledge of the American implements when I asked for help.

There are numerous other people I must thank collectively who helped me along the way either with positive suggestions or technical input.

Once again, Gail McKechnie must be congratulated for not only putting my handwritten drafts into digital format, but also for entering into the spirit of the text and doing her own bits of creative research. And a big thank you to Elaine Towns, the copy-editor, for her painstaking work and quiet suggestions. Unfortunately she is no longer with us to see this book completed.

Finally, thanks to Alison Harding for support and encouragement while writing *The Tractors in My Life*.

I'm trying this John Deere for size on a farm in Florida, where I bought a Hi-Crop 60 and a Linderman Crawler.

The Autobiographical Bit

Both my parents were born in 1910. My mother, Ivy, was the elder of two daughters. Her family name was Swindon; her father was a small-time builder, pretty conventional though perhaps slightly flashy in the style of furnishings in their house, but he did drive a Citroën and later a Bullnose Morris. I never knew my Grandfather Swindon, but my Grandmother Swindon was around into my early teens.

My father, Ambrose Alan (always known as Alan), had a younger brother, Tony. I never knew Grandfather Thorne either; I've been told he'd worked as a civil servant, but in what capacity I never knew. Grandma Thorne, I was told, was an orphan with the surname of Long. Like her husband, she had quite strong left wing leanings and a fascination

In the arms of my Grandfather Swindon, pointing to the future?

with books and music. Sadly, she died when I was about eight. As a little boy visiting with my parents I can still remember making a beeline for her neatly arranged bookshelves that had all the spines aligned exactly with the front edge of the shelves. I would proceed to push all the books inwards as far as they would go, thus destroying her aesthetic! I would then be reprimanded and told that I was a naughty boy and must not do it again, which of course I did on the next visit. This nonsense seemed, in fact, to amuse everyone, including me!

My parents married in 1936 (the year the Ferguson Type A was launched!) and I was born in May 1938, three weeks premature.

My father had a grammar school education in North London and matriculated in five subjects – a fact he frequently reminded me of when I was struggling with schoolwork. His brother Tony scored six subjects! They were quite competent amateur musicians – father played piano, Tony the flute and oboe. Their upbringing was left wing, this being made clear by Grandfather Thorne choosing to buy an early house on the Hampstead Garden Suburb development in north London: 13 Brookland Rise was the address. On getting married, my father bought a new house, 7 Devon Rise, also on the Hampstead Garden Suburb development, near East Finchley – these houses were a mile apart. I remembered from my childhood that it had an AC electrical supply, whereas 13 Brookland Rise had a DC supply. These later houses were built by a Mr Reece, whose daughter taught art part-time at my Primary School, Holy Trinity at East Finchley.

Devon Rise was an unmetalled road with sixteen semi-detached houses, most of them built in the Arts and Crafts style, but a few were in the modernist style, with curved glass to the bay windows. Just to emphasize this left-wing ethos, we were the only family in Devon Rise to have our milk delivered by the Co-op (London Wholesale Co-operative Society). I can still remember our 'divy' (dividend) number: 110180. All the other residents had their milk delivered by United Dairies (UD).

Hampstead Garden Suburb was run by a co-partnership (CoParts) tenants' lease holding company with restrictive covenants in place, in an attempt to ensure that the ethos of the development was not violated. My memory tells me that about half of the houses in Devon Rise were owned by Jewish families who had fled Germany before the start of the Second World War. There was a synagogue nearby.

The parish church where both my sister Margaret and I were christened was St Jude-on-the-Hill, part of the early development of Hampstead Garden Suburb, its architect being none other than Sir Edwin Lutyens. As a child I appreciated the design and quality of its construction as well as the pomp of the services, with incense being burnt in a censer swung by the rector. (Perhaps this is why I like to burn joss sticks sometimes?) My father sang in the choir and for a time was the church treasurer. He was not a religious man but I think he liked the music and theatre that was part of a High Church service.

The Second World War started in September 1939, followed soon after by the coalition government building air raid shelters at strategic locations for the general public, and for schools within their grounds. Several families in Devon Rise had their garages reinforced to create shelters, while others chose to have Morrison steel shelters indoors and some opted for Anderson shelters, which were set into the ground in the garden. My father, who had trained as a quantity surveyor (but as far as I know was never a member of the RICS), never bothered with air raid shelters, always remarking that if he was going to be killed, it would happen wherever he was. He did night-time fire-watching duties. He worked as a quantity surveyor for the London building firm of J. Styles and Son, who had an office on the first floor of a building in Jermyn Street, just off the Haymarket. Their workshop was at Kemps Court, adjacent to Berwick Street Market. Most of that building was destroyed by bombing early in the war, but a small group of staff were retained for the duration. My father's training as a quantity surveyor meant that he was in a reserved occupation, and he was seconded by

the government to work for the large construction company of George Wimpy, who were working mainly on airfield construction. Because of this he had the use of a car, a Hillman Minx, and coupons to buy petrol. By a strange coincidence his last airfield project was at Winkleigh, just seven miles from Coldridge. I've built several warehouses on that site and have even re-clad the only remaining hangar, which is used as a vintage bus store by the Shears family.

One 'amusing' encounter when I was about four years old is perhaps worth relating here. Just imagine this little boy who possessed one of those toy wooden mallets deciding to stand on the alighting board of one of his father's beehives on a nice sunny day and then proceed to give the hive a good working over with the mallet! The result was that I ran screaming to my mother who immediately plastered my face, arms and legs with calamine lotion and then told me to go and lie on my bed. It was not long before I couldn't see, as a result of the swelling face tissue. After more applications of calamine lotion and the elapsing of about twenty-four hours I began to be able to see again.

On odd occasions my father would take me on site visits: I can remember sitting on the lap of the driver of a Ruston Bucyrus 22RB and being allowed to pull the various levers, but with the driver in control, of course! On another site visit I was given a ride on a dumper truck, a Muir-Hill, I expect. I'm sure that this exposure fostered my early interest in machinery and construction.

My school career started in September 1943 at Holy Trinity, a church school built in 1847 at East Finchley, North London. This was about fifteen

My mother and father with our labrador, Sue, on a trip to Wales in the 1950s.

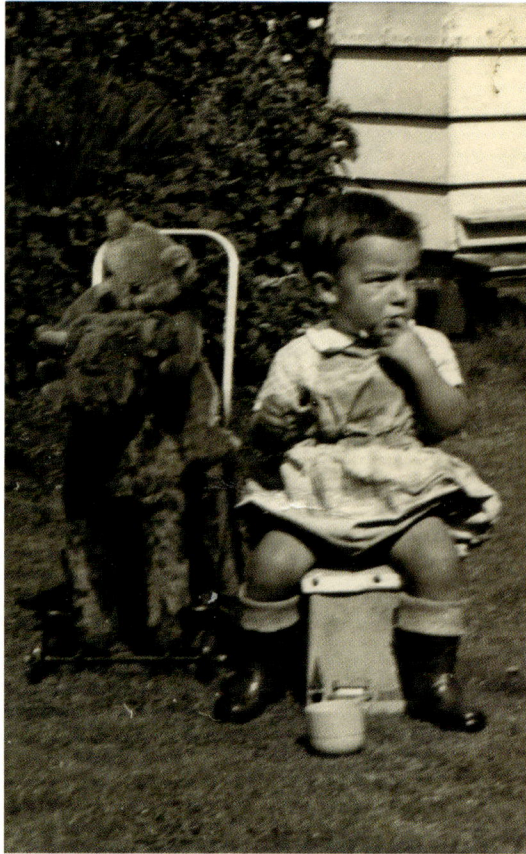

Me as a 2 or 3 year old with Toscar the dog on wheels and a Teddy bear. Note the bee hive with its alighting board.

A class photograph at Holy Trintiy. I'm at the top left.

bath partly refilled so that the contaminated pieces of clothing could be left to soak: the other clothes were taken to the kitchen and washed in the gas-fired copper (no washing machines in those days!). Next day I was back at Holy Trinity; to this day I put this sad saga down to fear!

Now a bit about the school. The main core of the school was divided in half to the roof, which originally would have been to cater for a class for girls and another for boys, with each section having its own entrance, one with 'Boys' carved in the archway of the porch and likewise the other having 'Girls'. These two classrooms were single storey with the underside of the ridge line exposed internally. Heating was a coke stove in each room, suitably guarded. The WCs for both boys and girls were in separate outside buildings. There were two other classrooms and the Head's Office within the original grand plan. The assembly hall was, I guess, just pre-war with its frame of precast concrete in-filled with block walls and windows. While at this school there were free ⅓-pint bottles of milk for each child each day. There was a rota in place that involved two boys from the top class 'delivering', in metal crates, the right number of bottles outside each classroom door – this job always appealed to me because it was an escape from the classroom and involved doing real work.

I missed out on big chunks of schooling in my early days at Holy Trinity because of poor health – ear infections, colds, etc, eventually diagnosed as an adenoids and tonsils infection (no antibiotics in those days, so at the age of six I was admitted to Dollis Hill Hospital in Middlesex to have them removed. My mother was not allowed to visit, but she bent the rules by appearing at a low window adjacent to my bed. Luckily for me, this procedure was a turning point as far as my general health was concerned, for although I was small (and still am) I became strong and healthy, with very little illness after that.

When I was about six our house was badly damaged by a flying bomb, a doodlebug, exploding about 60 yards away. All the tiles on the back of the roof were shed and all the rear leaded-light windows blown in. The blast didn't wake me, but my father did when he lifted me from my bed covered in glass. Margaret, my sister, and I were taken to Grandma Thorne's house at Brookland Rise for about a week. Somehow my father managed to get the windows re-glazed with plain glass and the roof covered with a tarpaulin.

Just prior to the start of the war my father had

minutes' walk from my home in Devon Rise. On my second day there I disgraced myself by messing my short trousers and had to be sent home. Needless to say, my mother was not pleased to see me at the front door in that sorry state. I was told to go to the bathroom, run the bath (the water was just lukewarm), take all my clothes off and get myself cleaned up. Having done that I was told to call downstairs, which I duly did. I was then inspected and dried. The dirty water was then run out and the bought two building plots, one across the footpath adjacent to our house and the other a bit further away. From the ages of 9 until 11 (when we moved house) I, with the help of a couple of school friends, built a 'house' on the nearest site with material gathered from bombsites. The only material we had to buy with our saved-up pocket money (6 old pence a week was mine) was cement. I drew a coloured plan of what we were intending to build, which in due course I showed to my teacher, Miss Morrison, of our top class. She was most impressed, which was quite a change from me always being reprimanded for bad spelling, poor handwriting, and for not paying attention. I have reproduced this plan as I remember it.

For years, the family had a small black-and-white photograph, sadly lost, of this 'house' with a monopitch roof. When we had completed it I decided to install an electric light, so we collected up all the suitable lengths of cable we could find, jointed them together with insulating tape, dug a little trench across the cinder footpath, buried a bit of scaffold tube to thread the cable through, and joined the supply cable to a plug in my bedroom and a bulb in the 'house'. We had light! A little later I had the idea of installing a telephone link between my bedroom and the 'house' after we had scrounged around to find enough cable. It's strange that my parents never seemed concerned about what we were up to.

Likewise with the loft space at 7 Devon Rise, where during the course of its construction my father had a dormer window installed, though to maintain symmetry he had to pay for a similar one in the adjoining property. Our loft space had a wooden floor over the usable area and a proper pull-down set of steps for access, an electric power socket and lighting. Prior to the war my father and Tony had fitted this space out as a woodworking area; they were both pretty good at making furniture. For my friends and me this became our 'playroom', and once up there we would pull the steps back up so that we were in our own world. We made a theatre complete with coloured lights. I tried to imitate a set-up I had seen at Gardeners of Highgate, the garage my father used for the Hillman Minx repairs and services. Basically, it was like a narrow pair of trolleybus wires running just below the ceiling for the full length of the workshop. Mechanics could, with a pole, connect their inspection lights to this power source, which was 12 volts. I was not aware of this at the time, so my system ran directly off the mains! Luckily no one was electrocuted.

My sister, Margaret, and I when I was about eight and she was about four.

During the war years toys were not being made, so parents had to find secondhand alternatives. In that vein my father bought a deed box full of Meccano, the early type that was nickel plated. He hid this deed box away in his wardrobe, the idea being that the parts would be dished out in small quantities at birthdays and Christmas provided I behaved myself. Needless to say, as little boys do and being nosey, I found this box and would occasionally help myself to the odd needed part – not too much, though, or it might have been noticed. I still have that Meccano, in the deed box, plus quite a bit more that I bought when it became available after the war. I played with this most educational toy until I was 16, making all sorts of ingenious contraptions, multi-speed gearboxes, differentials and so on.

I was given a secondhand Triang tricycle one Christmas, with pedals fixed to the front wheel, which was of a larger diameter than the rear wheels.

When I'd outgrown that it was passed down to my sister, but before it was given to her I decided to repaint it green – in my bedroom – which had a carpet of the same colour. I upset the tin of paint, but my mother and Grandma Swindon came to the rescue. They cleaned up the paint as best they could, took the furniture out of the room and turned the carpet so that the paint stain was hidden under the dressing table. My father never knew about this incident but it was typical of how protective my mother was towards me against my father's temper.

My next tricycle, again secondhand, was a conventional one with a chain drive to the rear axle; this I also repainted green, but in the garden this time! It too was eventually passed on to Margaret. My first bicycle was a secondhand Hercules with 18-inch wheels, but sadly I somehow broke the stem of the front forks riding on rough ground – mountain biking! My father was able to get this repaired by having it welded but the replacement ball bearings were just not available.

Another secondhand present given to me just before the end of the war was some pre-war Trix Twin 00 gauge model railway components, not a large set but enough track to make an oval, with two points, an 0-4-0 tank engine, a few goods wagons, a controller and a transformer. I added to the track and stock bit by bit, and still have it displayed at Coldridge, together with items I was never able to afford as a child but bought more recently.

My schoolfriend during the war years and just after was John Mason, who had a much more extensive Trix Twin layout, but for some reason

Burnhams, Totteridge Lane, where we moved in 1949.

he and I developed a fascination for manhole covers over drains and the smaller types used to access water main stopcocks. (I wonder what a psychologist would make of that!) So on our walks to school and back we would share the carrying of a small metal poker, the pointed end of which we'd bent to form a hook so that we could lift up the covers to make our inspections. Luckily for us there were several different routes we could take to and from school, but often we'd arrive late. The headmistress, Miss Gillet, was made aware of this and I was called into her office. She noticed that I was not paying attention to her and asked, 'Michael you are not listening – why are you looking over there at the window?' I replied, 'I'm looking at the lightning protector for your telephone line that is on the window frame, Miss.' She must have contacted my father about my lateness because the following morning my father told me, 'We had a policeman here last night telling me that you and John Mason have been reported lifting manhole covers and it has got to stop.' My hooked poker was confiscated.

We had our telephone line installed when I was about seven – it must have been half term so I was able to take a great interest in what the two GPO fitters were doing. We were outside and one said, 'Well, it's all finished now, sonny.' I replied, 'No, it's not, you haven't connected the earth wire to the copper spike.' The retort was, 'What a clever little bugger!'

I made my first crystal radio set when I was about nine, a simple bit of equipment that didn't need any power source, just a good aerial and earth, a 50 microfarad variable condenser, a pair of headphones, the quartz crystal, the 'cats whisker' and a coil of 26SWG enamelled copper wire on a 1½-inch toilet roll former. The first broadcast I picked up was from the BBC Third Programme, about brain leucotomy.

In 1947 my father was able to buy a brand new Austin 8 four-door saloon. He used to drive it like a racing car – that poor little sidevalve engine!

As the 11-plus exam loomed into view in 1949 there was pressure at school for pupils to perform well. At home my father paid for me to have private lessons on Saturday mornings in English and spelling. I would much rather have been helping the Co-op milkman with his deliveries from his Morrison Electric Milk Float (four-wheel type) which he would often let me drive – of course, that's why I helped him. Needless to say, all this pressure and expense was wasted as I failed the 11-plus. My father thought I should continue my secondary education at Watford Technical College, where they ran a teaching programme with a strong bias towards various trades including building and construction. So I was sent for an interview and had to complete a test paper. The outcome of this was as I expected – failure! The final possibility to be explored was to attend Clark's College, Wood Green, a fee paying co-educational school where most of the girls were taught secretarial skills like shorthand and typing. My father took me for an interview with the headmaster, Mr Scotney, a Quaker. This interview went without a hitch; another fee-paying pupil would help swell the profits!

The first stumbling block was that I had to change my style of writing. At Holy Trinity we had been taught italic using relief nibs. At Clark's College it was copperplate style, using very sharp pointed nibs. French lessons were a part of the curriculum that I did not take to at all, but I was able to get around that by being disruptive in the classroom. I was usually told by the teacher, Miss Tallow, 'Outside, Thorne, before you start.' Another new subject was algebra, which for the first term was completely beyond my comprehension. Luckily, the next term started with a new and younger teacher, Mr Shirley, who was a radio ham. He explained to me that by using formulae one could work out the required value of components in a radio circuit. Thereafter I took to algebra, trigonometry and logarithms – in fact Maths was the only GCE subject I passed while at school. Mr Scotney ran the art classes and was generally quite positive about what I produced, but I failed that GCE because I was in a huff over the black ink I had brought – it wasn't black enough – and I left the exam room. Mr Scotney was also supportive of my early interest in farming, and on a couple of occasions I went with him to the Smithfield Show at Earls Court.

Usually my end of term reports were pretty negative, and as it was the school's protocol that pupils had to take these reports home to their parents, who had to sign a counterfoil that they had been delivered, I cunningly got around this by not handing the report over and making a pretty good job of forging my father's rather flamboyant signature in black ink. I was frequently reminded of the expense my father was putting into my education, not just the school fees but other costs like transport and uniform.

My journey from our house, Burnhams, in Totteridge Lane to Clark's College at Wood Green was a two-part trip. Totteridge Lane was served by London Transport's single decker bus route 251,

which ran from Mill Hill to Arnos Grove Tube station. The buses were the RF (Regal Four) series with the body styling by Douglas Scott, who later went on to style the famous Routemaster. The Regal Four buses had chassis and running gear built by A.E.C. and the bodies built by M.C.W. (Metropolitan-Cammell-Weymann).

Arnos Grove, an above-ground station (now listed Grade II*) was designed by Charles Holden, as were the other seven stations on the Piccadilly Line extension from Finsbury Park to Cockfosters. Tube trains emerged from the tunnel just prior to drawing into Arnos Grove. Heading towards London, the first underground station was Bounds Green and the next Wood Green, my alighting point. Wood Green had a signal cabin that controlled a turning siding that would enable, if required, up-trains from London to terminate there and then be put on the down line back into London.

My schoolfriend, Bumberry, who travelled into Clark's College from Oakwood, the penultimate station on the northern end of this line, would often travel with me. We were both keen on railways so we made 'friends' with the signalmen in the cabin, which was at platform level; sometimes they would let us work the electro-pneumatic levers that set the signals and the points, under close observation, of course! Wood Green was also a point where train crews sometimes changed, and on one occasion a driver awaiting a train that he would take on to Cockfosters said, 'I expect you boys would like a ride in the cab.' His train arrived and he ushered us into the cab, which was pretty dark. He asked where we were going and I said Arnos Grove, and Bumberry said Oakwood, so he turned to me and said, 'Right then, you can drive to Arnos Grove, and your friend can drive from Arnos Grove to Oakwood.' What a thrill to stand at the controller with one hand on the brass knob of the dead man's

I went to college aboard an A.E.C. Regal Four, although this is the Greenline version.

handle and under instruction gently notch up the speed; the driver kept control of the brake lever. We soon pulLed into Bounds Green, the driver ensuring that the train stopped exactly where it should, then off again towards Arnos Grove, an above-ground station. Glimpsing the light of day at the end of the tunnel was a thrill, a perspective lesser mortals never have when travelling by underground. It was a most memorable experience.

Just one more wicked bit. A young teacher of English, Mr Pamerly (MA in Psychology), with Teddy Boy clothes and an Austin 7 Ruby, 'preached' individuality, which I naturally cottoned on to. For some reason he thought I should train to be a vet, but with my poor GCE results I needed to gain a few more, and some in the science subjects. He arranged for me to attend evening classes in Physics and Chemistry at the North London Polytechnic but there was a snag: students had to be over the age of 16 and I was only 15. He then fixed it for me attend these two evening classes under the name of Michael Denchfield, Pamerly having asked to borrow Michael's birth certificate in case it was needed as proof. Luckily, it was never requested and so I gained my first insight into adult education, which was a positive eye-opener compared to school.

When it came time for me to leave school at 16 my father asked one of his London customers, Noel Blake Ducker, who had a hairdressing salon in Dover Street in London, a hair dye manufactory at Harmondsworth, Middlesex, and a 1,000-acre mixed farm in Oxfordshire, if I could work on the farm for a year as a student prior to having a year at Oaklands, the Hertfordshire College of Agriculture, for the National Certificate of Agriculture course (the college also had a strong horticultural side). Ducker's farm was called Little Stoke Manor, situated about half-way between Wallingford and Goring-on-Thames. My pay was £3 per week but as my lodging was £2.10s, my father had to top me up slightly – or I had to get in some overtime. Once settled at the farm, I bought a brand new BSA Bantam motorcycle, JRD795, from a dealer in Reading (the basic model with no rear suspension and direct lighting), which my mother paid for, but I had to run it. I did pay her back. This I used four nights a week to attend evening classes in English, Chemistry, Physics and Biology. I tended to go home to Totteridge most weekends if there was no pressing farm work to be done. The bailiff was David Blomfield, with his wife Enid and their two teenage sons, Christopher and Nigel.

Arriving at this large mixed farm as a 16-year-old away from home for the first time was both exciting and a bit scary. About half the acreage was given over to cereals, hence the large coke-fired grain drier, and there were two herds of Aberdeen Angus beef cattle, a small dairy herd of about 25 Guernseys, and a large flock of sheep, Cheviots, I think.

I'll list the tractors and other vehicles on the farm at the time. It reads like a present-day vintage gathering:
• Two Fordson Standards, one with a high top gear, the other with an offset PTO
• Two American-made Allis Chalmers Bs
• Two R2 Caterpillars
• A TVO Minneapolis Moline GT
• International 10-20 and a 15-30
• Massey Harris 21 12ft Tanker Combine
• International Harvester 12ft trailed tanker combine
• Bean self-propelled steerage hoe with a Ford 10 side-valve engine
• Two Muir-Hill dumper trucks (based on the Fordson Standard skid units)
• Two pre-war Bedford Lorries, one a tipper (manually operated), the other a cattle lorry
• Two jeeps, one a Ford, the other a Willys
• A pre-war Morris van with the accelerator pedal placed between the clutch and the brake
• A new Fordson Major Diesel fitted with a Cameron Gardner Rear Loda
• A newish TE.D20 Ferguson with 6-volt electrics together with a Ferguson Post Hole Digger and a 3-ton Tipping Trailer.

Mr Ducker's personal transport was a Rolls-Royce, chauffeur-driven by Bert. The family had an Austin A40 Devon Countryman with a four-door coachbuilt body and a silver-grey Austin A40 Pickup, the early type with a floor-mounted gear lever. Bert had a well-equipped workshop including a Laycock pressure washer!

Johnny Vaughan, the farm mechanic, had his workshop in one of the farm's several beautiful timber-framed barns with tiled roofs. He did all the baling with a Massey Harris baler driven by a four-cylinder Coventry Climax petrol engine; I expect this was to ensure that he was on hand to fix any minor problems with the combines or baler in the field. There was an estate carpenter, Horace, and his son, a highly skilled joiner who tended to spend most of his time making fittings for the Dover Street shop. Albert Allaway was the shepherd, and also looked after the two herds of Aberdeen beef cattle, while Charlie Allaway was the cowman. They were related, but not brothers. The chap who ran the grain drier was Fred Appleton, a real character who also used to drive one of the Caterpillar R2s, usually ploughing or cultivating. Jack Vaughn was the main driver of the other R2 and was also a bit of a right-hand man for David Blomfield, the farm bailiff. Jack's son, Kenny Vaughn, was also a tractor driver, mainly using the 'high speed' green Fordson Standard. Yet another tractor driver was Fred Greenaway, who always drove the Minneapolis Moline GT, he was an ex-army lorry driver, so he was always very precise with his work. It was Patrick, whose surname I have forgotten, who always drove the Fordson Major Diesel, in which he took a great pride. Just as an aside – the farm's fertilizer requirement was brought in to our nearest railway station, Goring-on-Thames, about 3½ miles (5.63 km) away, in a covered British Rail wagon which was parked in a siding. From there it was transported to Little Stoke Manor using two of the farm's tractors with Patrick driving the Fordson Major Diesel towing a four-wheeled North Stoke wagon (the type with the front axle mounted under a turntable) his load was 7 tons (7.1 mt). The other tractor used while I was at this farm was the Ferguson TED20 with its 3 ton (3.04 mt) trailer, but always with a load of 4 tons (4.06 mt), and it performed impeccably! All these bags of Fisons fertilizer weighing 112 lbs (50.8 kg) had to be manhandled out of the railway wagon on to the trailers and then off-loaded and stacked in dry storage. All these people lived in tied cottages on the farm. The exceptions were the two gardeners, the horse-and-cart man and Fred Boughs, a general farm worker who drove each day from a nearby village on his Francis-Barnett two-stroke motorcycle with a pressed steel frame: he later bought Ducker's A40 Pickup complete with tonneau cover. The house staff included a cook and a butler.

After my year at Little Stoke Manor, I moved on to Oaklands, the Hertfordshire College of Agriculture, though it also had a strong horticultural facility, where it was not all classroom learning. My time there was really stimulating and we were treated like adults, though we sometimes regressed and got up to a few pranks. One could be working with pigs, horses, poultry, beef cattle, dairy cows or machinery, changing on a weekly basis. Students had to be up early to help with whatever tasks needed doing before breakfast; after that it was lectures until lunchtime. The afternoons were spent working and learning. It was while at Oaklands that I did

some horse ploughing – what an experience, two Suffolk Punches pulling a single-furrow plough, no noise of an engine, just the plodding of hooves and the sound of the plough cutting the soil. Later in my life I had a flight in a glider and the same peacefulness struck me. One of the projects we did in the farm workshop was to rebuild a David Brown Cropmaster Diesel, and a skill I learnt was to sharpen twist drills on a bench grinder.

The tractors at the time, as I remember, were a Field Marshall Series 3, a Fordson Major Diesel, a Ferguson TE.F20 with High Lift loader, and an International of some sort. The horticultural side had a Ransome Crawler. There were 27 students in my year and I managed to come sixth in the final exams, which helped to build up my confidence.

By the time I left Oaklands in early July 1956 my father had sold our house in Totteridge Lane because of financial problems, caused, I understand, by Westminster City Council making a compulsory purchase of J. Styles and Son's Kemps Court Workshops, but the Council failed to pay up promptly, so my father had to sell Burnhams to enable him to buy and set up a smaller workshop and office just off Fitzroy Square – a mews premises. This necessitated moving the family to Nicholls Farm House, Redbourn, in Hertfordshire, as a tenant. The house and farm was previously owned by L. F. Dove Ltd, a Ferguson Dealership. Nicholls Farm now has the M1 motorway passing through it. My job during that summer break was

An Austin A40 Pickup. There was an early model with floor-change at the Mr Ducker's Oxfordshire farm.

to rewire the house to my father's requirements and I was paid a modest sum, some of which I used to buy my first arc welder, an air-cooled unit that ran off a 13-amp plug with an output of 60 amps; it ran 14SWG rods! At a slightly later date my father suggested that I rent from BOC a couple of gas bottles so that I would have the facility to do gas welding and cutting: I bought the regulators and torches secondhand – Mike Thorne's first foray into steel fabrication?

I returned to work at Little Stoke Manor in September but this time I was lodging with the bailiff, his wife and family. This was a happy time. The two lads were bright but a bit wild. One prank they found amusing involved an old bicycle with the tyres removed from the wheels. They would set it off down the road (B4009) just to see how far it would travel before hitting the bank or a car! This fun came to an abrupt end when the driver of a police car had to swerve to avoid hitting it. On a lighter note, one of the boys was given a one-sixteenth scale Airfix model kit of a TE20 and I helped them to put that together and paint it grey (I wish that model was at Coldridge now!). I have just been given four model front wheels!

After about nine months I left Little Stoke in a huff. I can't remember what the trigger was, but it meant I was now back living at Nicholls Farm. I soon found myself another farm job, though, working for the Salter brothers, Ron and Joe, at Organ Hall Farm, Borehamwood, also in Hertfordshire, a 120-acre dairy farm that they rented from British Rail. Their father had a coal merchant's business at King's Cross in London. This was much more of a real working farm than Ducker's. They had 40 dairy cows milked in cowsheds, and lots of Landrace pigs as well as poultry. The eggs produced at Organ Hall sold well to passing trade and to some of the residents on the adjacent London County Council housing estate. When I first started working there, their two tractors were new-type Fordson Majors, one a very thirsty TVO model and the other a diesel; they also had, standing forlornly in the yard, an industrial Fordson Standard on small wheels.

The first season I was there the corn had been cut by a binder with the sheaves being stacked, so I was soon involved with thrashing, which was done by a contractor, Boughtons of Amersham. The driver's name was Frank Pratly, who was also from Redbourn, and a real character who owned a steam traction engine which he kept in the car park of a Redbourn pub. He gained many a free pint of beer by showing his machine to interested customers.

Working at Organ Hall Farm involved making a 20-mile round trip each day on my BSA Bantam. It is often said that a cat has nine lives, and maybe that observation can be applied to people too! Anyway, what follows represents my first life – more will follow as this story unfolds! I was travelling to work one morning on the A5 heading towards St Albans, riding near the centre line of the road and looking beyond a lorry I was planning on overtaking, I missed seeing a large lump of timber in my path which I hit, causing me and the motorcycle to capsize! The driver of the car following me was able to stop just in time! Three chaps got out, picked up the Bantam and helped me to my feet – asked if I was okay, which I was. I kicked up the engine and carried on to Organ Hall, where I checked my thermos flask in the pannier bag – it was quite sound. Following this experience I sold my BSA and bought a Jowett Bradford truck, which was powered by a flat twin engine and had a top speed of 48 mph. I learnt a lot about motor vehicles by doing a running restoration over time, but after 18 months I traded it in against a brand new Morris 1000 Pickup, registration XXM 572. This I collected from Henlys dealership in late October 1959, on the day that my father left home; I never saw him again. The Pickup cost me £386, plus £7.10s for the passenger seat. No direction indicators were fitted, nor was there a heater. I soon rectified these shortcomings, had a tonneau cover made, and fitted a removable bolster behind the cab. This Pickup gave me good service, clocking up 187,000 miles with two Gold Seal rebuilt engines, two Gold Seal gearboxes and a replacement chassis!

While at Organ Hall I studied A-level Zoology and Botany at evening classes at Watford College,

I sold my BSA Bantam to buy a Jowett Bradford truck, powered by a 1005cc flat twin.

THE BRADFORD LORRY

The ideal Builders' or Merchants' open truck with 27 square feet of loading space, drop sides and rear panel. Immensely strong. Extras: Painting in green, blue or grey; passenger's seat.

THE BRADFORD 10 CWT. LORRY

my aim being to train as a vet, but I only passed the Botany, though my real interest was in Zoology. I still did not have the English pass!

During my time at Organ Hall Farm I got to know the various MMB (Milk Marketing Board) inseminators who called when needed, and it dawned on me that if I was not going to make it as a vet, training to become an inseminator was an option. So I took a day off work to attend an interview at the area's main centre, at Little Horwood, near Bletchley in Buckinghamshire, conducted by the chief vet, Mr Forsythe, and the senior inseminator, Mr Thompson, if I remember correctly. The interview was successful, so I handed in my notice at Organ Hall and within a couple of weeks I had started my six-week training period, the first three being at the main centre. By then the Blomfield family (from Little Stoke Manor farm) had moved very close to Little Horwood, so I was able to lodge with them for the three weeks – very convenient and comfortable. The stock bulls were kept at Little Horwood, with the laboratory facilities on site. In those days, bulls' semen was 'fresh' on a daily basis, diluted to about 200:1 with egg yolk and then dispatched to the sub-centres for use on that day. Deep-frozen semen kept in liquid nitrogen was a rarity. Part of the training was handling and feeding the bulls. I seem to remember that the Jersey bulls had very bad tempers, while the big Herefords were usually quite placid.

The routine, when grazing was available, was that each bull was led out from the bull shed – the shed was just like a traditional cowshed but with larger and more robust partitions. To take a bull out to be tethered for grazing, a loop-ended rope would be passed up through the ring in his nose and then the loop passed around the base of each horn (I can't remember how we did it with the Red Poll bulls). The long end of the rope would be tied to the drawbar of a TE.D20 tractor and the bull towed slowly out to the field. I can remember carrying out this procedure with Porch Jumbo, a big mature Hereford, in tow and the engine running at a brisk tickover on petrol, when he decided to stop, and the engine stalled. I restarted and off we went in a most nonchalant way. I was very relieved that the bull did not become aggressive and charge the rear of the Ferguson. In a millisecond it reminded me of an occasion that I was involved in during my first year at Little Stoke Manor. The two herds of Aberdeen Angus had somehow got together and, of course, the two bulls had started fighting. Mr Ducker had noticed this while driving his open-sided Jeep: he

instructed me to get in the front passenger seat and then went on to explain how he proposed to deal with the situation. 'Michael,' he said, 'I will drive between the two bulls and head one off to another field.' I thought this a bit scary. He tried to drive the bulls apart but they were so engrossed in their fight that they just continued; the result was that they lifted the front wheels of the Jeep about two feet off the ground! At that point Mr Ducker announced he would retreat, and would instruct Blomfield (the farm bailiff) to deal with the situation. Needless to say, I was greatly relieved.

During this early training period I was sent to the abattoir at Bungay in Suffolk for a day to be shown the various organs of a bull's reproductive system. The ex-MMB bull was duly dispatched and the vet then proceeded to dissect the various organs and explain their function. Of course, I knew all about that anyway! Then he said, 'It's surprising what you can find in the rumen; do you want to have a search?' Well, yes, I did, and proceeded with the unpleasant task; my reward was that I found a ladies' silver necklace which I kept for years, but as often happens it disappeared eventually.

After three weeks at Little Horwood I was transferred to finish my training at the sub-centre from which I would ultimately work, Little Kingshill, near High Wycombe in Buckinghamshire. I was back living with my mother and sister by then, at Leverstock Green, near Hemel Hempstead in Hertfordshire. During my three years with the MMB I noted that, unlike modern quangos, it was run as a tight ship, very well organised and with all aspects strictly monitored.

At the time our cars were either Morris 1000s or Ford 105E Anglias. It seems appropriate at this point to explain how my 'second' life was lost. I was driving the Milk Marketing Board's Morris 1000 (colour Rose Taupe) early one winter morning from my home at Leverstock Green to the subcentre at Little Kingshill. On the last leg of the journey along the A413, between Amersham and Great Missenden, I hit black ice, the Morris veered across the road (luckily no traffic was heading in the opposite direction), mounted the wide grass verge and then started to slowly climb the adjacent bank. In a split second I wondered whether it was going to roll over, and yes, it did just that, on to its roof. I was crouched on the inside of the roof lining but was able to open the driver's door and crawl out unscathed. By that time a car had pulled up with three or four men in it; one asked if I was all right – which I was, physically. Another said 'We can't leave it here', so they proceeded to roll the Morris on to its side and then heave it on to its wheels again. I checked that no oil had leaked out of the engine but that was fine. I started the engine, thanked my saviours profusely and drove on to Little Kingshill. There I had to explain my lateness for work to Ian MacMillan, the senior inseminator, but there was no fuss there. Very little damage was done to this sturdy little car – just a slight depression in the roof panel and some scratches in the paintwork along the sides. I drove it for two weeks in this state until it was repaired by our local body shop in High Wycombe.

As I settled into 'my area' to the north and west of London I got on well with most of the farmers and I am sure this helped to build up my confidence further. As I built up a rapport with some I let it be known that I had skills other than inseminating cows; for example, welding with both gas and electric, electrical work and some plumbing, and that I had a small workshop at Leverstock Green. On my rounds I would sometimes pick up small welding repair jobs and was often able to deliver them back the next day – all very unofficial.

The MMB ruled that when men had completed their round of calls, their working day was finished. We all worked a rolling five-day week, including Saturdays and Sundays, and the days off gave more scope for my budding sideline business. The senior inseminator at Little Kingshill, Ian MacMillan, was ten years older than me, and like myself had a frustrated desire to go farming, so in 1964 we decided to buy a south-facing farm of 120 acres at Lower Whitsleigh, near Torrington in North Devon. This cost us £15,000 of which Ian put in £6,000 and I £2,000, the balance of £7,000 being provided by the Agricultural Mortgage Corporation (AMC) from their Taunton office.

Everybody who knew me warned that our project wouldn't work, and they proved to be correct, but we had to have a go! The farming went reasonably well here, milking about 30 cows, but we were grossly under-capitalised. My 'third' life went when I was on my back drilling some bolt holes with my Wolf Cub ¼-in drill to patch up our Massey Harris 726 Bagger Combine. I pulled the trigger switch and my hand 'froze' with an electric shock. I couldn't let go – luckily I was able to sling it by flexing my right arm violently. Shortly after, Ian appeared and asked if I was all right – apparently, I was as white as a sheet! After a year, one of Ian's relations in Sussex retired, sold his newsagent's shop and offered us some additional capital, but instead

of developing Lower Whitsleigh we bought the 57-acre Lower Park Farm at Coldridge, near Crediton, for £8,300. It was rough, with a fair bit of steep land. By this time we had 35 to 40 milking cows, mainly Friesian, so we moved them all to Lower Park. I moved into the dilapidated farmhouse and did all the milking six days a week. There was a Hosier Milking Bail and an Atcos Barn 45 ft long with a 22 ft lean-to along one side, which is now part of the Ferguson shed. After morning milking I usually travelled to Lower Whitsleigh to help Ian. The partnership eventually became strained, so we decided to put Lower Park on the market and go our separate ways, with the cows being returned to Lower Whitsleigh.

At this point in my life, with the ending of the partnership with Ian MacMillan and not having, until two years later, when Lower Park was eventually sold, my share of the money I had invested, I began to carry out a few car services for two or three people in the village of Coldridge, including one who never paid me! I did a bit of scrounging around at Lower Park and at a nearby rubbish tip to salvage any bits of metal I could find and then sell them to a man in the village who dealt in that sort of thing. He befriended me a bit by giving me the odd meal from time to time and occasionally an old washing machine or spin dryer he'd been landed with. I was able to put these back into working order and then sell them on for a few pounds. I remember surviving one week on only instant coffee and a few packets of biscuits – that was my lowest point. Some kind person in the village had noticed an advertisement in the Western Morning News placed by A. E. Watson of Exeter, who were looking for a fabricator/welder. I followed this up with a phone call to the workshop manager, a Mr King, who invited me to go along for an interview and welding test with the workshop foreman, Vic. This involved preparing two pieces of ½ in (12 mm) plate to be welded together full strength BUT welded in the vertical plane. I was allowed a little play-around to get the measure of their welding plant and the welding rods that were to be used. The test piece was duly scrutinized and then the weld was cut through: what Vic was looking for was any slag intrusions in the weld which would, of course, have weakened it. There were none: I had met their requirements, so I was offered a full-time job at six shillings per hour.

So I was able to get a full-time job as a welder with A. E. Watson at Marsh Barton in Exeter. This was a well-established business with an extensive drawing office, a template shop, and a large, well-equipped fabrication shop with a 5-ton travelling gantry crane with its driver sitting high up in an open cab. I worked there for nine months and it was like a compressed apprenticeship in steel fabrication. The quality of the welds was often monitored, either by ultrasound or X-ray. Quite a high proportion of the fabrication work was of a specialist nature: for example, large-diameter pipework for a British Gas sub-station, and the steel framework for a theatre at Sandhurst Academy, including cantilevered balconies. Another large and interesting project was the fabrication of an overhead conveyor and support trusses at Avonmouth Docks. This was a mile and a quarter long and made for the company Rio Tinto Zinc. It ran from the dockside where the ore was unloaded from a ship, and then went by conveyor to their smelter, which if I remember correctly was able to smelt zinc and lead simultaneously. The steel used in almost all the principal members was rectangular hollow section box in grade 50C, a higher tensile strength than the normal 43C. It had to be welded using low hydrogen welding rods, which have to be run at 80 volts as against the normal 50 volt setting. I worked every hour of overtime I possibly could, and there was a lot. After nine months I felt that I could do better for myself by going it alone, so I left despite the workshop foreman, Vic, offering to increase my pay to six shillings and sixpence per hour!

I was now on my own at Lower Park, living rent free in a rather primitive house with water coming through the thatched roof, which I patched up. In the barn at the west end of the house (now the kitchen) I concreted the floor with a cheap mix and made a pair of oak plank doors to keep it secure. This was my new 'workshop', equipped with a 180-amp welder, a couple of gas bottles, a bench, a box of tools and my trusty Morris 1000 Pickup. I took on any job the local farmers wanted me to do, provided I felt competent to do it, so there was relief milking, welding repairs, car servicing, electrical work, car body repairs and a few plumbing jobs.

My 'fourth' life went while I was attempting to drill a couple of holes on the inside of a very large stone-built chimney of a two-storey cottage at Partridge Walls near Winkleigh. The owner had asked me to make a metal bracket for the traditional open hearth where he could hang a large cast iron kettle. He thought it would look the part! He didn't want any fixing bolts to be visible when sitting by the fire.

I was using my Black and Decker ½ in (12 mm) drill which, by the way, was the cheapest in their range but it gave me fantastic service. As I pulled the trigger switch I got one hell of a belt off it; luckily this time it just fell out of my grasp on to the hearth. I completed the job by using a star drill and hammer, followed by fixing the bracket with two Rawlbolts. When I returned to Lower Park I tested the drill with a Multi-Meter – there was no indication of a leakage of current to its metal case. So the next test was to put the switch to 'on', clamp the drill gently in the vice, plug it into a 13 amp switched socket and turn it on – it ran perfectly. So I felt confident enough to touch it. All was well, so I can only put this experience down to a fault in the wiring of the cottage!

A good moneyspinner was making a three-tiered trolley with brushes attached to clean battery cage floors where the eggs roll prior to being collected; this idea of mine was the result of a poultry keeper asking if I could speed up the process by doing the three tiers in one pass. I sold a lot of these, but they were only suitable for Hatch houses (Hatch was the maker's name – from Cornwall). Thank goodness this obscene way of keeping poultry has now been outlawed.

By and large, this all developed nicely and steadily and after two years we were able to sell Lower Park Farm for £8,600 to a family by the name of Lowe. I had to move out so I bought a small secondhand caravan for £33 and was generously given permission to park it on a poultry farm (with Hatch houses) adjacent to Lower Park owned by Mr and Mrs Petty. These people had befriended me for a year prior to the move. Opposite their bungalow were two Second World War Nissen huts, the remains of a searchlight battery, on land known as Mount Evelyn, with a terrace of three cottages and a donkey stable built in 1875 by Lord Portsmouth. One of these Nissen huts was not being used, so the owners Mr and Mrs Coles offered it to me at a rent of 10 shillings a week provided I obtained planning permission from Mid Devon District Council to use it as an agricultural workshop. This was duly granted, with support from some local farmers. I had mains electricity connected and I wired the building for light and power. British Telecom provided a telephone line, Lapford 418, and the North Devon Water Board installed a meter for me.

I was soon able to employ a part-time helper, the late Bernard Tonkins, whose day job was at a nearby farm – he was ten years older than me but he took to welding like a duck to water. It wasn't long before Bernard came to work for me full-

Bernard using a 9-inch Metabo angle grinder in the Nissen hut. It's David Leach, the apprentice, in the background.

Lower Park farm house as it was when I bought it in 1977.

time. Later on I employed a full-time fabricator, the late Martin Petherick.

I feel I must own up to a bit of bad behaviour around this time. In late November, Martin, Bernard and I had been working flat out to finish various items farmers needed for their stock buildings to make them ready for overwintering their cattle. There was to be a folk-singing club meeting at Burton Hall in nearby North Tawton on the Saturday evening, which I was determined to attend – a bit of relaxation after so much hard work. I drove there in my trusty Morris Pickup, polished off a couple of pints of beer and then decided to buy a bottle of dry sherry, which I consumed during the rest of the evening. On leaving, slightly inebriated, I noticed that it had started to snow. My guardian angel must have been looking after me because I drove back to the caravan on automatic

pilot without incident – or so I thought. When I awoke late on the Sunday morning I noticed that my Avia watch was missing. I looked in the Pickup and phoned Burton Hall but there was no sign of my watch. Towards the end of that week I dreamt that it was in a 600-gallon rainwater tank next to my caravan. I mentioned this to Martin and his reply was, 'Well, us had better go and find out', so we emptied most of the water out with buckets and then tipped out the rest from the tank, and there in the sludge was my watch, just as in my dream. I must have caught my arm on the edge of the tank as I stumbled into the caravan. I wiped the watch off, wound it up, set the time and away it went; luckily, it was waterproof.

Not long after this episode, Mrs Petty was told by Mr and Mrs Coles, the owners of Mount Evelyn, a terrace of three cottages, that No. 3 was to become vacant. The Coles lived at No. 1. Perhaps it should be mentioned that these cottages were part of a large estate in this area owned by Lord Portsmouth. The cottages were built in 1874 with a high standard of craftsmanship and were of solid, well-detailed construction. Mrs Petty suggested that I might like to take on the tenancy. So following this wise advice I approached Mr and Mrs Coles, who were very happy for me to become their new tenant. Just prior to my moving in they had instructed our local builder to repaint it internally. Once installed there I made a few improvements, I built a stone fireplace to replace the tiled one, installed a bit of oil fired central heating on the ground floor as well as a wall hung toilet in the bathroom – which was adjacent to the kitchen. Having this cottage as my living space eventually allowed me to deal with improvements to the land at Lower Park before eventually moving on to make the house there more civilized.

I had the opportunity to buy a secondhand Kitchen & Wade 6 ft radial drill with the capacity to drill up to 1½-inch holes. The foundation for this had to be a 6 ft cube of concrete with the holding-down bolt cast in to exact dimensions. I had to hire a crane to lift it off the delivery lorry. Needless to say, this was placed outside the Nissen hut, so it had to be sheeted up when not in use. I also had to remove the three-phase motor and replace it with a single-phase type.

At this time we were making farmyard gates, cubicle partitions and feed barriers. We started to make a few low-loading bale trailers, similar to a Mole Valley design but better, and also a few 12-ton bulk feed bins – and my first steel-framed building, a 60 ft x 30 ft lean-to for a dairy farmer, the late Gerald

Palmer, of Chawleigh in mid Devon. He promptly followed this by ordering a 105 ft x 60 ft x 18 ft silage barn. The steelwork for this was shotblasted and zinc-sprayed, a treatment I used almost exclusively for years except when hot-dipped galvanised was specified. All the heavy steel sections had to be manhandled in and out of the Nissen hut. Bulk milk tanks were being introduced around this time, 1972, and I was asked to wire in several of these.

One incident that is worth mentioning at this point concerns a Hunter jet fighter flying on routine practice from RAF Chivenor, North Devon. Let me explain. It was a fine day, and Bernard and I were working in my Nissen hut fabricating the 30 ft (9.14m) rakers for Gerald Palmer's silage barn to be erected at Nutson Farm, Chawleigh. I had stepped outside to use the Kitchen and Wade radial drill, when I heard a swishing sound in the sky; I looked up to see a jet aircraft passing overhead – then I heard a loud pop and saw that the pilot had ejected while the jet continued flying. The pilot seemed to go quite high before his parachute began to open as he floated slowly towards the ground. I can remember thinking I hope to hell he has noticed the 33,000-volt grid line in the field he eventually landed in. Luckily, he was able to steer himself clear of that and landed in the field, which formed part of Mount Evelyn. Bernard and I ran across to make sure he was okay. He said that he was, apart from an injury to his back as the result of ejecting. He went on to explain that a helicopter with a doctor on board was on its way from his base at RAF Chivenor, where he was the station commander.

He was concerned that his abandoned aircraft would not kill or injure anyone, or cause damage. He told us he had set it to head towards open country. Bernard and I hung around until the helicopter had loaded the casualty and taken off.

Now the twist to this story. Yes, the aircraft did crash-land in open country – at Nutson Farm, Chawleigh, making a hole in one hedge bank, before coming to rest against the next hedge.

A few days later I had a letter from the pilot inviting me to visit the Chivenor air base. In my reply I thanked him profusely but turned down his kind offer as I could not spare time away from work. I have always regretted not taking him up on his offer – fantasising that I might have been given a short flight in some exotic piece of aeronautical engineering. What a strange combination of events!

By 1974 I felt well enough established to consider building myself a proper fabrication workshop, but first I had to buy the plot of land the Nissen hut

Here I am, working as a builder's labourer at Lower Park.

stood on plus an adjacent piece of land. Mr and Mrs Coles were happy to sell me the plot at a very fair price. With that hurdle negotiated I then had to deal with obtaining permissions from Crediton District Council, but the process went very smoothly, with the local councillor (a farmer) and others in the locality all being supportive. I asked a draughtsman from A. E. Watson to produce the application drawings, and once approved by the Council I was able to start making the frame. The building would be 75 ft long, 33ft wide and 15ft high to the eaves, with a centre hoist track and another to align with the bench of the radial drill. All the stanchions were 8ft offcuts from Gerald Palmer's silage building and were welded full strength.

As I wanted to make this workshop a bit of a 'shop window', I designed the front gable end to have a pair of 14ft-high offset sliding doors, with some of the infilling built to eaves height in local stone. I installed two full runs of roof lights and had an elevated office space at the far end of the south-facing side with a helical staircase leading to it. I did all the wiring myself and installed a couple of secondhand Westinghouse static phase converters to power the lower hoist.

In these early days we were making mainly yard gates, feed barriers, hay racks and cubicle partitions. It was also a time when the demand for bale trailers was increasing, so there was a move away from using secondhand lorry hubs to buying new axles and wheels from Belgium. I reckon we made just over 1500. Mixed with this was the fabrication and erection of steel-framed farm buildings. All this work went on in a gentle but expanding way.

Before moving on further I will explain how my

'fifth' life was lost. It was during winter time and I was laid up with mild 'flu for a few days, but work was going on as usual. The men in the workshop had loaded the TK Bedford lorry with steelwork for a farm building but as I was the only one licensed to drive it I was called out of my bed to drive it to site. As I approached the loaded lorry I noticed that they had not loaded two ladders, which annoyed me slightly so I stupidly climbed on to the steelwork loaded over the front and rear bolsters and asked someone to pass up the ladders – as they did, I slipped somehow and fell off the load on to the concrete yard. Luckily for me I only broke my right wrist, but had to be taken to A&E at Exeter hospital. I was in plaster for six weeks, by which time the plaster was covered with cheeky comments from well-wishers. Eventually, it was time for the plaster to be cut off and I erroneously thought that I would be straight back to working normally, but how wrong I was – I had to re-learn how to use my hand!

Around this time I felt that we needed a forklift on site. I found one advertised in *Exchange and Mart*, located in Essex, and took my TK Bedford truck to collect it. On my arrival I realised that I had come to a scrapyard and that the forklift was a non-runner and in very poor shape, but it was a Matbro Swing Lift. I should explain that these Matbros were of a unique design in that one can raise long steel beams in the normal way to about 4ft then slew the mast 90° so that the load is in line with the wheelbase of the truck – exactly what we needed with the layout of the workshop building. This particular model had

An early Michael Thorne bale trailer, built using second-hand rear lorry axle hubs, in this example from an Austin LD van.

a rated lift capacity of 4 tons.

The forklift had to be craned on to my lorry, and as it was being lowered I noticed that the aluminium floor was starting to buckle, so a large sheet of ¼ in (6mm) plate steel was placed on the floor and we tried again. Unfortunately, it was not until I'd left the yard that I noticed the forklift was slightly offset to the nearside, not a good omen with such a long drive ahead. I stopped at every motorway services to check the load binders but was worried the police would notice this rather lopsided lorry and I would be stopped and no doubt prosecuted for overloading! Fortunately, I made it back to Coldridge without incident. My friendly local farmer, the late Peter Bailey, of Westacott Farm, Coldridge, had a proper loading ramp at the top end of his lane and we were able to tow the forklift off the Bedford and down to my workshop.

A lot of work had to be invested in this forklift before it could be inspected and passed by my insurer's engineer. The diesel engine was as fitted to a Fordson Major E1A and had to be totally rebuilt. The Brockhouse torque converter shuttle transmission just needed a filter clean and fresh oil. The final drive to the front wheels was again from a Fordson Major E1A and was quite serviceable apart from needing the brakes relined and a couple of hub seals replaced. The rear steering axle needed replacement kingpins and bushes, which had to be specially machined. Most of the hydraulic rams were leak free, but we did replace all the hoses to be on the safe side. We fitted work lights front and rear. The machine passed testing and inspection and I was handed, by my insurer's engineer, a Certificate of Compliance. The machine gave useful service for two or three years until I decided to buy a new 6-ton swing lift from Matbro in 1987; that cost £27,500, the greatest sum of money I have ever spent on a machine, but it lasted a long time.

Around this time we started offering customers mass concrete walling, suitable for silage, grain and retaining walls. The late Harry Russell joined the firm at this point and this new venture was based on his expertise in the procedures involved. We even developed our own shuttering system, enabling 6 ft, 8 ft, 10 ft and 12 ft high walls to be constructed. This was a boom time as farmers could sign up with the Ministry of Agriculture (precursor to DEFRA) for a five-year farm development grant towards the cost. This scheme embraced buildings, concrete stockyards, fencing, drainage and so on. To be fair, it was also a boom time for those in rural construction.

MAMMOTH BALE TRAILER

MICHAEL THORNE TRAILERS

It so happened in the summer of 1977 that the owner of Lower Park Farm, which is located on the opposite side of the council road to my workshop at Mount Evelyn, called up there one Sunday morning while I was getting in some overtime. He had called to explain that he and his wife were planning on moving to Scotland and would I be interested in buying the property, which extends to 57 acres (23 hectares). His asking price was £68,000. The farmhouse I estimate to be dated to c.1650, while the adjoining part that was once my workshop is about 100 years more recent. The construction is typically vernacular in style – stone plinth with cob walls and a thatched roof. Everything about Lower Park was in a neglected state but I felt that his asking price reflected that and, of course, if I were to buy it he would not have to incur agents' fees! Well, at the time I had built up a reserve in a Building Society of about £38,000 so if I were to accept this tempting offer I would have to find someone prepared to lend me £30,000. I took the obvious approach by asking my bank manager at NatWest plc Crediton but was turned down. The next port of call was my solicitors, also in Crediton, where I asked if they might have a customer with that sort of money to invest, but this request also fell on stony ground. So during the following week I contacted the owner of Lower Park telling him that I had been unable to find the shortfall. I asked him if he would be prepared to sell me just the house and a bit of land. That was turned down because he didn't want to split it up, which, of course, is absolutely right. He did suggest, however, that he would be prepared to lend me the £30,000 to be paid back with interest over a three-year period. A deal was done on that basis. So I thought – Mike Thorne you will now have to turn the wick up and take on as much steelwork as possible.

I was lucky to be living, at this time, in the rented cottage at Mount Evelyn that I had made comfortable for my domestic needs, so although there was a lot of work and expense to be invested in Lower Park, I was not under any great pressure to move out of the cottage.

My plan was to set aside the first two years to sort out the farmland drainage, fences, hedges and gates, which in itself was quite a monumental challenge. This was duly achieved.

At the start of the third year I turned my attention towards the refurbishment of the house to my personal requirements. The house is not listed, though I feel it should have been: it is mentioned in the Domesday Book and is reputed to have been one of King Henry VIII's hunting parks.

A brief résumé of the work that took place over the third year may be of interest to readers. A total re-thatch of the roof was necessary (on the underside of the roof of the older part there is evidence of smoke blackening). Several custom-made wooden window frames had to be produced and installed to replace either rotten or inappropriate metal ones. A total replacement of all the plumbing and sanitary fittings: as part of this work I felt it prudent to install the pipework for a modest central heating system, but that was only made operational many years later.

An oil-fired AGA was included in the schedule.

Work underway on Lower Park Farm with demolition of the lean-to porch.

The restored linhay building at Lower Park which won a Country Land Owners' Award.

The electrical system was totally replaced to the then current safety standards.

Within the curtilage of the house and approach driveway about ten telephone and electricity poles were taken out and replaced with new underground cabling. At the time I was delighted that both BT and South Western Electricity Board did this work free of charge, but I did provide the trenches and back-filling after the cable runs had been installed. I remember giving the man from BT, who had handled their part, a bottle of wine on completion as a gesture of my appreciation of what had been achieved. He thanked me most heartily and then said, 'Well, I have worked on this sort of thing for BT for forty years and I have never been given anything like this!'

A new water main had to be installed in black polythene to replace the original steel pipe – about a 400 yd run (that in turn has just been replaced in August 2020, this time using blue pipe, apparently the earlier black was prone to perishing). A traditional type of oak plank front door with an adzed finish, and an adjoining open porch with a thatched roof was made. Quite a significant area of the cob walls had to be re-rendered with a scat finish to protect it. The soil abutting the wall at the rear of the house had to be dug out as it was causing damp on the inside. There was also some upgrading of the drainage system. When all of this had been completed, the final stage of the project was decorating inside, for which I chose just plain white, and for the outside render Barley White Snowcem. The window frames were painted in satin white paint. As this work was carried out by real craftsmen it lasted until 2008 with only minimal maintenance. That brings this project at Lower Park to September 1980. The previous owner had been paid according to the terms of our deal and I

was able to relinquish the rented cottage at Mount Evelyn and move myself and bits of furniture into Lower Park to start living there for the second time!

About a year later, 1981, I decided to build a single-storey extension to the east end of the house. This was to have its ridge line running at 45° to the rear corner of the house to embrace a utility room with adjoining double garage and storage space. It was built of local stone with plenty of glazing in the utility area using my own fabricated steel window frames, and the floor was of slate. The roof was clad with secondhand slates with a hip end: I purchased these slates from a customer where we had just erected a new steel framed farm building, even a few of the ridge tiles that were part of the deal had Thorne cast into them. I made the lift-up double garage door and clad it with black stained diagonal boarding which was supported when open by heavy gas struts. It was while the site was being prepared for this extension that I lost my 'sixth' life.

It was a Saturday morning, and having outlined to the digger driver, the late Nigel Beardon, how I wanted this area prepared, and then for him to move to digging out the driveway adjacent to what is now The Ferguson Shed. I left to visit a customer who required a quote for a farm building. Returning in the early afternoon to Lower Park I noticed that Nigel had placed a 6 ft (1.8 m) fibre cement ridge piece on the prepared ground: my reaction was 'What the hell is going on?' I thought I couldn't leave it there so I just walked across to pick it up and promptly fell into a freshly exposed well that was measured later to be 14 ft (4.2 m) deep. Luckily I instinctively saved myself by somehow grabbing one of the old suction pipes still in place – one lead and one steel. I scraped my back and arms, as being summer I had no shirt on. Nigel's digger was roaring away in the background so there was no point in shouting for help and one false move and I would be at the bottom – not good for a non-swimmer! I was able to lever my body up enough to place my foot on a bit of the suction pipe and scramble out. I walked around to where Nigel was working – he shut the engine down and exclaimed 'Cor be buggered!' We decided to call it a day, I made a cup of tea for us and bid him a good day before going for a good soak in the bath!

The next project, this time at Mount Evelyn, was to extend the workshop by 60 ft (18.2 m) to the rear of the existing one, with the same profile. Having fabricated the necessary steelwork and erected it, this was followed by the roof cladding, which was continued with the same layout as the first front

Site work underway for the new workshop. Note my Land Rover Series 2 in BMC Limeflower Green.

The GEKA hydraulic metal worker in action. Workshop foreman Danny Elgin (in green overalls) is notching plate steel while Graham Eastman, in blue, is punching holes.

A BOC straight-line cutter (a 'pug') in use.

The new office under construction.

pretty scary. I thought that I had better get home. As I walked/staggered across the field from the workshop to Mount Evelyn cottage I was making a big effort to breathe as deeply as I could and I remember thinking that this might be the last time I do this walk! Once home, I immediately phoned my local doctor, the late Bruce Marsden of Bow. His wife, also a doctor, answered my call and suggested that I sit down and continue deep breathing until I began to feel more normal. Luckily for me I felt able to walk back to the workshop after about half an hour. Needless to say, the block layer had packed up and gone home. Since this experience I have an absolute dread of fumes – a useful bit of body memory I guess!

When completed, this building enabled the heavier fabrication to continue in the front shop with its hoists, tracks and radial drill ready to hand. The 'new' extension would provide space for lighter fabrications and again a central crane track was installed. I bought a secondhand Kingsland cropper for the front workshop. This was a mechanical unit fitted with a heavy flywheel which enabled it to punch and shear up to ½ inch (12 mm) plate. This machine was a real boon and saved a lot of gas cutting and mess.

As time went on I felt that I needed a separate office, which was duly built on land at Lower Park opposite the workshop. It was also an excuse to design a bit of a quirky building, but with the walls built of local stone, and, of course, with a slate roof.

By this time the late Liz Abbotts, who had been working for me part-time dealing with typing, accounts, painting and welding was able to come on board full-time, hence the requirement for a new office. I am not an office type and much preferred working in the workshop, nor was I too keen on site work. The original elevated office was turned into a mess room.

Eventually the Kingsland cropper was replaced with a much more sophisticated machine that was able to punch and shear up to ¾ inch (20mm). This capacity was achieved by hydraulic pressure. It also had a computer-controlled system whereby, having been correctly programmed, the stops moved in a sequence to the appropriate hole spacing – the operator simply moved the plate to the stop and then depressed the punching pedal. It was a super bit of kit.

As time went on we decided to build a second extension of 60 ft (18.2 m) for use as a paint shop for fabricated steelwork, bringing the total length of the building to 195 ft (59.4 m). Access to this final

workshop. It was on a Saturday afternoon and I had a chap building the concrete block walls, and it was on this occasion that I lost my 'seventh' life. At one point in the afternoon he announced he had run out of petrol for his cement mixer and could I let him have some. My direct answer to that was that I did not have any to hand. So, rather than drive to our local garage in my Morris Marina van to get some, I decided to just siphon some out of the van's tank. I found a bit of hosepipe that was to hand, inserted one end into the tank and started sucking to try to get a flow going, but unsuccessfully! I was paying this man by the hour and did not want any hold up. I gave up when I began to feel faint and dizzy, it was building was through a 45 ft (13.7 m) side doorway.

I began to introduce Ian Rice to the role of running the day-to-day business of Michael Thorne Construction. Ian initially came to work for me part-time soon after I purchased Lower Park in September 1977. This part-time work went on for several months, and on odd occasions he would work full days on construction sites as well, taking to it like the proverbial duck to water. Eventually he gave up his farm job and joined me full-time, usually working with Paul Conibere, who also started working for me in August 1977 to follow an apprenticeship in agricultural engineering, which was in fact not ideal as a lot of his work was either steel fabrication or on site, erecting the building frames.

Ian had been a top student in his year at Bicton Agricultural College, Devon so it is not surprising that he proved to be a loyal and very competent person within the team at Michael Thorne Construction working a total of 33 years for the firm.

As the firm grew we needed more office space, so I extended the small one on Lower Park land with a two-storey addition, also designed to be a bit of a shop window. I was advised in 1985 to form the firm into a limited company, which, of course, was absolutely right and that is what I did. The directors I appointed were Ian Rice, managing; Paul Conibere, operations; Steve Glover, financial; and I was the chairman. Graham Easton and Robert Holland joined as directors in 1990.

I remember many years ago, when passing the Gregory Transport depot in North Tawton, thinking to myself that they would be good people to make a building for. Most of their existing warehouses had been built by Peter Horn Construction of Langtree, Torrington, but that firm had ceased trading. Then one day I got a phone call from Jack Gregory to say that he and his son, John, who had just joined the firm, would like me to submit a price for a new warehouse they were planning to have built. I visited their site to get the measure of what they were hoping for. This done, Ian and I worked out a full specification and price, including the Planning Application and Building Regulation Controls and the expected ground works needed. I then invited Jack and John to visit our site at Coldridge to view the building we had erected there. Towards the end of their visit Jack said to John, 'I think we have seen enough to place an order.' That was the start of a long and happy trading relationship with this prestigious transport and warehousing company. A few years later they expanded their

Part of the Michal Throne Construction fleet – a line-up of eight VW vans, all in BMC Limeflower Green

operation with the purchase of a large greenfield site at Cullompton. Again, we were asked to price Phase 1 of this development, which included office accommodation, vehicle workshops and, of course, warehouses, all surrounded by concrete yards.

One incident that happened very early on in the development of this site is worth recalling. A 2 ft diameter gas main that ran across the land had to be re-routed, so it was arranged that Graham Easton, with a JCB and driver, would go there to meet an official from British Gas, who had plans showing the line of this high-pressure main, the object of the exercise being to establish its depth. With the second bucket of soil a one-inch purging standpipe was broken off the main, which created a terrific noise and terrified the three chaps. The outcome was that the gas main had to be isolated and closed down promptly. The other properties on the adjacent industrial estate lost their gas supply,

The workers line up for a photo during the extension of the office building.

The Elephant House at Paignton Zoo, soon after occupation.

including Devon Grain, who at the time were operating one of their large gas-fired grain dryers! This was shut down immediately. A big panic, but no one was hurt, nor was there a huge claim by British Gas against Michael Thorne Construction Ltd. These standpipes are normally removed after purging is completed.

There seems little point in writing in detail of the various projects we were involved in so I will just list a few by name:

- Mole Valley Trading
- Gregory Transport
- RGB Builders' Merchants
- Crealy Adventure Park, Exeter
- The Elephant House, Paignton Zoo
- St Boniface Building, Crediton
- Yeo Valley Creamery, Somerset
- West End Engineering, Bideford
- Milk Marque, Cullompton
- The National Trust
- Teignmouth Docks
- Yeovil Land Rover

By early 2009 it was becoming clear that Michael Thorne Construction Ltd was heading towards insolvency. This was basically brought on by not being paid for a lot of work completed towards the end of a project run by a main contractor. Coinciding with this there was another sizeable project where we were the main contractor to build a small industrial estate complete with service roads etc., comprising about eight units that the developer was planning to rent out or sell on. At the end of this contract we never received the full and final payment.

So by November 2009, after 42 years of honest trading, the process of liquidation began. During the months prior to the final winding up of the business there were several grim and serious meetings that I had to attend. However, I found some positive respite in that I was able to get well into the writing of my second book for Herridge and Sons, about the Massey Ferguson 35/65 tractors.

Then on the night of 20 October 2009 I lost my 'eighth' life. Alison and I were sleeping at Pool Farm, my home, where the bedroom is reached via a stone helical staircase from the slate ground floor. I must have been sleepwalking (something I have never done before or since) and went head first down the treads, ending up on the slate floor unconscious with blood coming from my right ear. Luckily Alison was awakened by my moans and groans and called for an ambulance, then had to walk up to unlock the entrance gate and move the Land Rover so that the emergency vehicle could turn around. The lady operating the switchboard kept in contact with Alison all the time and reassured her until the paramedics arrived all the way from Barnstaple. Being unaware of what was going on, although I do have a vague memory of hearing gear changing while in the ambulance and shouting out 'What the hell is going on?' I eventually came around after two and a half hours, I was told, in a hospital bed. Looking at my body, it was black and blue in most parts! I was looked after there for four days before Alison came to take me home. While in the care of the hospital, I had some kind local friends come to visit me, which was reassuring. I made a pretty quick recovery after the bruising had subsided BUT it was nine months before I was able to resume the writing of the second book on the Massey Ferguson 35/65 tractors. Thanks are due to Alison, the paramedics and those at the hospital who cared for me I did not die or become a vegetable! Ever since this horrible experience I have made a point of jamming a large screwdriver into the latch of the bedroom door at the top of the staircase every night before I get into bed. After a week, resting and healing, I felt able to return to doing some steel fabrication in the workshop, which is something I always find uplifting and enjoyable.

Strange as it may seem, although greatly saddened by the liquidation of my company I was eventually able to 'crash on' with writing the text for my book on the Massey Ferguson 35 and 65: it was a kind of saviour, and after a year had passed I began to feel greatly relieved at not having the overall responsibility and my name on the company.

With the termination of Michael Thorne Construction Ltd in September 2010, Paul Conibere and Ian Rice were able to 'take over' the business under their trading title of C and R Construction (SW) Ltd. They rented my workshop and yard at Mount Evelyn, picking up projects from some of my former customers as well as developing their own trade contacts. By September 2018 Paul and Ian were able to sell C & R Construction (SW) Ltd as a going concern to Craig Furze, who I am glad to say, is now renting my workshops and developing his firm. I find all of this most heartening and in a strange way I feel as if Craig is the third 'generation': I wish him and his business partner, Will Dodd, well for the future. My time is now shared between looking after Pool Farm and Lower Park, where the Coldridge Collection is housed, and where my book writing for Herridge and Sons is done – this is book number four.

I also gain a sense of comradeship by helping friends with their projects AND sharing the Coldridge Collection with other tractor enthusiasts.

The Gregory Distribution hub at Cullompton.

The Coldridge Collection

I gave every tractor that came to Coldridge a number (usually!) and created a folder for all of its paperwork. When selling them, I often passed these folders on to the buyers as part of the deal. And so, In some cases, I have no records of some tractors and you will notice there are some numbers missing from the entries below. These were: No. 17 – A Case DEX 1948, No. 19 – 1939 Fordson Standard Blue, No. 20 – MF130, No. 25 – 1953 Ferguson TE.D20 (sold to make way for a better example), No. 27 – 1959 Ferguson FE35 TVO (sold to make way for No 49), No. 28 – 1942 International Model A, No. 30 – 1938 Bristol Crawler powered by an Austin 10 hp side-valve engine, No. 34 – 1960 MF65 Mk I (sold to make way for No.75), No. 42 – 1937 Case Model L, No. 43 – 1940 Allis Chalmers Model B, No. 50 – 1965 MF 130, No. 53 – 1943 International W4, No. 58 – 1944 International W6.

No. 1, Ferguson TE.D20
1950, Serial No. 124514

This is the one that infected me with the tractor collecting bug!

Late one afternoon in 1987, a friend, the late Jon Williams, called in at my workshop to tell me that earlier that day, while pricing up a scaffolding job at a large house near Tiverton owned by a solicitor, he had noticed a rough-looking Ferguson parked up in an open shed. Jon, being an inquisitive type with a mechanical bent, asked if he could have a quick look at it. The solicitor told him it was for sale, priced at £100. When Jon told me that, I decided I would like to buy it as I have always admired Harry Ferguson and his achievements, and those of his small team of engineers. Having used Ferguson tractors on the Oxfordshire farm, at Agricultural College and then in my short-lived

The first tractor of my collection: 1950 Ferguson TE.D20, Serial No. 124514. (Andrew Morland)

farming partnership, and just three years before having been given a copy of Colin Fraser's book, Harry Ferguson, Inventor & Pioneer, I rang the vendor saying I would like to buy it. I put a cheque in the post and told him I would arrange to collect it when I next had my flatbed TK Bedford lorry with HIAB crane in the Tiverton area.

The Sunday after I got the Ferguson to Lower Park I set aside some time to find out if it would start. I cleaned the plugs and points, put some fresh petrol in the tank and connected up a 12-volt battery from my Mini van (the tractor was wired for 6 volts). Lo and behold, it started and ran reasonably well so I took it for a drive. That was a high point in my life! The tractor was then put in the dry and the battery returned to the Morris.

Eventually, the late Ernie Luxton fully restored it for me and fitted it with a set of Ferguson Tyre Tracks I had acquired, made by Bombardier. This tractor is also fitted with an American Ferguson accessory, never marketed in this country, a PTO adaptor that brings the normal Ferguson PTO shaft of 1⅛in diameter up to SAE Standard of 1⅜in as well as bringing the end of the PTO shaft close to 14in from the centre hole of the drawbar, which is part of the Standard.

This tractor is displayed in the Ferguson Shed, of course!

Brief specification:
• Engine: Standard Motor Company. Petrol/TVO.85 capacity 127.4 cu in (2088cc) pi. Power output at belt: 25.4 at 2000 engine speed
• Gearbox: Four forward and one reverse
• Hydraulic system: Cat 1 three-point linkage, draft control only
• Tyre sizes: Front 400 x 19, 5.00 x 1.5 on the track idler wheels, rear 10 x 28
• Wheel base: 70 in (1778 mm)
• Weight of basic tractor: 2446 lbs (1110 kg)

No. 2, 1949 Allis-Chalmers Model B
TVO, British-built example, Now sold

This was the next tractor to arrive; an American design primarily intended to handle mid-mounted implements, of which several types were available. During my time at Little Stoke Manor there were two American-built examples of about 1940 vintage, brought to the UK under the Lend-Lease scheme. These had forged steel bow front axles and lever-operated independent brakes, whereas the UK-built Model Bs had an adjustable fabricated straight front axle and pedal-operated brakes.

My memory of using one of the Little Stokes tractors fitted with a mid-mounted mower was that this positioning saved one from having to look rearwards most of the time, but the long lever used to lift the mower out of work took some pulling. They were also devils to start, as they had a tendency to kick back while being hand cranked. No electric starter!

The example that stood at Coldridge for a while I purchased from a farmer at Witheridge, Devon. We repainted it before selling it on as part of my rationalisation.

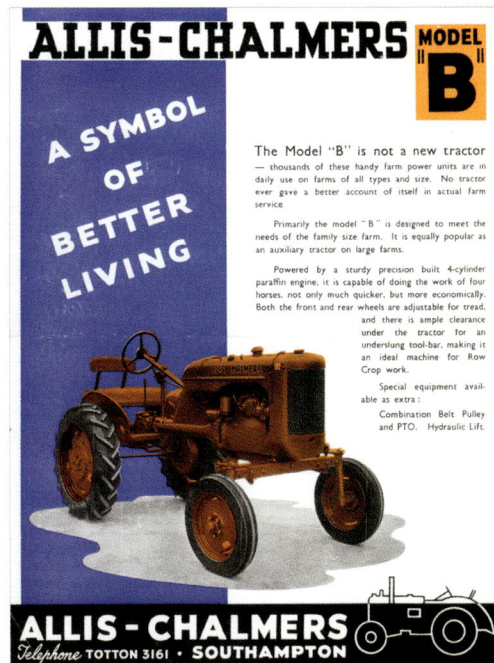

An advert for a British-built Allis-Chalmers Model B.

Brief specification:
• Engine: A.C. petrol/TVO, capacity 1900 cc; hand start; power output at belt 22.25 hp
• Gearbox: 3 forward and 1 reverse
• No hydraulic system but a range of special mid-mounted implements were offered that were raised/lowered by a manual linkage
• Tyre sizes: front 4.00 x 15; rear 9.00 x 24
• Wheel base: 73.4 in (1860 mm)
• Weight: 2060 lbs (934 kg)

No. 3, International F20
circa 1937, Sold

This was the third tractor I bought; I think it appealed to me at the time because of its nostalgic connotation, as it was an example of a model that had been at Little Stoke Manor, though theirs was fitted with a rear-mounted 6ft reciprocating knife mower. Some of the these could

The International F20 was fully refurbished by Ernie Luxton.

turn at 90º and continue cutting because they had a tricycle wheel layout and a cable-operated brake system which applied the appropriate rear brake but only when making sharp turns, thus assisting the manoeuvre.

This four-wheel version was refurbished by Ernie Luxton but it was, in due course, sold on to make way for more Fergusons. I can't remember the name of the person who bought it from me.

Brief specification:
• Engine: OHV 4 cylinder by International Harvester; petrol/TVO; capacity 220.9 cu in (3600 cc); power output at PTO claimed to be 26.67 hp, at belt (tested) 29 hp at 1200rpm engine speed
• Gearbox: 3 forward and 1 reverse
• Tyre sizes: front Vee twin arrangement 4.00 x 25, rear 6.00 x 40
• Wheel base: 85 in (2150 mm)
• Weight: 4400 lbs (1995 kg)

No. 4, Ferguson TE.A20
1948, Serial No. 57082, Registration No. KTT 82

I bought this tractor after finding it advertised for sale in the *Western Morning News* in the 1990s. It was owned by a smallholder living at

Black Torrington, not far from the offices of the publishers of this book.

It was in a tidy condition, having done very

1948 TE.A20 fitted with a Cameron Gardener Handy Loader. (Andrew Morland)

little hard work. It stood in storage for a few years and was later overhauled by Ernie, fitted with new Goodyear tyres all round and repainted by Peter Clark, to his usual high standard. At a later date I was able to buy a Cameron Gardner Handy-Loda complete with earth scoop. This was repaired and repainted prior to fitting it to this tractor, which is now protected by a genuine Ferguson tractor cover given to me by Colin Stevenson, a field test driver for Harry Ferguson.

Brief specification:
• Engine: Standard Motor Company; petrol 80 mm; capacity 112.9 cu in (1850 cc); power output at belt 23.9 hp at 2000 rmp engine speed
• Gearbox: 4 forward and 1 reverse
• Hydraulic system: Cat 1 three-point linkage with draft control only
• Tyre sizes: front 4.00 x 19; rear 10.00 x 28
• Wheel base: 70 in (1778 mm)
• Weight: 2500 lbs (1134 kg)

No. 5, Field Marshall Series III
1951, Contractor's model, Sold

My next purchase was this Field Marshall tractor, finished with green paintwork and, being a contractor's model, fitted with road lights and a high-ratio top gear to reduce the time taken travelling between farms. These models were used extensively by contractors to pull to site and then drive the traditional threshing drum and often a baler (these often had wire bindings). I am sure that what attracted me to this tractor was the note of its low-revving single-cylinder horizontal two-stroke diesel engine. Maximum engine speed was 700rpm.

My first encounter with Marshall tractors of this type was when I was attending the one-year National Certificate course at the Hertfordshire College of Agriculture. An incident I remember particularly well involved a fellow student starting up the Marshall after it had been parked overnight in an open-fronted wooden tractor shed. The power starting of these models was by using a 12 mm cartridge – like a 12 bore shotgun but without the lead shot. When starting by this method it was of paramount importance to align two arrows, one cast into the engine crankcase and the other on the flywheel. The student was not aware of this

The Contractor's model was fitted with road lights and high-ratio top gear.

procedure, fired the cartridge, the engine started and he put the tractor in reverse gear to back out. Instead, the tractor went forward and crashed through the weatherboarding of the shed. The engine was quite happily running backwards!

My next encounter with a Field Marshall, this time a Series III contractor's model, was during my first winter working at Organ Hall Farm, Borehamwood. My employers were brothers Joe and Ron Salter, and they called in the firm of Boughtons of Amersham, Buckinghamshire, to carry out the threshing of their 40 acres of barley, some of which might have been sold to the nearby London brewers for malting, or more likely used on the farm as the basis of a dairy ration for the 40 milking cows.

The grain was stored in 2 cwt sacks and then ground weekly through the autumn and winter using a large Massey Harris hammer mill belt-driven by a new-type Fordson Major diesel. The driver of this threshing outfit was Frank Pratly, a proper character and well-acquainted with steam traction engines.

Boughton were famous in their time for manufacturing heavy-duty winches for tractors, and in later years they diversified into producing a wide range of municipal and military specialised vehicles such as gully emptiers, high-speed crash tenders for use at airports, transmissions, 4WD conversions and many other pieces of equipment.

Anyway, I digress. The Field Marshall Series III was the penultimate model produced by the Marshall organisation. The last, painted orange, was designated the IIIA. Marshalls were originally the manufacturers of steam traction engines, but by the late 1920s sales had fallen off to almost nil. They decided to design a simple single-cylinder tractor, taking inspiration from the very successful Lanz Semi Diesel (hot bulb) engine which had acquired a good reputation in its native Germany. However, Boughton's design engineer, Samuel Dawson, chose to make his engine a full diesel by having a much higher compression ratio, in fact 15.5:1

Eventually these ideas became a reality and in 1930 production started with their 15-30, which had a bore of 8 in and a stroke of 10.5 in. These early models proved very problematic, though, so a revised model was manufactured, the 18-30; however, these also had serious issues. Marshall then developed the next generation, known as the 12-20, and introduced it in 1935. It proved to be a much better tractor, with a bore of 6.5 in and a 9 in stroke. These dimensions were retained on all future models. By 1938, a new model was made, known as the Model M, which had a slightly higher maximum engine speed of 700rpm. The M evolved into the Field Marshall by 1945, which had a certain amount of sheet metalwork to enhance its appearance and was known as the Series I, later becoming the Series II, which was in turn replaced in 1949 by the Series III. The great improvement here was the incorporation into the transmission of a high- and low-range gearbox as well as a PTO conforming to the Society of Automotive Engineers (SAE) Standard. The later models were widely exported and valued for their simplicity and reliability.

I bought my example from Lorna Mock, widow of the late Mervyn who had been a well-respected plant operator in North Devon. Following his early death, Lorna, knowing of my interest in old tractors, offered it to me and we agreed a price. I should mention here that Mervyn had been very helpful to me in my early days of steel fabrication, kindly recommending me to his farming customers and tipping me off when they were pricing up new farm buildings. I was often successful in getting the contracts, and gates and cow cubicle partitions followed in the wake of such work.

Soon after purchasing the tractor I took it to Clive Prosser at Yeovil for a repaint, which he did to a very high standard, and while this was being carried out I had the various chrome parts replated. When the Field Marshall returned to Coldridge I took it to a few local rallies but eventually decided to advertise it for sale. This resulted in a phone call from someone in Wales at about 6 pm one evening, who was keen to buy it. He said that he was setting off immediately with a friend, a 4 x 4 vehicle and a trailer. They duly arrived at Coldridge at about 10.30 pm. I offered to get them a starting cartridge from my house but one of them said, 'No thanks, don't bother, I'll start it by hand', which he did! A pretty strong chap! He did take the box of cartridges, though.

Brief specification:
• Engine: Horizontal single cylinder, water-cooled two-stroke diesel; bore 6.5in; stroke 9in; capacity 95.06 cu in (1550 cc); power output 40 hp at 700rpm
• Gearbox: main 3 forward and 1 reverse with a low/high range selection
• No hydraulic lift
• Tyre sizes: front 7.50 x 18; rear 14 x 30
• Wheel base: 72 in (1828 mm)
• Weight: including winch, approx. 7840 lbs (3556kg)

No. 6, Fordson Standard Row Crop Model
1938, Sold

This early purchase for the Collection was bought from Mr Norman Down of Spittle Farm, Chulmleigh in North Devon in the late 1980s. I guess it was its rarity and the fact that it was in tidy working order that influenced my decision to buy it. I kept it for quite a few years before selling it on to Tom Walling, a Ford tractor collector from the Exeter area. Prior to writing this piece I contacted Tom, who offered me the following details. He told me the rear wheels were made by French and I Leht, shod with 12.4/11-36 tyres. The single front wheel, 7.50 x 10, is a balloon type. He pointed out that the engine serial number dates the tractor to 1943, but the tractor has a number of earlier features suggesting it might have been an earlier model from the 1938/40 period, when Fordson tractors were finished in orange; it is likely that a replacement engine has been fitted.

It should be explained that these tricycle tractors had a braking system that operated one or other of the independent brakes when making sharp turns; these parts were missing when I owned the tractor, as were the driver's footplate and correct draw bar. Tom has informed me that he has now been able to find replacement parts, which he will be installing soon.

Brief specification:
- Engine: petrol/TVO, capacity 267 cu in (4380 cc), power output about 25hp flywheel at 1100rpm
- Gearbox: 3 forward and 1 reverse
- Tyre sizes: front 7.50 x 10; rear 12.4/11-36
- Wheel base: not known
- Weight: approx. 3600 lbs (1632 kg)

The Fordson Standard Row Crop Model was sold to Ford tractor collector Tom Walling.

No. 7, Ferguson Brown Model A
1936, Sold

I purchased this example from John Bownes Ltd, based in Winsford, Cheshire, who also offered me a two-furrow Ferguson plough of the same vintage for £100, which I also bought. He then went on to offer me a TE20, which I duly purchased, but which is now erroneously numbered 38 in the Collection – a Mike Thorne cock-up; more about that tractor later.

With the Model A and plough back at Coldridge I tried it out doing a bit of ploughing and it ran reasonably well, but the radiator was leaking water, not just from the copper core but also from the cast aluminium top and bottom tanks as well as the side panels. These had become corroded and porous as a result of electrolytic action between dissimilar metals, i.e. the cast iron of the engine block, the copper of the core and the cast aluminium coolant tank. So for a time this tractor was put into storage.

I then bought another Ferguson Brown, No. 39, on rubber tyres – but, of course, it had similar problems! Luckily, by that time Clive and Robert

John Chambers, ex-Ferguson Chief Engineer, sitting on my Ferguson Model A.

Lunn of Swinstead near Grantham in Lincolnshire had acquired, from the late Selwyn Houghton, a full set of original patterns for the cast aluminium components of the radiator. So I bought two sets as well as an aluminium quadrant for the hydraulic control lever and a cast aluminium steering wheel (the originals were pressed steel).

I had two replica radiator cores made up by Barnstaple Radiators, a most professional job. Now, with most of the parts we needed to rebuild both tractors I chose to start with the one with the rubber tyres, No. 39; more of that one later. The one with steel wheels, together with the new spare parts I eventually sold to Clifford Conibere of Crediton, Devon, a most capable self-taught engineer. Over time he has completely refurbished

this tractor himself including the machining of the new parts, and it now runs as Harry Ferguson had intended. From time to time he asks if my 16 in 1939 Ferguson plough is for sale – so far he has had a negative response!

Brief specification:
- Engine: Coventry Climax, petrol side valve; capacity 132.6 cu in (2175 cc); power output at flywheel 20 hp at 1400rpm
- Gearbox: 3 forward and 1 reverse
- Hydraulic system: Cat 1 three-point linkage with draft control only (pump only functions when the tractor is moving)
- Wheel base: 68 in (1727.2 mm)
- Weight: approx. 1848 lbs (8382 kg)

No. 8, Porsche Junior
1960s, Sold

I expect my motivation for buying this tractor stemmed from the fact that, at the time, I was driving a Porsche 924, the boys' model, which is now barn stored, and I was surprised to find that Porsche also produced agricultural tractors. I bought this example from a tractor collector living near Liskeard in Cornwall, who was selling off a few of his machines to raise some money to complete

the restoration of a steam traction engine he was working on.

The Porsche Junior was in a fairly poor state: its single-cylinder air-cooled engine needed a complete rebuild, which I entrusted to Chris at Kar Engine Services in Barnstaple, North Devon. Being a most competent machine shop man he was able to re-machine Fordson Major Diesel journal

The Porsche Junior came from a a tractor collector in Liskeard, Cornwall.

shells to fit the Porsche engine.

Robin Haughton and Peter Clarke resprayed the whole tractor and fitted it with new tyres, replacement lights, direction indicators and horn. An odd feature of these tractors was that the flywheel was oil filled. This, the makers claimed, smoothed out shock loads, and is not to be confused with fluid flywheels as fitted to vehicles with automatic transmission.

Perhaps I should mention that the range of four models produced by Porsche at the time all used the same cylinder block and head bolted to an appropriate crankcase with a corresponding crankshaft. This tractor, like the others in the range, had a mid-mounted PTO, or provision for it, used if necessary to drive a mid-mounted reciprocating mower.

I sold this and the other Porsche tractor in the Collection in early 2008 to a man living near South Molton, North Devon, who had a small collection of classic Porsche cars.

Brief specification:
• Engine: single cylinder air-cooled 4 stroke diesel; capacity 900 cc; power output at PTO 11.92 hp , at flywheel 15 hp
• Gearbox: 3 forward and 1 reverse compounded by high/low range
• Hydraulic lift: Cat 1 three-point linkage; position control only
• Tyre sizes: front 4.00 x 16; rear 8.00 x 24
• Wheel base: 60.6 in (1530 mm)
• Weight: 2575 lbs (1168 kg)

No. 9, Turner Yeoman of England
1953, Diesel, Registration PAF 425, Sold

I bought this tractor from the same man in Liskeard who sold me the Porsche. I bought it for its quirky V4 designed 4 stroke diesel engine, which appealed to me, and to some extent for its rarity – a bit of old England. When new, these tractors were nearly twice the price of a Fordson E27N. Their claim to fame was their quality, but in fact they suffered from many weaknesses and underwent no end of modifications.

This example was in a rather sorry state in that the engine needed a complete rebuild, which was carried out jointly by the late Ernie Luxton and Chris of Kar Engine Services, while the fuel injection equipment was overhauled and calibrated by Diesel Electric of Barnstaple. The exhaust silencer had to be remanufactured. The tractor was

Some autumn ploughing with the Turner.

repainted by Peter Clarke and eventually sold on to John Bownes of Cheshire.

Brief specification:
- Engine: V4, capacity; power output 36 hp at 1500rpm engine speed
- Gearbox: 4 forward and 1 reverse
- No hydraulic system
- Tyre sizes: front 6.00 x 19; rear 12.00 x 36
- Wheel base: 77.75 in (1975 mm)
- Weight: 4777 lbs (2175 kg)

The Turner parked by the front door of Lower Park house.

No. 10, John Deere Model B
1941 styled, Two-cylinder petrol, Sold

I bought this one because I was offered it! It was standing on a holding fairly close to the late John Moffitt's Hunday Collection in Northumberland. The man who owned it had bought an International Junior from a collector living near Market Harborough, Leicestershire. It was agreed that I would collect his 'new' International, take it up to his home, and then bring the John Deere

A John Deere Model B, similar to mine. This one belongs to Phillip Bragg's John Deere collection at South Moor Farm, Coldridge.

back to Devon. On arriving at his home we unloaded the International and loaded the John Deere. He then asked me if I would like to have a look around the Hunday Collection – what a great surprise, of course, yes I would, and what a thoughtful idea!

No work was done on this tractor back at Coldridge as it was a tidy example and obviously imported to the UK during the Second World War under the Lend-Lease scheme. I eventually sold it when I began to rationalise the Collection.

No. 11, Bristol Crawler
1948, Two-cylinder petrol, Sold

I suspect that my motivation for buying this little crawler was because it was powered by a two-cylinder Jowett Bradford horizontally-opposed petrol engine. The engine in the tractor was more or less the same as the engine fitted to the small Bradford lorry I once owned. That was my first four-wheeled vehicle and I learnt a lot about mechanics during the four years I owned it as a running restoration. In October 1959 I traded the Bradford in against a brand-new Morris 1000 Pickup, Registration No. XXM 572. I seem to remember that it cost £386 with no heater or any form of direction indicators, and that the passenger seat cost a further £7.10s. How basic can you get?

Back to the little crawler: I bought it from a retired smallholder living near Taunton who had decided to sell off his bits of machinery as at that time theft was an issue, his place being so close to Junction 25 of the M5 motorway. The tractor had Roadless rubber-jointed tracks and was eventually sold as part of the Coldridge 'sort out'.

Brief specification:
• Engine: Jowett horizontally opposed two-cylinder petrol side valve; capacity 1005 cc , power output 25 bhp

Brief specification:
• Engine: two cylinder OHV horizontal; water-cooled 4 stroke petrol/TVO; capacity 149 cu in (2400 cc); hand start; power output (claimed) at the belt 16 hp engine speed at 1250rpm. This engine is started by turning the flywheel by hand
• No rear linkage
• Gearbox: 3 forward and 1 reverse
• Tyre sizes: front Vee twin arrangement 3.25 x 22; rear 5.25 x 48
• Weight: approx. 3275 lbs (1485 kg)

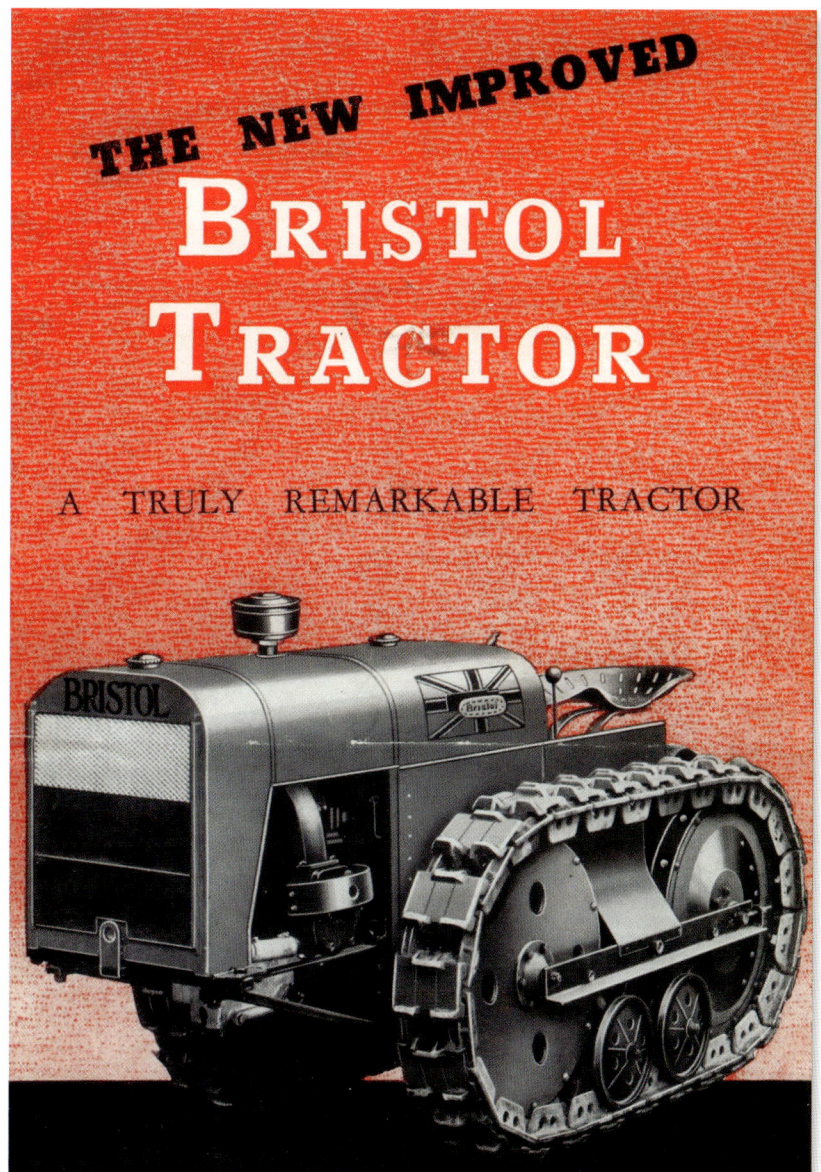

The Bristol Crawler was powered by the 1005 cc Jowett flat-twin engine.

No. 12, Oak Tree Appliances (OTA)
1950, Tricycle Model, Sold

I suspect that this appealed to me because OTA was one of many small firms trying to cash in on the expanding demand for tractors in the

The OTA was powered by a Ford 10hp sidevalve engine.

years following the Second World War. In my opinion, they all seemed to have over-optimistic sales projections. They had about the same chance of success as the proverbial snowflake in hell, especially with Ferguson producing the TE20 range at the same time. These little blue tractors were powered by a Ford 10hp sidevalve petrol engine coupled to a Ford three-speed and reverse car/van gearbox, which was compounded by passing the drive through a two-speed gearbox.

The radiator grille was of cast aluminium, and the steering of the single front wheel was linked to the steering column by wire ropes. Like others, I sold it to make way for more Fergusons.

Brief specification:
• Engine: Ford industrial Model E93A; petrol; side valve; capacity 71.49 cu in (1172 cc)
• Gearbox: 3 forward and 1 reverse compounded by 2-speed high/low range

All ready to go off to a rally aboard a Michael Thorne drop-side truck.

No. 13, Ransome Crawler MG2
1938, Sold

I can't remember whom I bought this example from, or why – maybe because it was the same vintage as me, or possibly because the horticultural side of the Agricultural College that I attended had one.

These little crawlers found favour with market garden owners because of their light weight and narrow width. This Ransome was powered by a single-cylinder air-cooled Sturmey Archer petrol engine (Sturmey Archer were more famous for their three- and four-speed bicycle hub gears). The tracks were made by Roadless Traction, whose patented rubber-jointed design was, of course, lighter than an all-steel design.

My most vivid memory of this little crawler is of getting it back to Coldridge, putting fresh petrol in the tank and cleaning the spark plug with the idea of trying out its capabilities on a steep hillside at Lower Park – but I never got that far. As I cranked the engine over it coughed once, which I thought was a good sign. The next time I pulled the handle up just very slightly, whereupon it kicked back violently, injuring my right wrist, which needed a visit to an osteopath to realign

A publicity photo of the Ransome MG2 Crawler.

it. Needless to say, I never bothered with the Ransome again and eventually sold it to my friend Robin Haughton, while making it quite clear what it had done to me! Interesting that it is numbered thirteen.

Brief specification:
• Engine: Sturmey Archer 'T'; 600 cc air-cooled 1 cylinder, output 6 hp

No. 14, Porsche Standard Star
1962, Sold

I bought this tractor from the collector near Liskeard whom I have already mentioned, to sit alongside the Junior.

The Standard Star models followed the same general outline as the Junior but were of a heavier build to handle twice the power. This was a well-equipped little tractor with lights, flashing direction indicators and the typical German-type adjustable-height and rotating rear draw bar, with mid-mounted PTO. It is fitted with a three-point linkage at Category I but is a simple lift type with no draft control. As with the Junior, the engine was totally rebuilt by Chris while Robin Haughton and Peter Clarke produced a fine paint finish, complemented by four new tyres.

I had one unfortunate experience with this when driving it to Coldridge Fete: the engine overheated because the thermostatically-controlled flap in the cooling air duct failed to open. As a result, the exhaust valve seat fell out of one of the cylinder heads, damaging not only the head but also the

piston. Luckily Chris of Kar Engine Services was able to sort it all out, but there was quite a bill to pay for that piece of work.

I sold this tractor in 2008 at the same time as the Junior, and to the same buyer.

Brief specification:
• Engine: Diesel twin cylinder air-cooled, 4 stroke, capacity 1800 cc; power output at flywheel 25 hp at 2000rpm engine speed
• Gearbox: 6 forward and 2 reverse
• PTO: Rear and mid-mounted PTO, both live in relation to ground speed
• Hydraulic system: Cat 1 three-point linkage, position control only
• Tyre sizes: front ; rear 11 x 28
• Wheel base: 79 in (2006 mm)
• Weight: 3420 lbs (1551 kg)
• Electrics: 12 volt, including lighting and flashing indicators

No. 15, Caterpillar R2
1944, Sold

This crawler came to the Collection for purely nostalgic reasons. The farm where I worked as a student, Little Stoke Manor, Oxfordshire, had two of them.

I noticed one in an open shed at Home Farm, Newton St Cyres, near Exeter, owned by Mary Quicke. My firm was there erecting a new cheese storage building for this well-respected farmer. Mary was happy to sell the crawler, informing me that it had been on the farm for a very long time. I suspect it was another Second World War Lend-Lease scheme import. I kept it around for a while in dry storage but later sold it to someone who was keen to buy it.

Brief specification:
• Engine: 4-cylinder water-cooled; petrol/TVO; capacity 221 cu in (3621.5 cc); hand start; power output at belt 31 hp; 1525rpm at full load
• Gearbox: 5 forward and 1 reverse
• No hydraulics
• Overall width: 40 in gauge model 52.75 in (1339 mm)
50 in gauge model 65.75 in (1670 mm)
• Weight: 40 in model 6120 lbs (2776 kg); 50 in model 6250 lbs (2835 kg)

No. 16, Ferguson FE35
1957, Serial No. SDF 52778, Registration No. YRL 668

This is a standard diesel model I bought from a dealer in North Cornwall in late June 1988. It ran but needed attention to the engine, brakes and wheel bearings, and of course it needed painting. All this work, apart from the fitting of four new tyres, was done by Robin Haughton and Peter

Clarke at Lapford, Devon.

On odd occasions it was called on to drive a 15Kw standby linkage-mounted alternator to power the workshop when there were electrical breakdowns in the days when we only had a single-phase power supply. It is now displayed with a Massey Ferguson

This is a standard model but at some point in its life it was fitted with a De Luxe seat. On the back is a Massey Ferguson fertiliser spinner. (Andrew Morland)

PTO-driven Fertilizer Spreader Type FE30. The hopper of these spreaders held 6.88cu.ft (0.95m3) of granular fertilizer. The joints in the drive shaft were Metalastic and were only able to accommodate small amounts of misalignment. Later types had a conventional PTO shaft.

Brief specification:
• Engine: Standard Motor Company; 23C indirect injection diesel; capacity 2259 cc; power output 35.9 hp at belt at 2000rpm engine speed; single clutch
• Gearbox: 6 forward and 2 reverse
• Hydraulic system: Cat 1 three-point linkage with draft and position control
• Tyre sizes: (on this example) front 600 x 16; rear 10 x 28
• Wheel base: 72 in (1828 mm)
• Weight: approx. 3150 lbs (1429 kg)

No. 18, Opperman Motocart
circa 1949

Well, this is the one that never got to Coldridge. Let me explain. I noticed this Motocart advertised for sale in *Tractor and Machinery* years ago at a site in Staffordshire. I paid the full asking price, which I seem to remember was £97.00, by cheque, but never got around to collecting the machine! So some lucky person still has a Motocart and my money, but that is entirely my fault. I expect the reason for my interest in it stems from having had a Dinky Toy model of one as a youngster, and I also tend to like quirky machines. For example, I once almost bought a Scammell Scarab and trailer from the late Colin Shears, who had the West of England Transport Collection based in the last remaining hangar on the old Second World War airfield at Winkleigh, Devon.

These little tricycle Motocarts were an attempt to replace a horse and cart with a mechanical unit. The single front driving and steering wheel was fitted with an 11 x 28 traction tyre and the machine was powered by a 6hp JAP (JA Prestwich) petrol engine driving through a clutch and three-speed and reverse gearbox. The driver stood to control it. The rear wheels were 7.50 x 16 and fitted with drum brakes. These Motocarts were highly manoeuvrable and could turn in their own length.

Opperman were a respected engineering firm with three sites near Borehamwood, Hertfordshire. I can remember as a young teenager my mother

had a rotary ironing machine that was designed and made by them. They also produced a range of rear wheel strakes for farm tractors to aid traction. They also attempted to produce a cheap rear-engined four-wheel motor car of very basic design; this was at the time of the Suez Crisis. The first and most basic design was named the 'Unicar' and their second attempt was a slightly more 'sporty'

My Dinky model of the Opperman Motocart.

version known as the 'Stirling' (perhaps so named as it carried sporting connotations, or because they had premises near Stirling Corner on the North Circular Road, London).

Brief specification:
- Engine: J.A.P (J.A. Prestwich); single cylinder; petrol; air-cooled; power output 8hp.
- Tyre sizes: front 11.28; rear 7.50 x 16
- Carrying capacity: 30 cwt (1524 kg)

No. 21, 1937 Mercury Tug Tractor
1937, Serial No. 3759, Age related Registration No. 415 YVH, Sold

I was attracted to this Tug, bought from Mr Nick Passmore, for two 'reasons': nostalgia, and the rarity of such a machine. On getting it to Coldridge I put it into dry storage for a few years until it was spotted by a visitor on one of our open days: Nate Hayes of Lapford, Devon, who took a fancy to it and bought it from me.

As for the nostalgia, this example was an ex-GWR (Great Western Railway) tug. I can remember as a child going to Paddington Station for our summer holiday trips to Cornwall and seeing these tugs, often towing up to six or eight four-wheeled trolleys loaded with parcels or passengers' luggage, snaking their way along platforms crowded with people — no flashing lights, as in those days just a strong blast on the loud horn by the driver was enough! The makers claimed a towing capacity of 7 to 8 tons.

When Nate became the owner he soon set about getting the tug into good working order so that he could take it to local rallies (slowly, as top speed was 10mph). Being a forklift engineer by trade

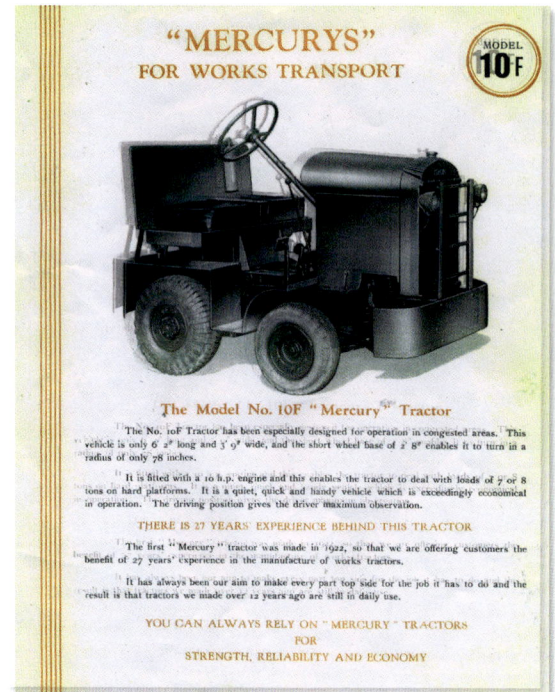

The ex-GWR Mercury Tug was sold to Nate Hayes, who has fully restored it.

"MERCURYS" FOR WORKS TRANSPORT — MODEL 10F

The Model No. 10F "Mercury" Tractor

he got stuck into the required work in his spare time. These heavy-duty little tugs weighed 23 cwt and had a pulling capacity of 7-8 tons. They are powered by a Ford 10hp industrial sidevalve petrol engine fitted with a B.W. Handy governor. Drive is taken through a dry clutch to the normal Ford three-speed and reverse gearbox. The rear axle is based on a Leyland Lion worm-gear type but built to a reduced track width. The brakes are on all four wheels and are cable operated. Tyre sizes are front 18 x 7 and rear 21 x 6. Electrics were originally 6 volt but are now 12 volt. Thank you for the use of the photographs, Nate.

Brief specification:
- Engine: Ford Industrial; 4-cylinder side valve; petrol; type E93A; capacity 1172 cc; power output 20 bhp at 2000rpm
- Wheel base: 2 ft 8 in (812.8 mm)
- Weight: 2576 lbs (1168 kg)

No. 22, Ferguson TE.F20
1953, Sold

I am sorry to say that I don't remember where this tractor came from, but I do remember my reason for selling it. It was in working order and stood at Coldridge for a few years. I was then able to buy a TE.T20 (see Coldridge Collection No. 65), a more unusual tractor, so decided to sell No. 22. The buyer was a budding young Ferguson enthusiast so I had the satisfaction of feeling that I was helping to foster his developing interest. I do wish I could remember his name...

Brief specification:
• Engine: Standard Motor Company; 2OC 4 cylinder indirect injection; diesel; OHV; capacity 2089cc (127.4 cu in); power output at belt 20 hp at 2000rpm
• Gearbox: 4 forward and 1 reverse
• Hydraulic system: Cat 1 three-point linkage with draft control only
• Tyre sizes: front 4.00 x 19; rear 10 x 28
• Wheel base: 70 in (1778 mm)
• Weight: 2700 lbs (1225 kg)

No. 23, French Austin
1928, Sold

I bought this tractor from Mr Coles, a tractor dealer based in Shaftesbury, Dorset, who also had a strong interest in vintage tractors. This Austin was powered by a 25 hp sidevalve engine, starting on petrol and then turning over to run on tractor vaporising oil (TVO). The steering wheel had a wooden rim and slotted side panels partially enclosed the engine.

Production of Austin tractors started at their Longbridge factory near Birmingham in 1918 but by 1923 an assembly line had been built at Liancourt, France. They built up tractors with parts supplied mainly by the Longbridge factory, but as time went on more components were sourced locally. Production continued until World War II, when the factory was taken over by the German armament giant Krupp. The director of the plant, Robert Rothschild, and some of the managers were shot by the Nazis, and all the records destroyed, or so I have read.

These tractors were very highly rated in the 1919 Lincoln Trials but their price of just over £300 made them expensive against the Fordson F, whose price was £225, but the Austin did have independent rear brakes to assist turning and like the Fordson it made use of unit construction.

Brief specification:
• Engine: four cylinder side valve petrol/TVO similar to the one used in the early Austin 20 hp car
• Gearbox: early models 2 forward, 1 reverse; later models 3 forward, 1 reverse
• Wheels: Steel front and rear with three types of bolt-on lugs for soil cultivation; steel spike lugs for grassland; rubber blocks for road use
• Weight: 3136 lbs (1422 kg)

No. 24, Ford 9N with Ferguson System
1942, 24hp TVO, Not registered

*A very smart restored 9N.
(Andrew Morland)*

Inoticed this tractor while my firm was erecting a steel-framed farm building for Fred Baulch, a dairy farmer at North Tawton, Devon. It was in a very sorry state, having been on his farm since 1942 as part of the Lend-Lease scheme. Nevertheless, I thought it would be a good idea to have one of these models in the Collection as it represents a significant development of the Ferguson system, brought about by the famous 'handshake' deal between Henry Ford and Harry Ferguson.

These models incorporated three important Ferguson patents that were not included in the Ferguson Model A. It is worth noting them here. First, the hydraulic pump on the Model A only operated when the rear wheels were turning. A Ferguson patent of having a constantly running layshaft in the gearbox (provided the clutch was engaged) meant that this shaft could run the hydraulic pump and power take-off (PTO) provided its clutch was engaged via its lever. The second patent was applied to the steering box and its double drop arms, which enabled the fitting of individual drag links to each front wheel swivel. The third patent to be introduced on these Fords with the Ferguson system was the swept back, adjustable-track front axle, whereby alterations could be made without disturbing the steering geometry. The key to this was that the central pivot point of the front axle is supported on a short shaft that allows the axle to move slightly fore and aft, but steadied by a radius arm on each side of the engine. This allows the front axle track to be adjusted in 4-inch (101.6 mm) steps from 48 in (1219 mm) to 72 in (1828.8 mm). To gain extra track width from 72 in (1828.8 mm) to 76 in (1930.4 mm) the front wheels have to be reversed on the hubs.

With Ford's expertise in mass production and the Ferguson's team with their innovative concepts, they were able to design and produce a most appealing tractor with the benefits just listed, plus, of course, draft control!

The head of its four-cylinder engine was taken directly from Ford's very successful sidevalve V8 petrol engine, and the differential was taken from a Ford truck. All the main dimensions of these models were carried over to the later TE20 and TO20 models. The Ford 9N in the Coldridge Collection is a later TVO model and has a slightly lower gear ratio between the engine and the layshaft to compensate for the reduced power output with the engine running on TVO. Harry Ferguson did not like the sidevalve engine, nor did he like the straight-cut gear wheels of these models, with selection being effected by the sliding gear principle. The later TE20s had a gearbox with helically-cut constant-mesh gears. The radius arms of these tractors were steel forgings, while the TE20s had a tubular fabricated type.

The electrical system was 6-volt positive earth. The starter was operated by a heavy push switch but had a linkage to the gearbox to ensure it would only operate with the gearbox in neutral. The dynamo's output could be adjusted by moving its third brush and had a built-in cut-out. The ignition coil and distributor were incorporated into one unit driven through the timing gear.

The 9N in the Collection would really benefit from a complete renovation. It was the first tractor I ever had painted, a cheap 'blow-over' by our local garage at my request! New Goodyear tyres were fitted to the front and some cheap

ones at the rear. Over time I was able to find a sound pair of steel rear wheels with lugs that are hardly worn. Also in the Collection are a couple of Ferguson Sherman two-furrow ploughs of the Ford Ferguson era, one general-purpose, the other a deep digger.

Brief specification:
• Engine: Ford; side valve; petrol/TVO; capacity 119.7 cu in (1962 cc); power output maximum at belt 17.5 hp
• Gearbox: 3 forward and 1 reverse
• Hydraulic system: Cat 1 three-point linkage with draft control only
• Tyre sizes: front 4.00 x 19; rear 10 x 28
• Wheel base: 70 in (1778 mm)
• Weight: 2140 lbs (970 kg)
• Note: 6 volt electrics fitted

No. 25, Singer Monarch
1953, Sold

These quirky little tractors were basically the same as the OTA (Oak Tree Appliances) tricycle models but were fitted with a conventional adjustable front axle that carried the smallish front wheels. These were introduced in 1952. My example was painted orange, which, I think, was the original colour. Singer took over the OTA business in 1953. No work was ever carried out on this tractor at Coldridge. I sold it on as part of the clearance.

Brief specification:
• Engine: Ford, 10 hp industrial; petrol, side valve; capacity 71.4 cu in (1172 cc)
• Gearbox: 3 forward and 1 reverse compounded by high/low range
• Weight: 1430 lbs (649 kg)

The Singer Monarch in storage at Coldridge.

No. 29, Oliver 80
1938, Sold

I can't remember from whom I bought this one, but it was in a clean and original condition. My guess was that it was imported into the UK during the Second World War as part of the Lend-Lease scheme. It stayed at Coldridge for a while until John French took a fancy to it and we eventually agreed on a swap; he had an FE35 diesel vineyard which was much more to my liking and suited the Collection much better (No. 47).

Brief specification:
• Engine: 4-cylinder petrol/TVO; capacity 298 cu in (4900 cc); power output belt 38.78 hp at 1200rpm engine speed; hand start
• Gearbox: three speed
• Weight: approx. 4800 lbs (2177 kg)

No. 31, John Deere Hi-Crop 60
circa 1954, Sold

I came across this tractor while on a week's visit to Florida with Michael Gibbings and his late brother, Tony. The Gibbings brothers were tractor and plant dealers based in Chulmleigh, Devon. It was their regular routine to visit a massive plant and tractor sale held in February at Kissimmee; I was told the site covered 350 acres. The sale didn't last for the whole week so we also had time to visit two or three tractor collections in the area.

One of the collectors offered to sell me this example and a further one (described next). This Hi-Crop 60 certainly caught my eye – its great height meant one had to climb up one of the rear wheels to get to the seat! The engine was a typical John Deere overhead-valve two-cylinder with a capacity of 32 cu in (5258 cc) which developed 38.2 bhp at 975rpm, with the benefit of electric starting, thank goodness. I eventually sold this on.

Brief specification:
• Engine: Horizontal twin-cylinder OHV; petrol/TVO; capacity 323.46 cu in (5300 cc); power output at belt 41.18 hp (tested)
• No hydraulic system on this example
• Tyre sizes: front 6.00 x 16
• Wheel base: 90 in (2280 mm)
• Weight: approx. 5600 lbs (2540 kg)

Ernie Luxton at the wheel of the Hi-Crop 60.

No. 32, John Deere BO Linderman Crawler
1938, Sold

As mentioned earlier, this tractor was also imported from America. These conversions by Linderman were based on the unstyled John Deere Model B tractors. I have a feeling I was told at the time I bought it that by 1940 John Deere had acquired the Linderman firm. I never used this Crawler so I can't comment on its driveability, but I guess they were generally used by vegetable growers and perhaps on steep vineyard sites. It was in a lightly restored condition. The Gibbings brothers bought several pieces of equipment at this Kissimmee sale, and these were shipped back to the UK along with my two items.

Both of these John Deeres stayed around at Coldridge for a few years but were eventually sold on to make way for another Ferguson MF.

During our stay in Florida we took a day off from tractor viewing and paid a visit to Walt Disney's Epcot Center, which I thought would have a theme park feel – but not a bit of it, I was most impressed!!

Brief specification:
- Engine two-cylinder OHV
- Bore 4.25 in (106.25 mm), stroke 5.25 in (133 mm), capacity 149 cu in (2.44 litres)
- Maximum engine speed 1150 rpm, output 16 bhp.
- Starting – by turning the flywheel by hand!
- Four forward gears and one reverse.

The Linderman Crawler came from the same sale as the Hi-Crop 60, opposite.

No. 33, Case Model L
1938, Petrol/TVO, Sold

This was an original tractor on rubber tyres which I bought from a friend, the late Ron Stanbrook, an ex-NIAE (National Institute of Agricultural Engineering) engineer. In the later years of his retirement Ron had used this tractor for road runs so it was in good working order. Eventually sold as part of my rationalisation.

Brief specification:
- Engine: Waukesha; side valve; capacity 132.7 cu in (2200 cc); power output belt 20.5 hp at 1425 rpm
- No hydraulic system
- Tyre sizes: front 5.00 x 15; rear 11 x 24
- Weight: 4150 lbs (1882 kg)

Ploughing with the Case Model L.

No. 35, International Mogul 10-20
1918, Not registered, Sold

Thousands of these robust tractors came to Britain during the First World War to aid food production.

Derrick Hackett and I shake hands on the deal.

This I acquired this tractor fairly early in my collecting days, from Derrick Hackett of Herefordshire, who over the years had accumulated some fine true vintage tractors. This example from 1918, if I remember correctly, had only been used occasionally over an eighteen-month period as it showed no sign of wear or rusting – just a nice age-related patination. It stayed around here for several years, much admired by visitors to our early open days.

Thousands of these robust and well-engineered tractors came to Britain during the First World War to help bring large areas of hitherto unploughed land into cereal production, thus helping to save the nation. I eventually sold this tractor to a keen collector in Cornwall.

Brief specification:
• Engine: Petrol/TVO; horizontal two-cylinder with exposed overhead valve gear, water-cooled by a large tank to dissipate heat
• Bore and stroke both 6.5 in (165 mm), belt horsepower 25 at maximum governed speed of 500rpm
• Clutch: hand-operated contracting type
• Gearbox: 2 forward and 1 reverse
• Weight: 7300 lbs (3311 kg)
• Width 60 in (1524 mm), length 147 in (3733 mm)

No. 36, Fordson Model F
1928–1932, Sold

I seem to remember buying this example from the late Colin Shears, who owned the West of England Transport Collection based at Winkleigh, Devon. I expect he sold it because his focus was vintage buses. (I'll let you, Reader, into a secret: I almost bought a Scammell Scarab and trailer from Colin that had been owned by the Exeter firm of Blatchford's International Removers.) I eventually sold this tractor as part of my great sort-out, but to whom I can't remember, though I understand it's still in Devon, at Honiton.

I have heard it suggested that Henry Ford took some of his tractor production to Cork to boost the economy of that part of Ireland, probably because of his Irish ancestry. Rumour has it that the long rear wings, each with a built-in toolbox at the rear lower end, were fitted to the tractors in an attempt to limit the degree of rearing up if the trailing plough were to strike an obstruction.

Brief specification:
- Engine: 4 cylinder side valve; petrol/TVO; capacity 268.5 cu in (4400 cc); power output at belt 21.09 hp (tested) at 1100rpm
- Gearbox: 3 forward and 1 reverse
- No hydraulic system
- Wheel base: 63 in (1600 mm)
- Weight: 3600 lbs (1632 kg)

The Fordson Model F at a rally.

No. 37, Allis Chalmers ED-40
1963, Sold

I acquired this fairly early on, the possible reason being that I thought that it would sit well with my Allis Chalmers B (No. 2 in the Collection). No doubt another influencing factor was that it was powered by the Standard Motor Company's 2260cc 23C diesel engine, which had an output of 41 bhp at 2250 rpm.

It had a single dry plate clutch, an eight-speed forward and two-speed reverse gearbox, and an independent PTO controlled by its own dedicated clutch operated by a hand lever. The hydraulic linkage system was constant running and referred to as having 'depthomatic' control. Although it was top-link sensing, the Allis Chalmers engineers must have been very careful not to violate any Ferguson patents; for example, control of the pump was on the output side. I used this tractor for a while at Pool Farm in the late 1990s; fitted with a homemade link box it worked quite well as a large powered wheelbarrow.

Brief specification:
- Engine: Standard Motor Company; 23C indirect injection (with heater plug in each combustion chamber); capacity 137.89 cu in (2260 cc); power output net 41 hp
- Gearbox: 4 forward and 1 reverse compounded by high/low range
- Hydraulic system: live with Cat 1; three-point linkage 'Depthomatic' giving draft and position control
- Tyre sizes: (on this example) front 6.00 x 16; rear 10 x 28
- Wheelbase: 76.5 in (1940 mm)
- Weight: approx. 358 lbs (1626 kg)

A sales brochure for the Allis-Chalmers ED-40.

No. 38, Ferguson TE20 Petrol
1947, Serial No. TE20 5148, Registration No. DUX 185

This tractor was bought from John Bownes of Cheshire in mid-1987, at the same time as the Ferguson Brown on steel wheels that is No. 7 in the Collection, so this one should have been No. 8! Mistakes happen even with the best of us, and there are a few more in the numbering sequence of the Collection.

It appealed to me because it looked like a reasonably complete example of an early Ferguson TE20, and those are few and far between.

In September 1987, Robin Haughton and Peter Clarke of Lapford, Devon, took on the refurbishment project for me. This involved decarbonising the engine, fitting new mudguards (ex-Army), new brake linings and a few oil seals; the expensive bit was repairing the radiator – £99.44 at the time. After Peter had completed the painting to his usual high standard, new Goodyear tyres were fitted.

It was a pity that one fault with the engine was not

The Continental-engined TE20 with with Mk1 tipping trailer. (Andrew Morland)

dealt with at the time, that being a slightly rattly camshaft. Unfortunately, on these Continental Z120 (their capacity in cubic inches) petrol engines the camshaft runs directly on bearings machined in the cylinder block, not on replaceable shells. It would have been an expensive process to sort that out. These engines have a pressed steel sump, an automotive type with no structural integrity. For a tractor application, Ferguson engineers had to overcome this shortcoming, so for speed and economy they chose the expedient of using a pair of ¾in (19 mm) diameter steel tension bars placed on either side of the sump. These were anchored at the rear to a pair of cast steel brackets bolted to either side of the bell housing, while at the front they were secured on the axle support bracket.

These petrol Continental engines were fitted with Marvel carburettors and 6-volt electrics. A quick identifying feature is the set in the down-swept exhaust pipe. It was claimed that these engines developed 23.9 hp at 2000rpm.

This tractor is now displayed in the Ferguson Shed, coupled to an early three-ton tipping trailer (F-J-A30), known retrospectively as a Mk I. Its design was an attempt to transfer part of the trailer's load to the rear wheels of the tractor. This concept was first exploited in the Ford Ferguson era, so it is not surprising that a similar arrangement was used in the early days of the TE20. However, as can be seen from the photograph,

It is a cumbersome system that Harry Ferguson and his customers were not happy with. The story goes that, to resolve this issue, Harry Ferguson asked Theo Sherwen, a talented inventor and industrial designer, to produce a better and more straightforward arrangement. He was given only ten days to complete the task but met the deadline, so it is him we have to thank for what is now the norm in tractor/trailer coupling.

I bought the trailer we now have at Coldridge from a retired farmer living near Wiveliscombe, Somerset. He was 94 at the time and had bought it new in 1947 along with a TE20, a two-furrow Ferguson plough and, later, a rear-mounted mower. Although the trailer was well worn with a half-rotted floor and missing side panels it was still in use and coupled to a Ford Dexta, so all the original hitching parts were in place – a great bonus. Because of the inherent problems of this early design and the fact that by that time all Ferguson trailers incorporated the Theo Sherwen patent, Harry Ferguson offered a conversion kit to update the early models. Therefore most were converted, but not this one!

On getting the trailer back to Coldridge it was clear that a new replica body was needed as well as an overhaul of the tipping ram and brakes, and a couple of new 7.50 x 16 tyres. I noticed that the towing bar was somewhat bent and happened to mention this to my friend, the late Harold Beer, whose response was, 'I have a brand new one you can have.' That cheered me up enormously. I gave the bent one to another friend, Ian Halstead, who was missing one for his trailer.

I did the fabrication of the new body myself but entrusted the painting of all the metalwork to Peter Clarke. The timber floors and sides on these early trailers were grey-painted softwood and can be seen on the previous page.

Brief specification:
• Engine: Continental; petrol, OHV.
Capacity 120 cu in (1966 cc); power output at belt 23.9 hp at 2000rpm
• Gearbox: 4 forward and 1 reverse
• Hydraulic system: Cat 1; three-point linkage with draft control only
• Tyre sizes: front 4.00 x 19; rear 10 x 28
• Wheel base: 70 in (1778 mm)
• Weight: approx. 2500 lbs (1134 kg)

The right hand side of the Continental engine showing the set in the exhaust pipe. (Andrew Morland)

No. 39, Ferguson Model A
Serial No. 88 Petrol, Not registered

This tractor was bought in 1986 from a man living in Dorset, but he told me it had spent its working life on the island of Jersey. When I viewed it we had great difficulty in trying to start the engine, but didn't spend much time playing with it; I just craned it on to my TK Bedford lorry and set off back to Devon.

Once back at Lower Park it stood around in dry storage for a few years until Ernie and I had a chance to fully evaluate what was required to bring it back to full working order. The list read something like this:

• Crankshaft regrind
• Main journals and big ends to be re-metalled and line bored, by a firm in Birmingham. Replacement cast aluminium radiator header and bottom tank and cast side panels, all supplied un-machined by Clive Robert Lunn of Swinstead, near Grantham, Lincolnshire
• New copper radiator core to be completely re-manufactured, including the correct fins, by Barnstaple Radiators
• New tyres; all the originals held air but were severely perished
• The BTH magneto to be overhauled
• Kingpins and bushes to be replaced.

So, Reader, you have an idea of the scale of the project Ernie was about to take on. Part-way through I felt it would be prudent to have a pair of rear mudguards made. These were, in 1937, optional fitments! Luckily, my friend Ian Halstead had a spare mudguard in his collection which he kindly loaned me as a pattern, so I asked Wildae Restorations to make up the sheet metal part, while the steel frames were made for me by James Kendrew, a most talented blacksmith from Dolton in Devon. At one point, Clive Lunn offered me a belt pulley and PTO drive unit, originally made as an accessory. Sadly, this example did not have the actual PTO shaft but nevertheless I bought it. It should be mentioned that Ferguson offered two types of belt pulley attachments: one a straightforward pulley, and the other incorporating a PTO drive selection controlled by a small lever on the casing, i.e. PTO, Neutral or Belt Pulley. I had the two petrol filler caps re-chromed along with the one for the radiator. After some deliberation I felt it would be better to leave this tractor unpainted, thus showing up the different metals used in its construction.

About 500 of the first tractors off the production line at David Brown's Huddersfield works were

The late John Chambers (Harry Ferguson's Chief Engineer of long standing) enjoying some ploughing with the Ferguson Model A.

powered by sidevalve Coventry Climax engines, with the design and dimensions closely following the American Hercules engine installed in the black prototype Model A built in 1933. On the Coventry Climax engines the spark plugs are not equally spaced. Later engines built by David Brown, who also made the tractors for Ferguson, had the plugs evenly spaced as well as a larger-capacity sump.

On all these models the hydraulic pump only operates when the rear wheels are turning. My tractor is displayed in the Ferguson Shed, fitted with a two-furrow plough of the same vintage. If I want to move this display I have to put the hydraulic control lever into the lift position, jack up one rear wheel clear of the floor, turn the wheel by hand and, hey presto, the plough begins to rise!

On one occasion I took this tractor with two others to a ploughing field day held in the Deer Park at Stoneleigh, Warwickshire. It was parked up on the headland at lunchtime with several of us gathered around it, including the late John Chambers (Harry

Ferguson's Chief Engineer of long standing). Two or three drivers wanted to take a photo of John on this Ferguson Model A, and this was duly done. I then suggested to John that he might like to do a bit of ploughing, his reply was 'Yes, I would like to do a couple of rounds.' Well, that was about 2:30 pm and he carried on until about 4 pm!

At the time he told me he had helped to assemble No. 88, the very tractor that he had been driving, and he was smiling like the cat that got the cream! Sadly, he died about nine months later.

Brief specification:
• Engine: Coventry Climax; side valve; petrol; hand start; capacity 132.6 cu in (2175 cc)
• Gearbox: 3 forward and 1 reverse
• Hydraulic system: Cat 1; three-point linkage with draft control only
• Tyre sizes: front 4.00 x 19; rear 9.00 x 24
• Wheel base: 105 in (2667 mm)
• Weight: approx. 1848 lbs (838 kg)

No. 40, Massey Ferguson 825
Serial No. 88, Diesel, Not registered

I came across this tractor when I was at the field day held at the Deer Park, Stoneleigh (see previous entry). I had taken along my Ferguson FE35 (No. 16), and my Ferguson Model A complete with its appropriate two-furrow plough (No. 39).

The MF825 was also taking part and I got talking to the owner, who lived in Derbyshire. He told me

The French-built Massey Ferguson 825.

he had been considering selling it, so I quietly made the point that if he did decide to go down that route perhaps he would let me know. We exchanged cards and carried on ploughing. He gave me a call about six months later confirming that he was now wanting to sell it and that he wanted it to go to Coldridge. I can't remember his asking price but I thought it fair bearing in mind that, although it was in working order, it would need quite a lot of work to bring it to a fully restored condition. However, it must be said that there are not many MF825s around in the UK.

Well, Derbyshire is a long way from Devon but I decided to drive up there with my Mercedes 1617 to collect it, on the way loading up a brand new 4WD Cherrypicker I had bought from the manufacturers not far from where the 825 was standing. I had an overnight stay and then back to Devon.

Most of the work that was needed on this tractor related to oil seal replacement, repairs to the sheet metal work and an overhaul of the electrical system. Two or three parts of the front bonnet trim were missing but my friend in France, Roland Pennaneach, came to my rescue and was able to find the parts needed, except for the centre vertical chrome trim – still searching for that.

These models were made in France and were in fact the precursors to the MF130. They were both powered by the Perkins indirect injection A4-107 engine. The version of the engine fitted to the 825 had an automotive pressed steel sump, so the French Massey Ferguson engineers had to develop a fabricated steel chassis that carried the front axle and engine; this in turn was bolted to the cast transmission case. For the MF130 a cast steel sump was fitted and the power output increased slightly. The gearbox was four-speed and reverse compounded by a high/low range; synchromesh operated on the four forward gears. Inboard dry disc brakes were fitted and the hydraulic system was built as an integrated unit that bolted to the top of the transmission case – so with the removal of 14 bolts the whole unit including the hydraulic pump could be lifted off.

As I have never used this tractor for work I can't comment on its performance or handling – sorry!

Brief specification:
• Engine: Perkins indirect injection; diesel A4-107; capacity 107.4 cu in (1753 cc); power output at flywheel 30 hp at engine speed of 2250rpm
• Gearbox: 4 forward with synchromesh and 1 reverse, compounded by high/low range
• Hydraulic system: Cat 1; three point linkage with draft and position control
• Tyre sizes: front 5.50 x 16; rear 12.4 x 28
• Wheel base: 71 in (1803 mm)
• Weight: 3115 lbs (1412 kg)

No. 41, Aerolift Small Forklift Truck, model 15 PH
Registration No. RFJ 999

Sales brochure for the Aerolift forklift.

I bought this small machine with a 1680 lbs (7620 kg) lift capacity from Beach Brothers of Exeter, who dealt in high quality timber but at the time also had a floor-covering side of the business. The truck had been taxed for road use and was even painted in their livery. I bought it because it was in good order, though not running, and thought it might be a handy little truck to have around the place. I hope that one of these days we shall return it to working order.

These little forklifts were powered by a Ford 10 hp industrial sidevalve petrol engine governed by a Handy governor to 3000rpm, giving an output of 26.8 bhp. Unusually for a Ford sidevalve engine, in this application it was fitted with an oil filter. The gearbox was simple, just forward and reverse, and drove the front axle. The rear steering wheels were independently sprung. Solid tyres were fitted front and rear. Hydraulic Lockheed brakes operated on the front wheels only. Hydraulic oil pressure for the lift and tilt rams was supplied via two control valves from an engine-mounted pump.

Brief specification:
• Engine: Ford; petrol, industrial side valve; capacity 1172 cc
• Gearbox: 1 forward and 1 reverse
• Tyre sizes: solid; front 24 x 5; rear 15 x 3.5 Dunlop
• Wheel base: 38 in (96.5 mm)
• Weight: 4100 lbs (1859 kg)

No. 44, Ferguson TE.D20 with Reekie Conversion
Sold

I can't remember very much about the background to buying this tractor apart from the fact that I bought it without viewing it first, which is not a clever approach! I had been told that it was a TE.L20 (Vineyard) on normal-size wheels. Well, when it arrived at Coldridge I immediately noticed that the commission plate had been tampered with: someone had tried to re-stamp the letters. It became clear that it was a Reekie conversion, and an early example because the trumpet housings had been shortened and then welded as the half shafts would have been (though I never inspected them) so all in all it was a bit of a disappointment. However, in due course someone came along who took a fancy to it, so that provided me with the opportunity to move it on.

Brief specification:
• Engine: Standard Motor Company; petrol/TVO; capacity 127.4 cu in (2088 cc); power output at belt 25.4 hp at 2000rpm engine speed
• Gearbox: 4 forward and 1 reverse
• Hydraulic system: Cat 1; three-point linkage with draft control only
• Tyre sizes: front 4.00 x 19; rear 10 x 28
• Wheel base: 70 in (1778 mm)
• Weight: 2400 lbs (1088 kg)

No. 45, 1950 Bristol 20 Crawler
Petrol/TVO, Sold

I don't remember from whom I bought this tractor, or to whom I sold it. There were two factors that influenced my decision to buy this compact little crawler. First, I felt it would sit well with the two Bristol Crawlers I already had: No. 11, with a Jowett two-cylinder horizontally-opposed engine; and No. 30, with a 10hp Austin sidevalve engine. The other persuading factor was

The Bristol 20 was powered by an Austin A70 car engine.

that this one was powered by an Austin A70 car engine, and my father had bought an Austin A70 Hampshire car in October 1949.

The basic car engine was modified for agricultural/industrial/marine applications by Newage of Manchester, who would install a belt-driven Weyburn mechanical governor and, if required, modifications to enable the engine to run on TVO. It is perhaps worth noting that the MH726 Combine was powered by a six-cylinder Austin/Newage, as was the MHF780 Combine, while the MHF735 Combine was powered by an Austin/Newage 1.5 litre engine.

Brief specification:
• Engine: Austin Newage; OHV; petrol/TVO; capacity 134.2 cu in (2200 cc); power output quoted at 22 hp
• Weight: 3000 lbs (1360 kg)

No. 46, 1964 Nuffield 10-60
Sold

I bought this tractor fairly early in my collecting mania phase, from a semi-retired farmer at Black Dog near Crediton in mid-Devon. At the time it was looking forlorn, with flat tyres, in one of his sheds. The owner explained it had been new when the family bought it and was used for many years, then at some point it had been involved in an accident (I can't remember the details) and the family decided they would park it up in the shed and not use it any more. Then I came along expressing an interest in it, so it duly passed into my hands. My interest was based on nostalgia, having used a Nuffield Universal TVO for a bit of ploughing at Nicholls Farm, Redbourn, Hertfordshire, back in the late 1950s. I had a memory of it being a very smooth running tractor – much more refined than a Fordson E27N. And, of course, I quite like BMC stuff.

This particular tractor, dating from the mid-1960s, had a BMC diesel engine, designated type 0EE (bore 100 mm, stroke 120 mm) with a capacity of 3.77 litres. Maximum torque of 170 ft/lb was produced at 1200rpm. Power output was just under 60 bhp at 2000rpm. These tractors had a primary two-speed gearbox forward of the five-speed and reverse main box, i.e. a high/low selection.

The hydraulic linkage incorporated top link sensing, giving draft control, as Harry Ferguson patents had by then expired. Twin Plessey hydraulic pumps mounted in tandem powered the system. I am pretty sure they were fitted with a mechanical lift lock to the rear linkage, thus taking the strain off the hydraulic system when in the transport position.

An unusual feature for a tractor of this period was a dashboard-mounted two-pin socket which would accept the two-pin plug of a Lucas inspection lamp. These were often found on quality cars of the period; in fact, the early Range Rovers were similarly equipped.

The Nuffield 10/60.

Brief specification:
• Engine: BMC diesel; capacity 230 cu in (3800 cc); power output at PTO 55.3 bhp at 2000rpm engine speed
• Gearbox: Splitter gearbox in front of the main gearbox gave a high/low range to the main gearbox with 5 forward and 1 reverse ratio
• Hydraulic system: Cat 2; three-point linkage with twin pumps and Nuffield's own type of top link sensing
• Tyre sizes: front 7.50 x 16; rear 16.9 x 30
• Wheel base: 78 in (1980 mm)
• Weight of Deluxe Model: 5040 lbs (2280 kg)

No. 47, Ferguson FE35 Vineyard Model
TVO, Serial No. VNM 281425, Registration No. 44 PYB, sold

This FE35 Vineyard model was restored by new owner, Mark Glover.

I bought this tractor in 1988 from the owner of a holding in Somerset because it was a fairly rare model, but I sold it when I had the opportunity to acquire as a swap a diesel variant (No. 52 in the Collection). The new owner was Mark Glover of North Devon, who, being a lecturer in automotive engineering, has now made a first-class job of restoring this example.

There is a question as to why this TVO tractor carries a commission plate indicating it is fitted with a Perkins A3-152 diesel engine, i.e. V = vineyard, N = A3-152 and M = dual clutch? All the other features of the tractor appear to be correct: fuel tank, dash panel with ignition warning light in exactly the correct positions. The Somerset registration PYB was introduced in April 1962.

Brief specification:
• Engine: Standard Motor Company; petrol/TVO, capacity 133.4 cu in (2186 cc); power output at PTO 27.5 at engine speed of 2000rpm
• Gearbox: 6 forward and 2 reverse
• Hydraulic system: Cat 1; three-point linkage; draft and position control
• Tyre sizes: front 5.00 x 15; rear 9.00 x 24
• Wheel base: 76.6 in (1945 mm)
• Weight: 2863 lbs (1928 kg)

No. 48, Massey Ferguson MF35X Vineyard Model
Serial No. VND 306832, Registration No. 523 PBW

I am sorry to say that I can't remember from whom I bought this tractor, but having the original registration document to hand I can say that it had been owned by a firm trading as Evesham Glasshouse Produce Ltd of Boat Lane, Offenham, Worcester (now trading as EVG) and first registered on 3 May 1963. One can only speculate that these growers chose a vineyard model to work between rows of vegetables, and possibly within the confines of, one would hope, a well-ventilated greenhouse!

I seem to remember being very pleased to find this example of a fairly rare variant of the MF35X. It was in a clean condition, but for me the downside was that it was fitted with standard-sized wheels and mudguards. This did not put me off buying it, though, so before any refurbishment work started I found a pair of the correct 10 x 24 rear wheels, though for the fronts the only wheels I could find

This 35X Vineyard model is displayed in the heptagonal tractor shed, fitted with a MF723 Post Hole Digger. (Andrew Morland)

at the time were 5.50 x 15, the correct size but factored equivalents which unfortunately did not exactly match the type MF would have used. The next big challenge was to find a pair of smaller shell mudguards. This had to wait quite a time until I was able to purchase No. 61 in the Collection, a TEL20, the Vineyard model. This was complete with its smaller wheels and mudguards, so the only option I had now was to ask Wildae Restorations of Braunton to help. I was on good terms with the proprietors, David and Bill, as my firm had built them a workshop and showroom to enable them to extend their facilities. I took a mudguard from the TEL20 as a pattern and asked if they could make me a pair of 'skins': I felt capable of making the brackets myself (the easy bit!). Needless to say, they produced a perfect pair, but they did have a few quiet moans about having to use such thick sheet steel!

Ernie overhauled the Vineyard's engine, fitted new clutch and brake linings, and several oil seals in the usual places. A friend of Ernie's sorted out the starter and dynamo, and Peter Clarke did the painting. We had a few bits either re-chromed or zinc plated. A new set of Goodyear tyres was fitted, along with a new battery, a new wiring harness and four new track rod ends.

The modifications made to achieve the dimensions of these vineyard tractors from the standard-width tractors relate mainly to the axle components, i.e. very short trumpet housings and half shafts. Likewise, the front axle beam is much shorter, necessitating sets in both radius arm and steering drag links so that these components clear the engine.

The vertical front side panels of the bonnet are cut away to give clearance for the swivel arms when they move from lock to lock. The other modification is the placement of the hydraulic control quadrants. These are arranged singly on either side of the driver's seat with the position control to the right and the draft control on the left. Vineyard models were usually fitted with a downswept exhaust.

This particular tractor is displayed in the heptagonal tractor shed, fitted with a MF723 Post Hole Digger, a Ferguson design made by Steels Engineering Products Ltd of Sunderland, Co. Durham. This PTO-driven implement is still occasionally used for the odd bit of fencing repair. Mine is the later model, with a spring-loaded slip clutch to protect the machine should the auger strike a large root or rock. The earlier Ferguson

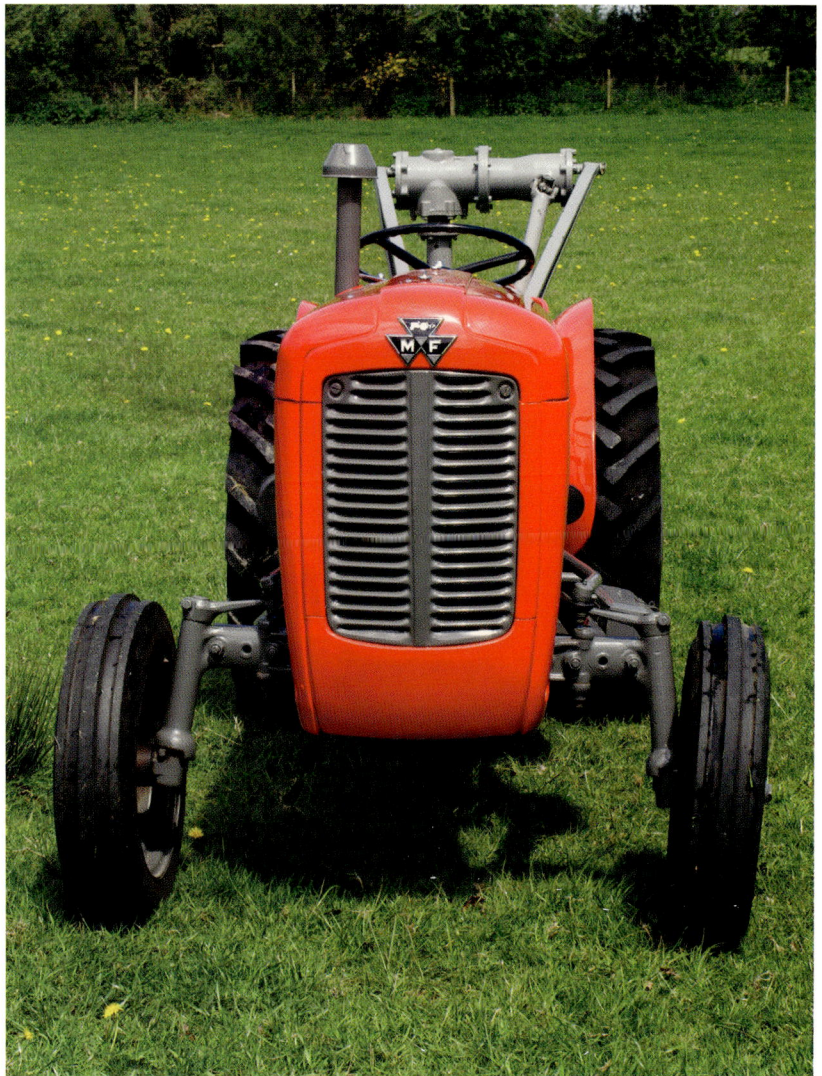

models had shear pin protection. We have the full set of different diameter augers at Coldridge: 6 in (152.4 mm), 9 in (228.6 mm), 12 in (304.8 mm) and 18 inch (457.2 mm).

I wonder if a tractor-mounted post hole digger was a Ferguson innovation, as they were being sold during the era of the Ford 9N.

Brief specification:
• Engine: Perkins direct injection; diesel; A3-152; capacity 152.7 cu in (2500 cc); power output at PTO 41.5 hp at 2250rpm engine speed
• Gearbox: 6 forward and 2 reverse
• Hydraulic system: Cat 1; three-point linkage with draft and position control
• Tyre sizes: front 5.00 x 15; rear 10 x 24
• Wheel base: 76.6 in (1945 mm)
• Weight: 3225 lbs (1472 kg)

The photograph makes it appear that the tractor is wider at the front. Front and rear track are almost the same. (Andrew Morland)

No. 49, Ferguson FE35
1957, Serial No. SKF 52100, Registration No. XTA 464

Around the middle of June 1995, a storeman at our local MF dealership, Medland Sanders & Twose (later MST Group), told me this tractor was up for sale. He made the point of saying that it was a most original TVO example, and that several people were itching to buy it. That comment got me fired up. This particular tractor had been owned from new in August 1957 by a lady farmer, Kate Hookway, who farmed near Exeter Airport. Following her death, her executors had ensured that someone was put in charge to keep an eye on things until the farm and its equipment were sold off.

I made an appointment to view the tractor and yes, it was in very nice original condition and was complete with a Ferguson Mid-Mounted Mower (MF779). I noticed its top link hanging on a nail nearby; it had never been used and there was still bronze paint on the ball ends. The rear tyres were Dunlop Fieldmaster originals, 98% good. The man in charge told me that the fronts were replacements because the originals had perished, and that the tractor had only ever been used for grass cutting. He also informed me that I would have to put in an offer to the executors. The quality of this tractor and the fact that the mower was included made me decide to put in a serious offer, which in due course was accepted, to my great relief.

I collected the machine and brought it back to Coldridge, where I fitted a new battery, cleaned the plugs and carburettor, and put fresh petrol in the tank and water in the radiator. The engine fired up almost at once, and when warmed up ran like the proverbial sewing machine. After running it for a while Ernie noticed a leak from the water pump – not surprising as it had stood dry for quite some time. We decided to fit a new pump and repair two small dents in the bonnet.

Now for my big mistake: in retrospect, I feel that this tractor should have been treated to an Oily Rag restoration but instead I was keen to have Peter Clarke respray it. At that time no paint supplier sold the correct shade of metallic bronze paint; the nearest match I could find was a BMC colour called Reynard which as it turned out was

A well-equipped FE35 TVO ready to cut the grass and to turn it.
(Andrew Morland)

The mid-mounted mower was bought attached to the tractor. (Andrew Morland)

way off the mark. A pity.

The tractor is now coupled to a British-built Ferguson Side Delivery Rake D-E-20. This implement is PTO driven and is very well engineered, with roller bearings at each end of the six bars that carry the tines.

In 1999 The Ferguson Club was invited to have a display stand at the Bath and West Showground. Four Southwest Club members volunteered to take on the challenge, and I was one of them. I made the suggestion that it would be pretty dull just to have a line-up of tractors and implements: what was needed to draw attention to the Club's presence was a working exhibit.

As it happened I had recently been given a photograph by an ex-Ferguson friend of mine, the late Keith Base, who had been an instructor at Stoneleigh and for a time had worked in New Zealand setting up a training facility at Norwoods, the main Ferguson dealership there. He was involved in the preparations for Edmund Hillary's expedition to Antarctica and was at the launch of the Ferguson FE35 range. The photograph Keith gave me was entitled 'The Ferguson Hydraulics and the Egg'. It showed a promotional stunt thought up by Keith in 1956 using the new tractor and a Ferguson Side Delivery Rake DE.F20, and the

ensemble was duly put together by the late Gary Billington. It was designed to highlight the fine control of the Ferguson hydraulic system. With the tractor engine running at a brisk tickover, the rake would slowly cycle up and down with one of the castor wheels apparently touching an egg at its lowest point. Of course, in reality there was a small gap between tyre and egg! My idea was to recreate this for our stand, all agreed and I had a FE35 and a rake.

Well, it is all very well having bright ideas but how does one turn the tractor's normal hydraulic system into one that goes through an up-and-down sequence automatically? 'Simple,' I thought: the position control lever is moved over a centre spring loaded like the toggle of a switch for up and then flicked back over centre at the top end of the lift for down. It was Ernie's dedication to a challenge that turned the idea into reality, which worked to perfection. We recreated the signage Keith had used all those years ago on his display, fenced the whole piece off to ensure no visitors got caught up, set the engine running at a brisk tickover, engaged the PTO, adjusted the height of the egg (which was not hard boiled but set in sand so that the castor tyre of the Side Delivery Rake just cleared it!). What was good was that, on the lift, the engine opened up slightly under the control of the governor, and on lowering, the reverse happened, so there wasn't a continuous note to the engine's exhaust; this is what attracted the attention of the visitors.

The Club was awarded second prize in the trade stand class. The HSE (Health and Safety Executive) took the first prize, which I felt was well deserved, but we had done our bit free of charge and not at the taxpayer's expense!

Brief specification:
• Engine: Standard Motor Company; petrol/TVO; 87 mm; capacity 133 cu in (2186 cc); power output at PTO 27.5 hp at 2000rpm engine speed
• Gearbox: 6 forward and 2 reverse
• Hydraulic system: Cat 1; three-point linkage with draft and position control
• Tyre sizes: front 6.00 x 16; rear 10 x 28
• Wheel base: 72 in (1830 mm)
• Weight: this basic model, 2890 lbs (1311 kg

No. 51, Ford Dexta Narrow Model
1959, Serial No. 957E 35258, Registration No. 346 YUY, Sold

I bought this tractor from my friend John French when he lived in North East Scotland. At that time it was pretty rough and the engine was totally worn out. It stayed around Coldridge for a few years and was eventually bought by my friend Andrew Green, who has a good collection of Ford and Fordson tractors at his farm in the parish of Coldridge.

Well I'm glad to say that he and his mechanic, Ron Leach, have brought this unusual model back to fine working order.

It is worth mentioning that the modifications necessary to bring the overall width back to 52 in (1320.8 mm) were carried out by Stormont Engineering of Kent. They were supplied by Kent Ford Dealers (KFD), of which Stormont was one.

These early Ford Dextas were powered by an F3-144 diesel engine, 144 being the capacity in cubic inches. The head, block and sump were cast by Ford at their Dagenham foundry and then sent to Perkins of Peterborough for machining and assembly. The crankshafts were forged in chrome molybdenum steel, with the journals induction hardened. The injection equipment was by Simms and featured an inline pump. The later Super Dextas had a similar engine but of increased capacity to 152 cu in, very similar to the Perkins A3-152.

Brief specification:
• Engine: Ford F3; diesel indirect injection; capacity 144 cu in (2360 cc); power output 32 hp at 2000rpm engine speed
• Gearbox: 6 forward and 2 reverse
• Hydraulic system: Cat 1; three-point linkage with Qualitrol (draft) and position control
• Tyre sizes: front 4.00 x 19; rear 10 x 28
• Overall width: 52 in (1320.8 mm)
• Wheel base: 73.5 in (1870 mm)
• Weight: 2950 lbs (1338 kg)

The Ford Dexta was sold to my friend Andrew Green, who has restored it. It is shown fitted with row-crop rear wheels.

No. 52, Ferguson FE35 Diesel Vineyard
1958, Serial No. VDF 74050, Registration No. SSR 121

Two views of the Ferguson FE35 Vineyard model. Note the cut-away bonnet sides to allow full movement of the swivel arms. (Andrew Morland)

This tractor came to Coldridge as the result of a direct swap of tractors between my friend John French and me. I had, at the time, an Oliver 80 (Coldridge Collection No. 29) and John had a rather tatty FE35 Vineyard, which I was very keen to have in the Collection, while John was eager to own an Oliver. Today we know the whereabouts of twelve FE35 Diesel Vineyard models; more may yet come to light.

About six years went by from the time that we swapped before Ernie made a start on the refurbishment of the tractor. Although it was well worn, it was complete, with the correct smaller wheels and corresponding mudguards. The engine needed a total rebuild. A new single clutch was fitted, new oil seals all round, new track rod ends, new brake linings, a new wiring harness, new battery, and a set of Goodyear tyres all round. The instruments were overhauled and the chrome parts replated. The painting of the body of the

tractor was done in a metallic bronze but that gave Ernie a problem. At the first painting we used Sparex Metallic Bronze, which when we had used it in the past had been a very good match to the original colour, but this time it turned out to be far too light. At the second attempt, using Massey Ferguson paint, it turned out better but still on the light side so it has been left at that, but it always irks me. This tractor is not yet fitted with an implement but one day I may come across something that would be appropriate.

Brief specification:
• Engine: Standard Motor Company; indirect injection; diesel 23C; capacity 137.8 cu in (2259 cc); power output at PTO 34 hp at 2000rpm engine speed
• Gearbox: 6 forward and 2 reverse
• Hydraulic system: Cat 1; three-point linkage with draft position control
• Tyre sizes: front 5.00 x 15; rear 10 x 24
• Wheel base: 76.6 in (1949 mm)
• Weight: 2866 lbs (1300 kg)

No. 54, Massey Ferguson 65 MkII Industrial
Late 1964, Serial No. JAY614176, Registration No. HCJ 826D

The MF65 MkII Industrial model lives in the heptagonal tractor shed. The radiator grilles are removed to show the power-assisted steering arrangement.

My 'reason' for buying this tractor was that it was an industrial model complete with front loader and bucket, and was equipped with the MF Instant Reverse Shuttle type transmission with four speeds, both forward and reverse.

I bought it from a fencing contractor operating near Leominster, Herefordshire, in late December 1992. It was all in working order, as the contractor had been using it to drive a linkage-mounted posthole digger, and had found the front bucket handy for carrying fencing stakes. He pointed out to me that having the Instant Reverse Shuttle meant that when the appropriate operating pedal was depressed to give reverse and the gear selection was in neutral, the PTO would turn backwards. This ,of course, would prove disastrous for most PTO-driven machines, but it was handy if the auger were to jam against roots or rocks as it could be wound out under power.

I remember my friend Robin Haughton and I collecting this tractor from his yard on New Year's Day 1993 with my Mercedes 16-17 lorry.

After a few months we set about dealing with the oil leaks, which necessitated removing the loader and its frame (not yet refitted). The gauges were sent away for repair. The sheet metal components and the wheels were all repaired and repainted.

New tyres were fitted front and rear. At one point I acquired a Bristol Duplex air compressor, which I have always intended to mount on the rear of this tractor. It would complement the front loader if that was fitted. One day, maybe...

These MKII 65s were fitted with the Perkins A4-203 direct injection engine that gave a PTO output of 54.96 bhp at 2000rpm engine speed. They were fitted with a single HD (Heavy Duty) 12 volt battery (2 x 6 volts on the MKI) thus enabling the fuel tank capacity to be increased to 14.5 gallons (65.9 litres). This example, being an Industrial, was equipped with mechanically operated drum brakes at the rear wheel hubs which were controlled by the handbrake: the normal inboard dry disc brakes were retained. Also, to comply with Road Traffic Act requirements, a horn was fitted.

This machine is now displayed in the heptagonal tractor shed with the radiator grille set to one side so that visitors can view the power steering arrangement.

Brief specification:
• Engine: Perkins A4-203 direct injection; diesel; capacity 203.5 cu in (3335 cc); power output at PTO 54.5 hp at 2000rpm engine speed
• Gearbox: Instant reverse shuttle with 4 speeds in each direction
• Hydraulic system: Cat 2; three-point linkage with draft and position control
• Tyre sizes: front 7.50 x 16; rear 16.9 x 28 12 ply
• Wheel base: 84 in (2133 mm)
• Weight: a bit over the standard Agricultural tractor, which is quoted at approx. 4158 lbs (1886 kg)

No. 55, Caterpillar D2
1940, Sold

My guess is that I bought this model to complement the Caterpillar R2 that was in the Collection at the time. The diesel models were very similar in specification to the TVO crawlers, apart from the engine, of course. The makers claimed a 31hp draw bar pull. To start these diesel engines Caterpillar employed a horizontal two-cylinder petrol engine, the coolant of which was common to the main engine, so in extremely cold conditions the petrol starting or donkey engine could be run for a while to preheat the diesel. As my example had a broken donkey engine I never had it running, and eventually sold it to a keen and enthusiastic buyer.

Brief specification:
• Main engine: diesel, capacity 221 cu in (3622 cc), power output at belt 31.9 hp at 1000rpm; Starting or Donkey engine: two-cylinder horizontal petrol develops 10 hp at 3000rpm, engages with main engine flywheel through multiple disc clutch and helical gears
• Steering: by lever operated clutch on each rear axle output shaft, aided by foot operated band brake
• Gearbox: 5 forward and 1 reverse
• Width: Standard was known as 50 in gauge, i.e. 5 ft 5¾ in; Optional width known as 40 in, i.e. 4 ft 7¾ in

No. 56, Allis Chalmers D270
1955, Sold

I bought this tractor because it was in working order and I thought that it would sit well with the other two Allis Chalmers tractors I had at the time. I did use it for a bit of carting for a short while, until it was sold as part of my rationalisation plan. The example we had at Coldridge was powered by the Perkins P3 144, 144 being its capacity in cubic inches. These units produced 31 bhp at a governed engine speed of 1900rpm. Also available at the time were a petrol-engined model rated at 30 bhp, or a TVO (tractor vaporising oil) model rated at 26 bhp, both at

1900rpm engine speed. The gearbox was four-speed and reverse, while the final drive to the rear wheel hubs was via reduction drop boxes. A novel method of providing independent PTO was by not having a dual clutch but instead, on the right-hand side high-speed shaft from the differential, a manually operated clutch controlled by a lever. With this disengaged, the right-hand wheel just ceased driving so that the tractor came to a halt but the PTO continued to drive. Front tyres were 5.00 x 15, rears 10.00 x 24, and PAVT rear wheels were optional – an Allis Chalmers patent.

Brief specification:
• Engine: Perkins P3-144 indirect injection; diesel; capacity 144 cu in (2359 cc); power output 31 hp at flywheel at 1900rpm engine speed
• Gearbox: 4 forward and 1 reverse
• Hydraulic system: Cat 1; three-point linkage with position control
• Tyre sizes: front 5.00 x 15; rear 10 x 24
• Wheel base: 75 in (1905 mm)
• Weight: 3500 lbs (1587 kg)

The D-270 was restored by Wildae Restorations of Braunton, North Devon. This company is a world-class vintage and classic car restorer. They bought it from me because a Belgian customer of theirs had recently bought a farm and needed a tractor.

No. 57, David Brown Cropmaster
1951, Registration MOD 198, Sold

I bought this tractor from a man who was a Rolls-Royce trained engineer and lived at Bovey Tracey, Devon. I think my motivation for buying it was because I had previously owned one for a short time in my early years of being self-employed – 1968/9. The mistake I made when buying No. 57 was not asking for it to be run up. Anyway, when it arrived at Coldridge it was put into dry storage and left at that. I eventually sold it to my friend Paul Delahoy in 1996 and delivered it to his home. Sadly, when he filled it up with coolant he soon found that

The Cropmaster loaded and ready to go off to new owner Paul Delahoy.

the cylinder block was cracked. Needless to say, Paul was soon on the phone to me, not a happy bunny! I apologised profusely and explained that I was completely unaware of this fault. I reassured Paul by telling him that there were two options I could offer. He could have his money back or I would have it professionally repaired. He chose the second option so I collected the tractor and took it to Ernie's workshop so that he could weld up the crack. That was the start of a super friendship with Paul that has developed over the years.

During Paul's ownership he tidied up the paintwork and sorted other minor issues, took it to several local rallies and went on a few road runs. He sold the David Brown in 2015 as he needed extra space in his workshop to make way for a massive restoration job on a Triumph Spitfire Mk III two-seater sports car, which he has now completed to a very high standard.

Brief specification:
• Engine: David Brown; petrol/TVO; capacity 154 cu in (2523 cc); power output at flywheel 31.7 hp
• Gearbox: 6 forward and 2 reverse
• Hydraulic system: Cat 1 and Cat 2 positions
• Tyre sizes: front 6.00 x 19; rear 11 x 28
• Wheel base: 74.5 in (1879 mm)
• Weight: 3740 lbs (1696 kg)

No. 59, Lister Gold Star
Approximate year 1960, Sold

I can't remember how I came to buy this tractor, but prior to my ownership it had been used as a towing tractor to launch gliders at a small airfield in Lincolnshire.

The story goes that Lister built up five prototypes and 30 pre-production examples (which were sold to Iran) at their facility at Stamford in Lincolnshire. The model was intended to be a simple tractor for developing countries.

My example was powered by a Lister HB2 engine, air-cooled, two cylinders, hand-crank start with automatic release to the decompressor. I seem to remember that they claimed it developed 21 bhp at 2000rpm. The clutch was a 9-inch (228.6 mm) Borg & Beck. The gearbox had six forward speeds and two reverse, and the rear axle featured inboard disc brakes, a differential lock and PTO, all marked ZF. It had a Category I hydraulic lift three-point linkage but no draft control. I have a feeling that the transmission and rear axle were taken from an Eicher tractor. The front axle was a fabricated adjustable unit, 44 in to 64 in (1117.6 mm to 1625.6 mm), in 4-inch (101.6 mm) steps track setting. The front tyres were 6.50 x 16 and the rears 11.00 x 28; to my eye, both front and rear wheels were Massey Ferguson types. The sloping bonnet was of reinforced fibreglass and hinged forward, while the front was shaped to allow the optional fitment of Lucas 7 in (177.8 mm) headlight units. I can remember visiting a man in South Devon who owned a Gold Star fitted with these lights as well as electric starting.

Progress would have been slow with the Lister and an MF35 aboard!

Posing for the camera with the Lister at a tractor rally near Dursley in Gloucester.

When I bought this tractor it had been painted all over with gold paint except for the wheel rims, which were red. During Ernie's full refurbishment of it we found that the bonnet had at one time been painted green, so that is what we chose. I eventually sold it in 2008 but unfortunately can't remember the name of the buyer.

Brief specification:
• Engine: Lister HB2; air-cooled; two cylinders, 21 bhp at 2000rpm
• Gearbox: 6 forward and 2 reverse
• Hydraulic system: Cat 1; three-point linkage but no draft control
• Tyre sizes: front 6.50 x 16; rear 11.00 x 28

No. 60, International Titan 10-20
1918, Serial No. TV1940, Petrol/TVO, Sold

I bought this tractor from Robert Coles, a vintage tractor enthusiast and dealer in modern farm machinery based in Shaftesbury, Dorset. It's thought that it was imported from Canada. When it arrived at Coldridge it was reasonably complete but needed quite a bit of work to get it running and presentable. I eventually sold it to Vivian Hockeridge of Landsend Farm near Crediton, a dairy farmer with a passion for old machinery. Being a capable self-taught engineer he was able to take on the challenge and over time sorted out the engine so that it ran as it should.

The major part of the work he had to carry out was the fabrication of the new sheet metal gear covers as well as some sensitive repairs to the mudguards. The other issue he had to deal with concerned the re-manufacture of both the front wheel hubs and bearings.

New owner Vivian Hockeridge, of Landsend Farm near Crediton, restored the Titan.

He certainly achieved his objectives, as the photograph shows.

It's reckoned that about 3,000 examples of this model were imported to Britain during the First World War to help boost food production. Of the 180 farm tractors operating in Kent at that time, 112 were Titans, a clear indication of superior performance.

Brief specification:
• Engine: 2 cylinder horizontal with a 6.5 in (165 mm) bore and an 8 in (203 mm) stroke which ran at 575rpm producing 10 hp at the drawbar and 20 hp at the pulley; capacity 326.76 cu in (5354.6 cu cm); starting on petrol and running on TVO
• Gearbox: 2 forward and 1 reverse, with exposed chain to the rear wheels
• Cooling from a large header tank holding 39 gallons of water
• Weight about 6000 lbs (2721.5 kg)

No. 61, Ferguson TE.L20
1954, Serial No. 214969, Registration No. RYC 244

I bought this vineyard model on 16 April 1992 following a tip-off that it was for sale. The vendor was a Mr Gillman, who owned a fruit farm at Washford in Somerset. Needless to say, I was keen to have this example in the Collection so I promptly drove to Washford with the Land Rover and trailer (perhaps not the best way to get a good deal as it gave away my level of interest in buying it!), but two trips to Washford would have cost time and money. Mr Gillman seemed glad it was going to be refurbished and displayed with a collection to be shared with others. If you look at the photograph taken when it came to Coldridge you will be able to judge its condition – well, cosmetically anyway.

Before going on to look at the work that first the late Ernie and then Peter put into this tractor, I think it will be worthwhile to outline the engineering modifications that had to be made to achieve a front track width of 37 in (940 mm) and rear 32 in (813 mm) while at the same time creating a machine that was reasonably stable. This was achieved by lowering the centre of gravity by having 5.00 x 15 tyres front and 9.00 x 24 rear. To enable the front wheels to clear the bonnet when put on full lock, the bonnet hinge bracket was extended by 3.75 in (95.2 mm) and the same amount of sheet metal was added at the rear of the bonnet to ensure that it closed down to meet the dash panel; the fan guard was also extended by a similar amount. I think that this bit of extra bonnet length and its lower height improves the aesthetics of the tractor but then, as they say, 'beauty is in the eye of the beholder'.

Both the centre and the two outer sections of the front axle beam are much shorter than standard. Both of the radius arms as well as the track rods have pronounced sets in them. The

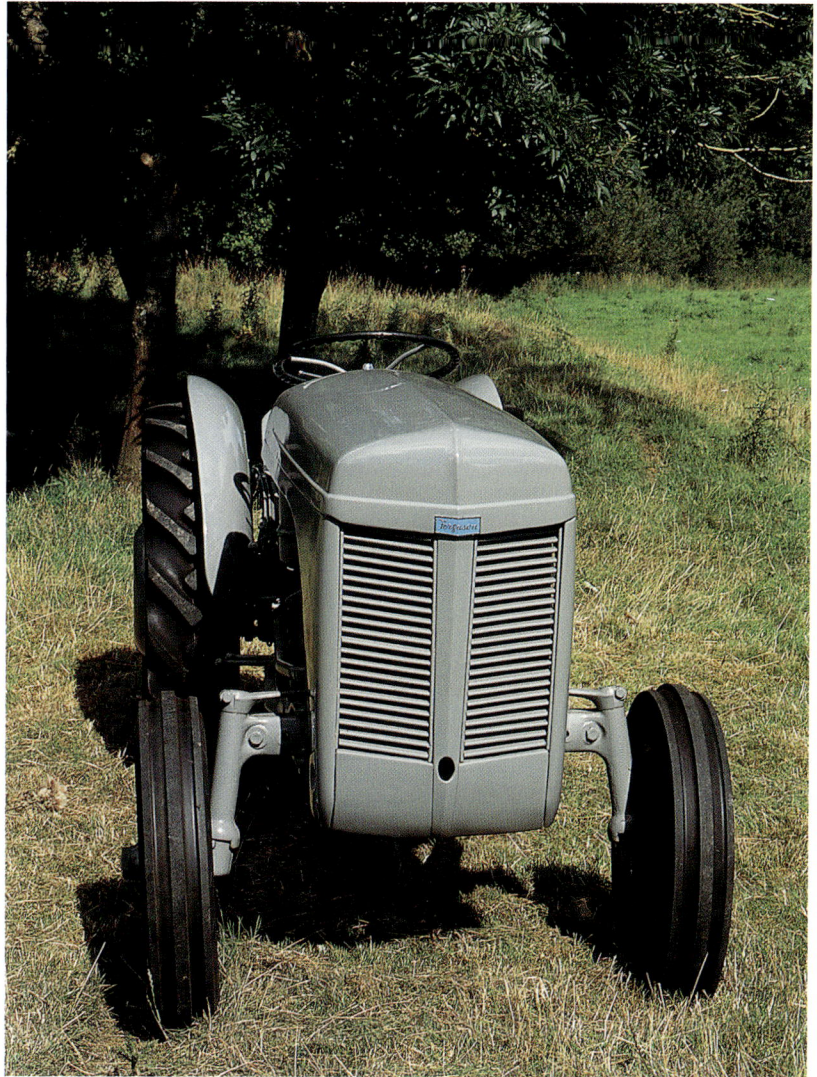

My TEL20 showing off how slim it is. The front track is 37 inches, the rear is a little narrower at 32 inches. (Andrew Morland)

Showing the features of its rear linkage. The hydraulic lift arms are straight and the lower links have sets near the rear ball ends. A special 9-hole draw bar was produced for these models. (Andrew Morland)

two swivel arms are 1 in (25.4 mm) shorter than standard. Both trumpet housings and half shafts are shortened by 9 in (228.6 mm). The hydraulic lift arms are straight and the lower links have sets near the rear ball ends. A special 9-hole draw bar was produced for these models, with an effective length of 16 in (406 mm). The standard is 26 in (660 mm) but the holes at each end are slightly countersunk on each face, intended for the attachment of special implements. Yet another change is that the levelling box crank handle was extended so that it cleared the mudguards, which were specially fabricated to take into account the smaller rear wheels. The mudguards were made longer on the front leading edge to give protection to the driver's feet, bearing in mind the close proximity to the tyres. The hubs for the front wheels do not have the normal projecting 1 1/16 in (27 mm) square ends but are made flatter with a hexagonal shape of 2⅛in (51mm) across the flats. I wonder if Ferguson ever produced a spanner of that size – or perhaps that is why an

adjustable spanner was included in the tool kit. The brake pedals are very similar to the standard type but were made more or less straight to keep them close to the transmission case. The final modification to note is that the dynamo had to be moved closer to the engine, which necessitated a cut-out in the aluminium heat shield.

To bring this somewhat unusual tractor back into good condition, Ernie rebuilt the engine, fitted a new clutch and brake linings as well as numerous oil seals, adjusted the steering box and fitted four new track rod ends. An overhaul of the starter and dynamo was carried out and a new wiring harness was eventually installed. All the sheet metal work and wheel rims and centres were shot blasted prior to Peter doing the respray to his usual high standard. New Goodyear tyres were fitted front and rear.

I forgot to mention that this tractor had been fitted with a Howard reduction unit, so with that engaged and its smaller rear wheels it would stand a very good chance of winning a slow-speed race. These units were designed primarily to enable TE20s to operate the Howard Rotovator they had designed specifically for the grey Ferguson. This was a very neat unit installed within the transmission case directly behind the gearbox, and replaced the normal drive shaft to the rear axle. The reduction was achieved by the engagement of sliding spur gears, selected by a lever mounted on the right-hand side of the transmission case, which is mounted on a special circular casting that replaces the standard type that holds the dipstick; obviously, this feature was retained in the Howard version. The only drawback to this accessory is that excessive torque can give rise to broken gear teeth within the unit. There is no overload protection. You have been warned...

Brief specification:
• Engine: Standard Motor Company; Petrol/TVO (85mm); capacity 127.4 cu in (2088 cc); power output at belt 25.4 hp at engine speed of 2000rpm
• Gearbox: 4 forward and 1 reverse. This example is fitted with a Howard reduction gear, i.e. high/low
• Electrics: This example has 12 volt electrics
• Hydraulic system: Cat 1, three-point linkage, draft control only
• Tyre sizes: front 5.00 x 15; rear 10 x 24
• Wheel base: 75 ins (1905 mm)
• Weight: 2480 lbs (1125 kg)

No. 62, Massey Ferguson 1020 Compact Tractor 4WD
Serial No. 4058, Registration No. B684 BFJ

I bought this tractor in the summer of 2000 from Donald Ladd of Crediton, Devon; a gunsmith by profession but a man who has always dealt in a small way with light farm machinery and workshop equipment. He has, over the years, sourced odd bits of equipment for me and his prices have always been fair.

I bought this because it's a handy working tractor and had very low hours on the clock – and it is 4WD. Donald had bought it new from our local Massey Ferguson dealer, Medland Sanders & Twose of Tiverton. At first it was used mainly to drive a small grass topper at my home, but now it is occasionally used with a link box for log collection.

Massey Ferguson introduced a range of three compact tractors in the late 1970s, designated MF1010, MF1020 and MF1030. They were the result of an agreement between the makers Toyosha of Japan and Massey Ferguson, and were styled to tie in with the then Coventry-built tractors. Although the photograph shows the tractor without a cab I do in fact have one, but sadly it is missing a door.

Brief specification:
• Engine: Toyosha 3-cylinder, indirect injection; capacity 68.7 cu in (1126 cc); power output at flywheel 21 hp at 2350rpm
• Gearbox: 12 forward and 4 reverse
• Hydraulic system: Cat 1 three-point linkage, position control only; constant running pump
• Tyre sizes: front 8.50 x 25 Turf; rear 8.3 x 24 Turf
• Wheel base: 56.5 in (1435 mm)
• Weight: approx. 1898 lbs (861 kg)

My friend Rupert Gill on the MF1020 with his son on my lap (he's now finishing university) coming to terms with my Kubota G18 diesel grass cutter.

No. 63, BMC Mini Tractor De Luxe Model
Serial No. 16D3097, Registration No. YTA 179E

Posing outside the heptagonal tractor shed on the BMC Mini Tractor.

I added this tractor to my Ferguson collection in the mid-1990s because I had just established that it was Tractor Research (part of Harry Ferguson Research) that had been responsible for the design and development of the early prototypes.

I felt it would sit well in the Collection following a rebuild by Ernie Luxton. It was finished in Ferguson Grey to emphasize the connection, rather than the correct BMC orange. Little did I know then that one day I would be able to buy the first of a batch of four prototypes produced and evaluated by Tractor Research for the British Motor Corporation (BMC) (Coldridge Collection No. 92).

I first saw this tractor when it was on display at Thornfalcon Classics near Taunton, Somerset, a business specialising in buying, restoring and selling interesting older vehicles and related artefacts. My memory of it then was that it was in a tidy condition, though the tyres were pretty worn. However, it had been fitted with a BMC A Series 948cc petrol engine, obviously taken directly from a road vehicle as it was not fitted with a governor, just a direct linkage from the hand throttle on the dash to the carburettor – not really suitable for agricultural applications!

Steve of Thornfalcon Classics eventually sold the Mini Tractor to another dealer, who in turn sold it to a market gardener in the Torquay area. Later, Steve somehow learned that it was up for sale again and took the trouble to contact me with its price and location. This time I decided to buy it even though it had the wrong engine. So I went to collect it, found it standing in a polytunnel, and brought it back to Coldridge. It should be noted at this point that BMC did offer a petrol engine as an alternative to the normal diesel, but that engine was not an automotive unit. It was in fact a conversion of a diesel to run on petrol. The block, sump, crankshaft and connecting rods were all as per the diesel, but it obviously had a different head, special pistons, and induction/exhaust manifolds. It had a Zenith 26 VME carburettor, a Lucas distributor and a cable-driven Weyburn governor, its drive taken off through a special right-angle drive gear from the front of the timing cover.

Now back to the tractor. Luckily for me it was still in reasonable shape apart from having the wrong engine and worn tyres. I was able to source a replacement diesel engine as a box of bits from Wyard Scott near Bury St Edmunds, who at the time specialised in BMC Mini Tractors. On checking the contents of the box, all the wearing parts needed machining or replacing: crankshaft, dry liners, pistons, etc. However, there were no major parts missing; a positive start.

The engine work was carried out by Chris of Kar Engine Services of Barnstaple, while Ernie dealt with other necessary repairs: brake discs, sorting out the hydraulic lift which, by the way, bolts as a single unit to the rear axle casing. This unit does not incorporate draft control but does use an early Ferguson System of having five different height settings for the forward ends of the lower links. This arrangement, according to ploughmen who use Mini Tractors, seems to work pretty well. There is a lift lock on the three-point linkage.

Brief specifications:
Basic model
• Engine: water-cooled four-cylinder of 2.478 in (62.94 mm) bore and 3.0 in (76.2 mm) stroke, capacity 57.9 cu in (948cc), compression ratio 22.5:1
• Power output often mentioned as 15 bhp
• Heater plugs fitted to each combustion chamber (it needs a lot of pre-heat to start it!)
• AC fuel lift pump, injector pump CAV DPA type
• Fuel tank capacity 6.5 gallons (29.6 litres)
• 12-volt electrics, 67AH battery, positive earth
• Lucas pre-engaged starter, dynamo and control box, 4 heater plugs with warning light. Ammeter, oil pressure warning light, Tractormeter
• Steering and front axle have the normal Ferguson layout, with track adjustable from 3 ft 3 in (990.6 mm) to 5ft 8 in (1727 mm), in 4 in (101.6 mm) increments
• Clutch: Borg & Beck single plate 9 in (22.86mm)
• Gearbox: three speeds and reverse, constant mesh unit with integral high, medium and low ranges
• Final drive, spiral-bevel gear and heavy duty spur reduction hubs, differential lock controlled by hand lever
• Dry disc brakes controlled by three pedals, one for each rear wheel and the third balanced for both rear wheels; parking latch provided
• Wheels/tyres: front 5.00 x 15, rear 9.00 x 24; swinging draw bar.

In addition, the Deluxe model has Category I three-point linkage PTO, full electric lighting and ploughing light. Extras listed include pick-up hitch, rear belt pulley, heavy duty 109AH battery, tipping trailer kit, front wheel weights inner and outer, rear wheel weights, and alternative tyre sizes and tread patterns.

It has to be said that this was a good little tractor but grossly underpowered. Why such a small engine was developed and used always baffles me, since at the time BMC had a proven B-Series diesel of 1.5 litres (2.64 pts) producing 24.9 bhp at 2500rpm which was in fact introduced at the Smithfield Show in December 1968, just three years after the BMC Mini Tractor was introduced. The new model was designated 4.25, i.e. 4 cylinders, 25 bhp. By then BMC had merged with Leyland. This engine was 2 in (50.8 mm) longer than the 948cc units, so the radius arms and drag links had to be made longer, and the bonnet needed to be extended at the rear edge. Very few BMC Minis, or 4/25s for that matter, found use on farms, most models sold being bought by local authorities for park and sports field maintenance work, while some found favour with large private garden owners; one could say they were in fact the precursors of the compact tractors of today.

I must own up and say that I have never used mine for any real work, though it is nice to drive and the controls are well laid out – but it is a bit of a gutless wonder!

No. 64, Ferguson TE.E20 Narrow Tractor
1951, Serial no. 172038

This tractor came to Coldridge in 1993; it was bought at the Richard Smith collection auction. I didn't attend the auction for the simple reason that I don't like them, but my friend, the late Harold Beer, did, so he bought it on my behalf and no doubt several other items for himself. This example was in very nice original condition, including the tyres. I was told that it had been owned by a lady farmer in Somerset, who was obviously a careful driver because the hubcaps fitted to the front wheels of these models were still in place; one perfect, the other with just a small dent in it.

It was fairly early on, in 1947, that Ferguson offered a narrow model. A few were built with the petrol Continental engine and designated TE.B20. The later ones with Standard petrol engines were prefixed TE.C20, while the TVO models were marked TE.E20 and the export lamp oil models TE.J20. No diesel version was ever made at Coventry, but they were produced in France.

To achieve a track width of 42 in (1067 mm), compared with the standard 48 in (1219.2 mm), several engineering changes had to be made. It must be noted that when set to 42 in these models were less stable than a standard Ferguson, but their track could be extended back to the normal. The changes to the front axle involved shortening the centre section from approximately 38 in (965.2 mm) to 34 in (863.6 mm), while the two outer beams were reduced from approximately 20 in (508 mm) to 15in (381 mm). Sets had to be put in both radius arms and in the left-hand track rod. The independent brake pedals are different, to bring them in closer to the transmission case, while the standard circular foot pads are replaced by a straight flat metal pedal with an upturn at the far end near the wheel. The trumpet housings and half shafts forming the rear axle are also made shorter, by about 5in (127mm).

The narrow TE.E20 as it is equipped today. (Andrew Morland)

The lower links have sets in them at the forward ends, while the normal cranked handle of the levelling box is replaced by a tommy bar because of the restricted space. The point of attachment for the check chains near the PTO has a slotted arrangement to allow the chains to rise slightly as the lower links move upwards.

After my example had been overhauled by Ernie and repainted by Peter I decided to replace the standard rear wheels with a pair of row crop wheels shod with 4.00 x 36 tyres.

I already had in the Collection a Ferguson Low Volume Sprayer S-LE-20 that had been completely restored, minus the correct type of rubber hose; this was coupled up to the Narrow Tractor and I feel that together they form an interesting exhibit. Slightly later, Ian Halstead kindly gave me an Alman speedometer that included an odometer calibrated in furlongs. As it turned out, this is a pretty unusual accessory. It is mounted on the top of the left-hand side of the swivel hub and is driven off the inside wall of the front tyre. The drive can be disengaged by turning the drive pulley away from the tyre, rather similar to the system used on old bicycle dynamos!

Alman produced two versions of these speedometer instruments. The early type had a speed reading up to 15 mph (24 kph), while the later type, as fitted to No. 64, reads to 20 mph (32 kph). There really was a need to have a speedometer so that a forward speed of 4 mph (6.4 kph) could be maintained accurately, thus ensuring that the rate of application of the sprayed chemical was correct.

So who were the customers that required a narrow TE20? Perhaps large private gardens before the compact tractors of today arrived, vegetable growers, owners of apple orchards and vineyards. They were sometimes also found operating on industrial sites with restricted roadways. Why this Somerset lady farmer had one remains a mystery.

Brief specification:
• Engine: Standard Motor Company; petrol/TVO; capacity 127.36 cu in (2088 cc); power output at belt 25.4 hp at 2000rpm engine speed
• Electrics: This example has 6 volt electrics
• Gearbox: 4 forward and 1 reverse
• Hydraulic system: Cat 1, three-point linkage with draft control only
• Tyre sizes: front 4.00 x 19; rear 4.00 x 36 on this tractor
• Wheel base: 70 in (1778 mm)
• Weight: approx. 2397 lbs (1087 kg)

No. 65, Ferguson TE.T20 Diesel
1953, Serial No. 350692

I bought this tractor from Richard Smith in Somerset. It was in very poor condition but luckily it had retained its original front and rear wide mudguards, which were in surprisingly good condition. Ernie rebuilt the engine, and the starter, dynamo and fuel injection equipment were all overhauled. Most of the oil seals were replaced, as were the four track rod ends. The most difficult bit was sourcing the correct seals for the brake master cylinder and wheel cylinders, but Ernie's painstaking research eventually proved fruitful. To meet the Road Traffic Act requirements of the time, tractors used for road repair work had to be fitted with two independent braking systems, in this case one hydraulic and the other mechanical, front and rear mudguards as well as a horn, and this tractor meets all those requirements. The industrial models were fitted with wide foot

The TE.T20 with 3-ton industrial tipping trailer. (Andrew Morland)

The TE.T20 is fitted with a Tractormeter. (Andrew Morland)

Wide rear brake drums hide two sets of brake shoes – one set for the mechanical system, the other for the hydraulic system. (Andrew Morland)

boards and a tip-up seat.

This tractor still had the supplying dealer's nameplate affixed to the dash panel: Reigate Garage Ltd. There was evidence of yellow paintwork on the sheet metal work, so I would assume that it had been used by Surrey County Council on road and park maintenance, and for fun I have applied that lettering to each side of the bonnet. During its restoration, a Ferguson Tractormeter that I happened to have was fitted, as well as a lighting set.

This tractor is now displayed coupled to a three-ton Ferguson tipping trailer which features over-run brakes as well as a handbrake, leaf springs to the rear axle, and quarter mudguards to the rear of the wheels, again to meet Road Traffic Act requirements.

During the extensive restoration of this trailer I refitted rear lights and direction indicators as there was evidence of these having been installed in the past.

Why did I buy it? These industrial models are a bit of a rarity, so visitors to the Collection have the opportunity to view one.

Brief specification:
• Engine: Standard Motor company; indirect injection diesel 20C; capacity 127.68 cu in (2092 cc)
• Gearbox: 4 forward and 1 reverse
• Hydraulic system: Cat 1; three-point linkage with draft control only
• Tyre sizes: front 6.00 x 16; rear 10 x 28
• Wheel base: 70 in (1778 mm)
• Weight: approx. 3320 lbs (1506 kg)

No. 66, Ferguson FE.35
1957, Serial No. JDM 20515 (J = Industrial, D = Diesel, M = Dual Clutch)

I know nothing of this tractor's history. I was told of its existence by Richard Smith, a Ferguson collector from Somerset, who had bought it from a ground-care operator who looked after a playing field near High Wycombe, Buckinghamshire. Richard had paid for it but had never collected it and he offered it to me in early June 1993. I paid him his asking price of £700. Having paid for it and knowing that it was standing on an open playing field I was keen to get it back to Coldridge. I set off with my friend Robin Haughton in my Land Rover IIB Forward Control with ramps, a spare well-charged 12-volt battery, long heavy duty jump leads, and a new can of Easi Start! Our thinking was that even if the engine would not start we could override the safety start and wind it up the ramps on the starter, using the jump leads to charge up the battery on its way up the ramps. Luckily for us the engine did fire up and just about ran, so we were able to load using bottom gear. As we were strapping the tractor down we noticed the glass in all the gauges had been smashed. We took

turns driving back to Devon.

On getting it back to Coldridge, it was offloaded it was then left in a shed for about five years before Ernie began any repair work on it. As can be seen from the photographs, it had retained its wide front and rear industrial mudguards, a great bonus. The engine required a complete rebuild, and a new clutch, four sets of brake shoes and several replacement oil seals were fitted. The front axle and steering all required attention, with new bushes and track rod ends fitted. The fiddliest job was sorting out the hydraulic brake cylinders, but Ernie found a motor factor that had the right seals on the shelf. When he had dealt with all the mechanical aspects we had the sheet metal shot-blasted and primed prior to Peter working his magic touch with the painting. He used Massey Ferguson paint for the light grey and we found that Sparex produced the best match for the metallic bronze. New tyres were fitted, with grassland-type treads on the rear; unfortunately the old types of industrial rear tyres were not available. New

The 1957 FE.35 Industrial model. Note the front wheel weights. (Andrew Morland)

The MF737 fork-lift was made under licence by Fewsters of Stocksbridge, Northumberland. (Andrew Morland)

Goodyear tyres went on the front.

A quick résumé of the special features of the Industrial FE35 models. The wide mudguards were generally specified, and to meet Road Transport Act requirements a dual braking system was a statutory requirement. This was effected by having the footbrake operate the main brake shoes hydraulically. The independent brake pedals and the handbrake mechanically activate a second set of slightly narrower shoes within the same wide brake drums. In addition a Lucas horn was fitted to meet legal requirements.

When all the parts had been put together with great care we had a shining example of a fairly unusual Ferguson, so my next quest was to find an appropriate Ferguson industrial attachment to mount on the tractor. This issue was solved when a friend and Ferguson collector, Ian Halstead, offered me a Ferguson Forklift 737 made under licence by Fewsters of Stockbridge, Northumberland. This had a lifting capacity of one ton, but the front wheel weights were essential and we fitted them, but since this tractor arrived with a weight frame I tended to add a few 'jerry can' weights to be on the safe side.

When I purchased the Forklift from Ian it was in a tidy condition but sadly missing its tilt ram and all of the quick-release linkage that fits to the long pin and a special bracket under the driver's seat; it also forms one attachment point for the tilt ram. Luckily, Ian had another Ferguson forklift in working order mounted on one of his TE20s. He kindly loaned me all the parts mine was missing and I was able to commission Derick Lane Hydraulics of Exeter to manufacture an identical tilt ram. While this was going on I put my fabrication skills to use to produce the other missing parts. It all worked out very well, and after double checking that every part fitted I returned Ian's parts to him.

I really appreciated his help.

I also asked Derick Lane Hydraulics to overhaul the spool valve chest and supply a tailor-made set of replacement hoses. It should be noted that the tractor's lower links are not used to attach the forklift, and are substituted by a pair of shorter-length and heavier-section steel items without ball ends. There is also a facility to fit a trailer pick-up hook so that trailers may be towed with the lift in place, but the lift tines have to be folded forward into their transport position first.

The Ferguson Dealers publication No. 630, *Information for Your Business*, makes the point that if a 3-ton (3048 kg) Ferguson trailer is operated behind a tractor and forklift combination, the maximum load, evenly distributed, must not exceed 2.5 tons (2540 kg). There is no mention of this important fact in the operator's instruction book, bearing in mind that the point of attachment is 13in (330mm) further away from the normal coupling point for a trailer.

I have used this combination of what is probably the precursor of the rough terrain forklift and it does the job, but the steering is pretty heavy when driving without a load on the tines. The attachment, somewhat ahead of the times in farming perhaps, makes them quite rare today.

Brief specification:
• Engine: Standard Motor Company; indirect injection 23C diesel; capacity 137.89 cu in (2259 cc); power output at PTO 24 hp at 2000rpm engine speed
• Gearbox: 6 forward and 2 reverse
• Hydraulic system: Cat 1; three-point linkage with draft control and   position control
• Tyre sizes: front 6.00 x 16; rear 10 x 28
• Wheel base: 72 in (1830 mm)
• Weight: approx. 3200 lbs (1452 kg)

No. 67, Ferguson TE20 with Perkins P3 Diesel conversion
1947, Serial No. 2632, Registration No. CFX 408

There were two very good reasons for buying this tractor. The first was that it was a pretty early model that would originally have been fitted with a petrol Continental Engine but had been converted to a Perkins P3 unit. This was the early type, fitted with a CAV coaxial starter motor; later conversions had the engine fitted with the normal Lucas pre-engaged starter. The second reason for acquiring the tractor was that it had been fitted

with a Ferguson Epicyclic Reduction gearbox, model number A-TE-118, serial number 196.

When I bought the tractor it was in a very sorry state both mechanically and cosmetically, so it was necessary for Ernie to carry out a full engine rebuild, with parts machined where needed by Chris of Kar Engine Services of Barnstaple. Parts for these older Perkins engines are difficult to find, and when found tend to be expensive.

This photo gives a good indication of the extra height of the Perkins engine. (Andrew Morland)

However, Ernie's competence enabled the engine to be rebuilt to its original specification. A rebuilt and recalibrated injector pump and three reconditioned injectors were fitted. The starter motor was overhauled by a friend of Ernie's, likewise the dynamo and the Ki-Gas pump part of the Cold Start system (which I have never needed to use, instead simply using the excess fuel button on the injector pump).

During the restoration I decided to reconnect the Ferguson gear lever starting arrangement. As part of the conversion kit a button switch had been provided on the dash panel, along with a similar one for the heater element fitted to the induction manifold.

The brakes needed relining and new oil seals were fitted to the axle hubs. Four new track rod ends were fitted, along with new steering swivel bushes and a new pin and bush for the front axle pivot bearing. This sorted out the steering.

The main gearbox was okay and the Ferguson Epicyclic Reduction unit was in good working order, luckily for me.

The sheet metal work needed quite a bit of attention but new skins were fitted to the rear mudguards. The body repairs and the respray that followed were carried out by Peter Clarke, who was highly skilled in this area; in fact it was he who repainted most of the tractors in the Coldridge Collection.

The genuine Ferguson Epicyclic Reduction box (A-TE-118) is a rather unusual accessory and deserves further description. These units were installed on all three converted TEA20 tractors that Sir Edmund Hillary and his team drove to the South Pole and back in 1957/58.

This epicyclic unit is 4¾ in (120.6 mm) long, built to the same profile as the gearbox casing and fitted directly behind it. Accordingly, the brake rods have to be lengthened, achieved by fitting

short, screw-on extensions to the brake rods. This was all part of the kit, and the box requires the addition of four pints of oil to the transmission. These units not only gave a reduction option of 3:1 throughout the gear range but also had the benefit of having Live PTO and hydraulics in the low range. This was one of the first LPTO systems; I think one was available for retrofit to the Ford E27N tractors, but this was produced by an outside manufacturer.

On this unit, the brake band that is applied to the epicyclic hub to bring it into operation is activated hydraulically by oil pressure from the unit's own dedicated small, single-cylinder pump. This pre-set pressure ensures that the transmission cannot be overloaded by excessive torque because the brake simply slips and no damage is done to any other components. This is a better engineered installation than the Howard Reduction arrangement, which is dealt with elsewhere in this book.

There is another slight benefit gained when these Ferguson Epicyclic Reduction units are fitted to a tractor, in that its stability is improved by its extended wheelbase, not to mention making a bit more room for the driver. A Ferguson publication relating to this accessory makes the obvious point that the Manure Loader, High Lift Loader, Disc Terracer or Earth Mover cannot be fitted to a TE20 tractor that has been fitted with this type of reduction unit, because of the extended wheelbase.

The bonnet line of the tractors fitted with the Perkins P3 engine is higher than usual because the engine is taller, so part of the conversion kit is a sheet steel pressing to close off the gap that would otherwise be apparent between the top of the dash panel and the bonnet adjacent to the steering wheel. It is worth noting that the earlier Standard petrol engine had a power output of 23.9bhp, while the Perkins P3 engine produced 34bhp and with better torque characteristics!

This tractor is fitted with a Hydrovane belt-driven rotary compressor A-UE-20, marketed by Ferguson as 25C-FM. This example's serial number is 402. These compressors were designed primarily to operate one of two types of Marples handheld air-powered reciprocating hedge cutters. The larger model has a cut of about 32 in (812.8 mm) and is designed to trim farm hedges; at the far end of the knife there is a short saw to deal with thicker branches. It has its own clear Perspex guard to cover the blade when not in use.

The other unit is much lighter, intended to deal with garden hedges and topiary trimming. Of course, these compressors could also be used to drive other air tools, and for tyre inflation. What is missing, sadly, is the governor, which made the tractor's engine respond to air demand.

I have fitted this tractor with the Ferguson Dual Rear Wheel Kit A-TE-78 so that visitors can view this rather unusual accessory for themselves; I have not fitted extra rear wheels as that would take up too much room!

Brief specification:
• Engine: Perkins P3 indirect injection; diesel; capacity 144 cu in (2360 cc); power output 34 hp at flywheel at 1800rpm
• Gearbox: This example is the normal 4 forward and 1 reverse compounded with the Ferguson Reduction gearbox
• Hydraulic system: Cat 1; three-point linkage with draft control only
• Tyre sizes: front 4.00 x 19; rear 10 x 28
• Wheel base: 74.75 in (1890 mm)
• Weight: not known

No. 68, Steyr
Sold

I guess I bought this one because of its quirky appearance. Painted green and with a sloping (Snoopy) bonnet, they were often referred to as Frogs. I suspect I also bought it for its rarity in the UK and its unconventional two-cylinder water-cooled diesel engine. The other unusual feature was the sprung front axle. This was achieved, if I remember correctly, by having a conventional forged steel front axle with the wheel hubs attached to it by kingpins. A stout, semi-elliptical multi-leaf spring pivoted at its centre point to the front casting of the tractor. Each end of the transverse leaf spring was bolted near to the ends of the front axle adjacent to the kingpins. Sorry to be a bit vague about this one but, yet again, it was sold as part of my rationalisation!

Brief specification:
• Engine: Steyr; diesel 2-cylinder, water-cooled; 26 hp at 1500rpm
• Gearbox: 5 forward and 1 reverse; dry disc
• Tyres: front 5.00 x 16; rear 9.00 x 24
• Electrics: 12 volt battery
• Brakes: dry disc

The Steyr aboard a Mike Thorne Construction Mercedes lorry, ready for the journey back to its new home in Coldridge.

No. 69, Ford Super Dexta with Roadless Four Wheel Drive Conversion
Sold

This rare example, one of only 27 made (I have been told on good authority), was sold to me by a man from the Tedburn St Mary area of Devon.

I bought it for its rarity rather than its condition. It was in a very poor state, with a broken differential in the front axle, a worn-out engine, and very rusted sheet metal work. It languished in what is now the Ferguson Shed for a couple of years until one day a delivery lorry driver called at Lower Park, noticed my tractors and asked if he could have a quick look at them, which, of course, I was happy to agree to. He saw this rather sad-looking Dexta 4WD in bits and told me he had a friend in Lancashire who was building a small collection of 4WD Fords. I told me this one was for sale. The result was that his friend bought it,

and has now restored it. Some parts of the front axle were missing or broken, so the new owner had to have them re-manufactured. I had the opportunity to view this restored tractor several years ago and that made me feel it had gone to the right person. It is a pity I can't remember the man's name. Sorry!

Brief specification:
• Engine: Ford Super3, indirect injection diesel; capacity 152.7 cu in (2500 cc); power output at flywheel 39.5 hp at 2000rpm
• Gearbox: 6 forward and 2 reverse
• Hydraulic system: Draft (Qualitrol) and position control
• Tyre sizes: front, not known; rear 10 x 28

The Super Dexta with Roadless Four Wheel Drive conversion following restoration by its new owner.

No. 70, Standard Motor Company Prototype Tractor
Serial No. X671 or X672, Model Zero I

This is one of my favourite tractors because I like prototypes for their pioneering qualities and because this one is unique. I became aware of its existence at the 1993 AGM of the Ferguson Club, which that year was held near Bromyard, Worcester. The tractor was owned by a Club member, David Lockhart, who at the time was refurbishing certain MF tractors to an agreed standard set by MF prior to them being exported to Third World countries. David sold me this tractor and the remains of a

second prototype of the same design, but all that was left of that one was a rusting transmission case. Also included in the deal was a nice set of archive photographs David had obtained from the British Motor Museum at Gaydon, Warwickshire. These photographs illustrated Zero I undergoing field tests, both ploughing and forage harvesting, as well as some pictures of styling mock-ups.

David told me the story of this pair of tractors. The Standard Motor Company had sold the pair

to a scrap dealer in the Midlands, but on the way back to his yard the dealer sold them to a factory in Wolverhampton. At a later date they were sold to a farmer by the name of Dickson in Shropshire, who used them for twelve years and then laid them up for a further three years. They had obviously been worked hard, because the engine of the remaining tractor was not only very worn but also had severe cracks in the strengthening gussets at the flywheel end of the crankcase.

When Ernie Luxton rebuilt the engine we decided to replace the block with a second-hand unit, but I forgot to record the engine number marked on the original. If I had I could have worked out its correct commission number from Standard records with the information I now have. This was all in the spring of 1994. It should be noted here that Standard did go on to produce two more prototype tractors, known as Zero II, which were of a totally different design apart from being powered by the 23C diesel engine. These were numbered X677 and X678, the latter being owned by Robert Crawford of Lincolnshire.

The background information I have been able to glean from company archives and other sources is worth setting out briefly. Harry Ferguson sold out

to Massey Harris in 1953. Massey Ferguson (MF) purchased F. Perkins of Peterborough, the world-famous diesel engine manufacturers, in December 1958. Prior to that, MF had produced, on Friday, 1 March 1957 at Banner Lane, Coventry, an MF35 powered by a Perkins A3-152 engine which, by the way, had a single clutch. According to Massey

Unloading with my Climax Forklift.

Standard Motor Company prototype Tractor, Zero I, following restoration by Ernie Luxton.

Ferguson records, the last MF35 powered by the Standard 23C diesel engine was produced on Wednesday, 2 March 1960.

By the middle of 1959 MF had bought the Banner Lane manufacturing facility from the Standard Motor Company, who then moved their engineering development department to Canley, Fletchamstead North; while their engine manufacturing continued at Canley Road, Coventry. The 23C engines produced there were being installed in a few Standard Vanguard cars and vans as well as in some Triumph Atlas vans and pick-ups. They were also sold to outside manufacturers such as Allis Chalmers for installation in the ED40 tractor, in ungoverned form in some London taxis, and in the Jen Tug, a small, four-wheeled vehicle similar to the three-wheeled Scammell Scarab. Some of these 23C engines were also installed in Commer Superpoise delivery vans and pick-up trucks.

Anyway, back to Zero I. Following the Standard Motor Company's move to Fletchamstead North they very soon started development work on their own tractor, the Zero I. The design team was headed by none other than John Chambers and Trevor Knox, both ex-Ferguson men, and the workshop was run by Graham Stanley. The tractor was powered by the Standard 23C diesel engine. It is generally accepted that this engine has bad cold-starting characteristics. It was designed for Standard by Arthur Freeman Sanders in collaboration with Standard's own engineers. The cylinder head was of the Ricardo type, with heater plugs in each combustion chamber. This was considered too expensive for the engines installed in the Ferguson FE35, so the cold-starting aid became a single Thermostart device made by CAV and installed in the induction manifold. Generally, for other installations the four heater plugs were retained, as they were on Zero I. It may interest readers to know that on my prototype I have never had cause to use the heater plugs even when starting at 0ºC, so I wonder if the combustion chamber is of a different shape. In retrospect, I wish now that I had made a comparative study when Ernie was rebuilding the engine.

To move on from the engine, the clutch is of the dual type similar to that offered on some MF35s. The gearbox has four forward and one reverse ratio compounded by an epicyclic box at the output end. What is interesting is that both the gear selection and the operation of the reduction unit are controlled by the same lever. Great care is needed when making changes as there is a tendency for things to become jammed up. There is a feature to ensure that the gear lever is in neutral before the starter solenoid will operate. The rear end of the transmission is, in my opinion, very over-engineered but similar in layout to the MF65. Zero I has a distance of 11½ in (292 mm) between the axle trumpets, whereas the MF65 has just 9 in (228 mm). The brakes are dry disc, slightly different from an MF65. The PTO is two speed as well as ground speed, all controlled by one lever on the left-hand side of the transmission case. Immediately adjacent to this are the following cast-in markings: Stanpart 300007 (from what I can make out) and the Bean logo with the number 402504. Bean Cars had been taken over by Standard long before, but they continued as casting manufacturers, obviously for Standard but possibly also for others.

The hydraulic system offers both draft and position control virtually the same as the Ferguson system, but the two functions are controlled by the same lever, the mode of operation being determined by which of the two quadrants the lever is moved in: a nifty idea. There are tappings for external services, which can be brought into operation by a dedicated valve.

The front axle beam is taken directly from the TE20 parts bin, but the radius arms are not bolted in the usual position, instead being located by bolts passing through drilled holes in each of the outer sections of the front axle. The arms fixed to the top of the steering swivels are special forgings giving a distance of 5.5 in (139.7 mm) from centre of swivel to centre of track rod ball joint. On normal Fergusons this measurement is 6.5 in (165 mm).

The steering arrangement is an interesting one, and I suspect it was designed to circumnavigate Harry Ferguson's patent in that the steering box has only one drop arm instead of two, but it does have steering rods either side of the engine as per a TE20. The solution to this obstacle was achieved by Standard's engineers using an EnFo (Ford) single-drop arm unit to activate a lever that passes through a gap in the transmission housing, the ends of which are attached to the steering rods, and on the left-hand side via a short drag link to the single drop arm of the steering box.

The sheet metal work of the rear mudguards and footboards are taken directly from a Ford Dexta, the seat is an MF35 tip-up type with cushions. The bonnet looks, at first sight, to be a Ferguson TE20 but it is interesting to note the slats in the grille number 21 on each side and are welded in place, whereas the TE20 grille has 22 slats per side and are crimped into place. The bonnet hinges forward and is retained in the closed position by rubber straps on either side. The fuel tank and battery are covered by

the bonnet, but to achieve this the rear part is flared out, with the fuel filler protruding slightly above the bonnet line.

Not having done any field work with this tractor I can't comment on its performance.

To complete this piece, readers may like to know a little of the two later Standard prototype tractors known as Zero II with commission numbers X677 and X678, produced in 1961. These were powered by the 23C diesel engine and had a dual clutch, but in every other way were quite different. The transmission incorporated a forward and reverse shuttle box, with a four-speed main gear box as well as high and low range. The brakes were inboard dry discs on the output side of the differential, with spur gear reductions to the rear hubs. A two-speed PTO was fitted, as was a differential lock. However, the takeover of Standard-Triumph by Leyland Motors in 1961 sounded the death knell for any future tractor development, as Leyland had its own line-up of various tractors.

Brief specification:
- Engine: bore 84.14 mm (3.31 in), stroke of 137.89 mm (5.43 in) to give 2259 cc, (137.85 cu in) compression ratio 20:1, output 35.9 bhp at the belt at 2000rpm engine speed
- Tyres: front 6.00 x 16, rear 12.4 x 28
- Wheel base: 74 in (1879 mm)
- Weight: Not known

A nearside view of the prototype's Standard 23C diesel engine.

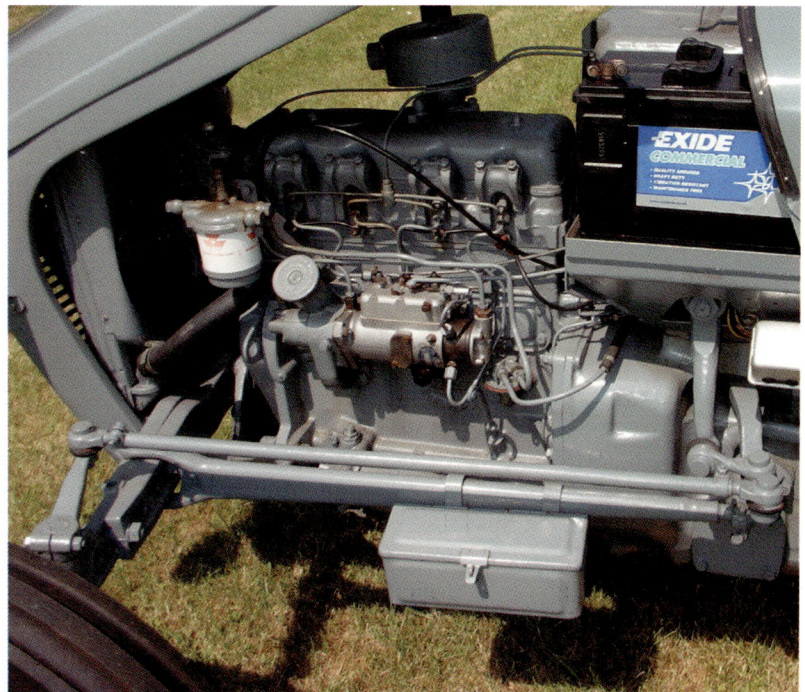

No. 71, Ford 8N 195 Petrol/TVO
1950, Not registered

I remember buying this tractor from my friend John French, who lived for a while in the North East of Scotland, which is where he bought it. Later, John and his wife moved to Devon, bringing his collection of tractors with them. These American-built tractors were never sold into the UK but were sold in the Republic of Ireland, and obviously a few 'escaped' across the Irish Sea. It's my guess that this example was shipped over to Scotland from Northern Ireland.

I bought it because the Ford 8N had become known as the 'Lawsuit Tractor'. I'll explain. The 8N was introduced in 1947 but was intended for introduction in 1948, hence the 8 designation. It was the result of Henry Ford's grandson (Henry Ford II) issuing an instruction to engineers to upgrade the previous model, which was the result of collaboration between Henry Ford and Harry Ferguson and their famous Handshake Deal. On the other hand, the 8N resulted in the famous five-year lawsuit in which Harry Ferguson eventually won a US$9.25 million settlement from Ford for violation of his patents.

Let us first consider the enhanced aspects of the 8N against the earlier 9N. Ford claimed that the 8N incorporated 22 new features, but here I shall list the major differences. The first was the provision of both draft control (which was an infringement of Harry Ferguson's patents) as well as position control. The selection of either mode was made by moving a small lever on the right-hand side of the hydraulic top cover. Thus draft or position was controlled by the same lever moving in a quadrant. Another improvement over the 9N was that the bonnet could be hinged forward to clear the radiator, just as on the TE20, but there was an openable panel in front of the steering wheel that gave access to both the petrol and TVO filler caps, the battery, and behind that a toolbox. A tip-up seat was provided, as were step boards to either side so the driver could stand if desired.

This tractor will need quite a bit of work to bring it back to working order, so my feeling at the moment is to keep it as it is.

Brief specification:
• Engine: Four-cylinder sidevalve petrol/TVO with steel sleeves, bore 3.188 in (80.97 mm), stroke 3.75 in (95.25 mm), capacity 119.7 cu in (1961.5 cc), compression ratio 6.5:1, belt hp 23.16 at 2000rpm engine speed. Cast steel three-bearing crankshaft, aluminium pistons with two compression rings and one oil-control ring
• Wheelbase: 70 in (1778 mm) (the same as Ferguson TE20 tractors)
• Draft and position controls
• Tyres: front 4.00 x 19, rear 11.00 x 28
• Overall length 115 in (2921 mm), overall width 64.75 in (1644.6 mm), height 54.5 in (1384 mm)

The Ford 8N – the 'Lawsuit Tractor'. Harry Ferguson won a $9.25 million settlement from Ford for violation of his patents.

No. 72, MF35 Experimental 32hp
1957, Not registered

An experimental Industrial MF35. It was obviously well-used at Banner Lane. (Andrew Morland)

I know very little about the background of this tractor, but will share what little I have been able to establish. The late John Popplewell, Ferguson enthusiast and dealer, offered it to me, indicating that it was an experimental model he had bought from a Massey Ferguson employee based in Coventry. I accepted this and bought it.

Later, I had the opportunity to buy a pre-production TEF20 with commission number EXP11 (Coldridge Collection No. 84). The vendor of EXP11 told me he had heard of a similar model, numbered EXP16, being owned by an ex-Massey Ferguson employee living in Coventry, and he gave me his name and phone number. I contacted this man and found that he still had EXP16, and it was he who had sold the experimental MF35 to John – a good bit of alignment there.

The former MF employee went on to tell me that the two FE35s were taken from the assembly line, one to be fitted with a Perkins P3 (TA) engine while the other (now mine) was fitted with a Dexta F3 engine. It is worth mentioning that the Ford foundry at Dagenham produced the head, block and sump castings for these engines. These components were then transported to Peterborough, machined and built up by Perkins, then returned to Dagenham ready for installation on their assembly line. The F3 engine is very similar in many respects to Perkins' own A3-152, the most obvious difference being that the F3 is fitted with Simms injection equipment while the Perkins

It is fitted with a Ford Dexta F3 engine, Note the traces of Ford blue paint. (Andrew Morland)

unit has injection by CAV. My own observation is that the CAV equipment, with its mechanical governor, gives a smoother running engine, while the Simms, with its pneumatic governor, tends to 'hunt'. Ford devotees may not agree.

Just to highlight the main differences between the engines, the Ford F3 is an indirect-injection unit with a capacity of 144 cu in (2360 cc), the same as the Perkins P3 (TA) engine. The Ford engine was fitted with cast iron liners, whereas the Perkins P3 liners were of chrome alloy. Ford claimed that their F3 developed 32bhp, the same as the Perkins P3. The Perkins A3-152 that was eventually fitted to the diesel MF35 had direct injection, a capacity of 152 cu in (2.5 litres) and an output of 45.5 bhp at 2250rpm. The capacity was the same as the later Ford Super Dextas.

This tractor was used for yard work around the Banner Lane factory at Coventry. Perhaps that is why it is painted yellow. There is a warning plate affixed to the rear right-hand mudguard, reading, 'No unauthorised person to operate this vehicle'. You have been warned! On the dash panel there is a serrated quadrant just below the hand throttle, as fitted to most industrial variants.

Brief specification:
- Engine: Ford F3; indirect injection diesel; capacity 144 cu in (2360 cc); power output 32 hp at flywheel at 2000rpm
- Gearbox: 6 forward and 2 reverse
- Hydraulic system: Cat 1; three-point linkage with draft and position control
- Tyre sizes: front 6.00 x 16; rear 12.4 x 28
- Wheel base: 72 in (1828 mm)
- Weight: approx. 3185 lbs (1445 kg)

No. 73, Massey Ferguson 135 Narrow
1968, Serial No. 96793

Another tractor I bought from my friend John French in 1997. He had bought it from Lunan Fruit Farms of Arbroath in Scotland. My reason for buying it was twofold: it would make an unusual addition to the Collection, and I also felt it would couple well to a 5-foot grass topper I had bought from John Popplewell. When the tractor arrived at Coldridge it was in a rather sorry state, and was fitted with a Duncan cab. As it was my intention to use it for grass topping among low trees I decided to remove the cab, which I sold on to a keen buyer.

Before the tractor could be put to work, Ernie Luxton totally rebuilt the Perkins A3-152 engine, relined the brakes, fitted some new oil seals where

Ernie Luxton rebuilt the Perkins A3-152 engine of the Narrow 135. It features Power Adjustable Variable Track (PAVT) wheels. (Andrew Morland)

needed, sorted out the electrics, and gave it a full service. The rear Power Adjustable Variable Track (PAVT) wheels were cleaned up, painted and fitted with new Goodyear tyres; the fronts (4.00 x 19) were well worn but left in place. At this time, the bonnet was resprayed but not to a high standard as this was going to be a working tractor both at Lower Park and at my home at Warkleigh. This Narrow Tractor is now displayed in the heptagonal shed along with the other MF100 series tractors.

The following modification was necessary to reduce the track width of these models. The rear axle trumpet housings and half shafts were reduced to 18 in (457 mm) overall, whereas the standard width tractor had trumpet housings of 22.5 in (571.5 mm). The front axle was, of course, made narrower, necessitating sets in the radius arms and the draglinks so that the front wheel did not foul them.

Brief specification:
• Engine: Perkins direct injection; diesel A3-152; capacity 152.7 cu in (2500 cc); power output at flywheel 45.5 hp at engine speed of 2250rpm
• Gearbox: 6 forward and 2 reverse
• Hydraulic system: Cat 1; three-point linkage with draft, position and pressure controls
• Tyre sizes: (on this tractor) front 4.00 x 19; rear 11.00 x 28, with PAVT centres
• Wheel base: 72 inc (1829 mm)
• Weight: approx. 3200 lbs (1541.5 kg)

The Narrow 135 is wider than the Vineyard model. (Andrew Morland)

No. 74, Massey Ferguson 130
1965, Serial No. SNMY 372598, Registration No. EUE 173C

These tractors were the smallest in the Red Giant range introduced in December 1964, and were imported from the MF manufacturing facility at Beauvais, France. This particular example was supplied new to a Mr W. F. Adcock of Wainsbury Wood Farm, Finham, Warwickshire, on 17 May 1965 – the day before my 27th birthday! I bought it in November 1995 in a rough condition from Peter Hawken, who lived near St Austell, Cornwall.

A huge amount of work was carried out by Ernie to bring this tractor up to its present condition. These models were powered by the Perkins indirect injection diesel engine A4-107, which sadly had a weakness in the cylinder head leading to cracking; mine had exactly that! We were lucky enough to find a sound second-hand replacement taken from a portable air compressor, so Ernie was able to totally rebuild the engine.

The brakes on these models were another weakness that had to be dealt with, along with new steering joints and the replacement of numerous oil seals. At the time that this tractor was refurbished, parts for the nose cone and radiator grille panels were available from our local MF dealer.

A positive feature of the MF130 was the hydraulic system, which was built as an integrated unit bolted directly to the top of the transmission case, so with the removal of 14 bolts the complete unit, including the pump, could be lifted off.

The reason why relatively small numbers of these MF130s were sold in the UK is perhaps explained by comparing the December 1964 price of £660 for a Deluxe model to that of a Deluxe MF135, which cost £740, so for an extra £80 one could buy what, in my opinion, was a much more robust and reliable tractor.

The only time my MF130 was put to work was in 2005, when I was involved with Old Pond Publishing in producing a DVD, *Early Massey Ferguson Tractors 1956–1976*. Part of this programme shows my tractor hitched to a two-furrow Ferguson disc plough, 2-P-AE-20, and I must say that it performed very well considering the hardness of the soil; it is a very nice little tractor to drive. I was asked later to write the script for this DVD, so I took on the challenge on the understanding that if they were not happy with my efforts I would not be upset. Well, it all fell into place nicely.

Brief specification:
• Engine: Perkins indirect injection; diesel A4-107; capacity 107.4 cu in (1753 cc); power output at flywheel 30 hp at 2250rpm
• Gearbox: 8 forward and 2 reverse
• Hydraulic system: Cat 1; three-point linkage with draft and position control. Also a facility to control the rate of response when operating in draft control mode, and another to adjust and preset the rate of drop, not only in relation to the three-point linkage but also that of external rams
• Tyre sizes: (on this tractor) front 6.00 x 16; rear 10 x 28
• Wheel base: 72 in (1830 mm)
• Weight: approx. 2900 lbs (1320 kg)

The MF130 in front of Lower Park house. (Andrew Morland)

No. 75, Massey Ferguson MF65 MkI
1959, Serial No. SNY 51078, Registration No. 935 CTT

I bought this tractor in May 1996 from Jason Esmond-Cole of Goodleigh, Devon. It was in a well-worn state at the time, but pretty complete. Once it was back at Coldridge, Ernie and I were able to evaluate just what work and parts would be needed to bring it back to a nice restored condition.

A full rebuild of the Perkins A4-192 indirect injection engine and its auxiliaries was needed and the dual clutch would have to be rebuilt. Luckily, the gearbox was fine, as was the rear axle apart from needing new oil seals all round, eight in total. The hydraulic pump needed a set of replacement wearing parts and, of course, new disc brake linings would be fitted. The dash panel instruments were sent to Speedograph Richfield of Nottingham for refurbishment. A new set of radiator hoses, a new

wiring loom, a pair of six-volt batteries and a set of new Goodyear tyres more or less completed the list.

The sheet metal work was in reasonable shape, and following some careful repairs by Peter Clarke it was eventually refitted, the exceptions being the perforated radiator grille panels and the air intake bezel, which were factored parts. A lot of dedicated work by Ernie and Peter was required to bring this restoration to completion. The paint used was synthetic MF Red and MF Metallic Flint Grey supplied by our local Massey Ferguson dealer, MST of Tiverton.

There were a couple of changes made to this tractor's specification during its restoration. First was the fitment of power steering, which had in fact been optional during the years of production.

The MF65 Mk1 was fully restored by Ernie Luxton. (Andrew Morland)

The other change I chose to make was to ask Double S Exhausts Ltd of Cullompton to fabricate a downswept system – again an option at the time of production. I feel the tractor looks better with an uncluttered bonnet line. I have never used this tractor for any serious farm work apart from driving it around towing an empty Ferguson Manure Spreader when filming the Old Pond Publishing DVD, so I can't really comment about its performance, but I must say I'm glad we fitted the power steering kit.

Brief specification:
• Engine: Perkins indirect injection; diesel; A4-192; capacity 192 cu in (3146 cc); power output at PTO 46 hp at 2000rpm engine speed
• Gearbox: 6 forward and 2 reverse
• Hydraulic system: Cat 1; three-point linkage (Cat 2 ball ends optional extra); draft position and response controls
• Tyre sizes: front 6.00 x 16; rear 12.4 x 32
• Wheel base: 84 in (2133.6 mm)
• Weight: approx. 4010 lbs (1819 kg)

It was repainted using synthetic MF Red and MF Metallic Flint Grey supplied by our local Massey Ferguson dealer, MST of Tiverton. (Andrew Morland)

No. 76, Massey Ferguson MF165 4WD
1971, Serial No. 605226, Age related Registration No. VTT 709J, Sold

This unusual conversion by Four Wheel Traction Ltd was bought from an agricultural engineer, Richard Pears, in July 1999. He had recently obtained it from a contractor who operated in the hilly parts of South Devon and who obviously appreciated the benefits of 4WD.

The tractor was in a well-worn condition when I bought it, apart from the Perkins A4-212 direct injection diesel engine, which had been rebuilt some time earlier. The earlier MF165s were powered by the Perkins A4-203 with the exhaust on the left-hand side until November 1967, when the A4-212 engine was introduced with the exhaust on the right-hand side. The bonnet and mudguards were badly damaged but I found second-hand replacement parts in pretty good condition.

The only time I used this tractor for 'work' was in 2005, when Old Pond Publishing were filming the DVD. On this occasion it was rolling a field at Coldridge. This tractor is no longer in the Collection as I swapped it in 2015 for a pair of Ferguson prototype flat-four cylinder car engines: one an overhead valve unit designed for the 4WD Ferguson prototype car R4, while the other was an overhead camshaft unit as fitted to the later prototype estate car R5.

The MF165 4WD was swapped for a pair of Ferguson prototype flat-four car engines

Brief specification:
- Engine: Perkins direct injection; diesel; A4-212; capacity 212 cu in (3470 cc); power output at flywheel 60 hp at 2000rpm
- Gearbox: 6 forward and 2 reverse
- Hydraulic system: Cat 2; three-point linkage with draft, position and response control
- Tyre sizes: on this example, front 10 x 24; rear 13 x 28
- Wheel base: 87.25 in (2216 mm)
- Weight: 5544 lbs (2514 kg)

No. 77, Massey Ferguson 35 Industrial
1963, Serial No. not known

A very sorry MF35 Indutrial model.

This must be the saddest tractor in the collection. I bought it from an agricultural engineer in North Devon where he had stored it for a few years under a tree, and I am ashamed to say that during its fifteen years at Coldridge it has been stored in a similar fashion. Since it carried a Cornish registration I guess that it was operated by Cornwall County Council. There is evidence of the fitment of a MF35 front loader. It has the dual braking system. I hope I might get around to sorting it out one day.

Brief specification:
- Engine: Perkins direct injection; diesel; A3-152; capacity 152 cu in (2500 cc); power output at PTO 41.5 hp at 2250rpm engine speed
- Gearbox: 6 forward and 2 reverse
- Hydraulic system: Cat 1, three-point linkage with draft and position control
- Twin braking system
- Tyre sizes: front 6.00 x 16; rear 11.00 x 28
- Wheel base: 72 in (1830 mm)
- Weight: approx. 3185 lbs (1445 kg)

No. 78, Massey Ferguson 175
1967, Serial No. 718432, Present Registration No. YTA 159E

As bought in 1999, the MF175 with Multipower. (Andrew Morland)

I bought this MF175 in March 1999 from a customer and friend, Robert Purvis, who farms near Taunton. He had bought it a few years earlier and had commissioned a Massey Ferguson trained engineer to totally refurbish it. This he did to an extremely high standard, fitting new Massey Ferguson parts where needed. During this work Robert had it fitted with twin spool valves so that he could use the tractor to operate modern implements on his arable farm. It had been owned from new by the Berkshire Institute of Agriculture at Hall Place near Maidenhead, registered as OJB 205F.

For some obscure reason the DVLA insisted on it being given an age-related plate which has the correct suffix for a mid-1967 vehicle – E. Perhaps the explanation is that the tractor was not registered until 1968. I have two rear number plates, one for legal road use and the other for display!

In my opinion, the MF175 is a very capable tractor. It was the top of the Red Giant range introduced by Massey Ferguson at the 1964 Smithfield Show. These Coventry-built models are powered by the direct-injection Perkins A4.236 engine, capacity 236 cu in (3867 cc), which develops 66.4 bhp at 2000rpm. They are fitted with a dual clutch as standard, and a six-speed and two-reverse gearbox with Multi Power doubling the number of ratios

available, with the live power take-off being driven at a speed proportional to the engine or, if selected, at a ratio to forward travel. The front wheels have cast centres, as do the rears, but they also had the benefit of being the Power Adjustable Variable Track (PAVT) type.

The only time I have really put this tractor to any serious hard work was in September 2005 when I was involved with production of the Old Pond Publishing DVD. On this occasion I was ploughing with an MF86 five-furrow semi-mounted plough on hard soil, and I must say that it performed remarkably well – the engine note was impressive!

Brief specification:
• Engine: Perkins direct injection; A4-236; capacity 236 cu in (3867 cc); power output at flywheel 66.4 hp at 2000rpm engine speed
• Gearbox: 6 forward and 2 reverse, plus Multi Power giving overdrive to these ratios
• Hydraulic system: Cat 2; three-point linkage with draft, position pressure and response, and response control
• Tyre sizes: front 7.50 x 16; rear 16.7 x 30 with PAVT (on this tractor)
• Wheel base: 84 in (2134 mm)
• Weight: approx. 6500 lbs (2948 kg)

No. 79, Massey Ferguson MF20 Industrial
1976, Serial No. 808252, Registration No. ODV 313P

The Coldridge Collection MF20 is an ex-military tractor.

This style of Massey Ferguson badge was fitted to all MF construction equipment. It represents a digger bucket.

There is a farmer and dealer in second-hand tractors based near Witheridge, Devon, by the name of John Lake. His display area usually offers modern, well-presented tractors of differing makes, with a few wheeled diggers thrown in for good measure.

When I pass his site I tend to scan what he has on offer, and it was back in late May 1996 that I noticed this ex-army MF20 painted in khaki. I stopped, introduced myself and had a good look at it. Being the industrial version of the popular MF135 it had the usual Tractormeter, showing 1,573 hours, and a combined speedometer and odometer showing only 2,676 miles. It was clear that this machine had done very little work, and his asking price, I felt, was very fair for such a tidy tractor, so I bought myself a belated birthday present!

The army had sprayed it all over with khaki paint, leaving only the instrument glasses and the various light lenses unpainted. Typical, I thought, for a government organisation to sell off a machine that was only just about run in. Before going on to relate the work that Ernie and Peter put into this tractor to bring it back to something like its original condition, it makes sense to outline the features of these models that set them apart from the agricultural MF135s.

As already mentioned, they have a speedometer

fitted. They are also equipped with a full lighting set that includes brake lights and direction indicators, as well as a horn. They have a dual mechanical braking system, a legal requirement under the Road Traffic Act. To meet the braking legislation, the brake drums are made wider so that two sets of brake shoes can be accommodated concentrically but operated independently. The running brake shoes are 2in (50mm) wide, operated by two pedals latched together for road use or independently for field work. The other set of brake shoes, 1½in (40mm) wide, are controlled by the parking brake lever. A nice little touch is that MF industrial machines of this era feature a miniature profile of a digger bucket on the radiator grille rather than the usual Triple Triangle emblem. Luckily, the khaki paint had preserved the chromium plating!

This tractor, being a late example, has a straight front axle. Its precursor, the MF2135, had a swept-back front axle. Another important change in 1971 to the Perkins A3-152 engine was the introduction of a large-diameter lipped oil seal to the flywheel end of the crankshaft; the earlier type was a two-part rope seal which tended to leak; not what is wanted in the clutch housing!

The mechanical repair work was basically the replacement of a few oil seals, fitting new light units where necessary and sourcing a replacement for the little gearbox that takes the drive from the rear axle to the flexible driveshaft to the speedometer, which is now showing 2,837 miles, while the Tractormeter reads 1,610 hours. The readings show that since being at Coldridge in my ownership we have covered only 161 miles: equating to an average speed of 4.35mph.

Obviously, Ernie removed all the sheet metal work and wheels so that these items could be shotblasted prior to being primed and painted by Peter to his usual high standard. If I remember correctly, paint stripper was used on the cast parts to remove the khaki paint. New tyres were fitted all around with turf treads on the rears.

This is a very well balanced tractor to drive.

Brief specification:
• Engine: Perkins direct injection; diesel; AD3-152; capacity 152.7 cu in (2500 cc); power output at flywheel 45.5 hp or at PTO 42.9 hp at engine speed of 2250rpm
• Gearbox: 6 forward and 2 reverse
• Hydraulic system: Cat 1; three-point linkage with draft, position and response control
• Two independent mechanical braking systems
• Tyre sizes: front 6.50 x 16; rear 11.00 x 28
• Wheel base: 72 in (1830 mm)
• Weight: approx. 3528 lbs (1601 kg)

The blanking plate to the right would be replaced with a temperature gauge to monitor the transmission oil if it were fitted with an instant-reverse shuttle. Notice also, top left, the cigarette lighter – the only one in the Coldridge Collection!

No. 80, Massey Ferguson 130 Vineyard
1968, Model No 130-8-VNMY Made in France, Serial No. 438807, Registration No. NTF 516G

I bought this rather sorry-looking tractor from the late John Popplewell, Ferguson enthusiast and dealer. I bought it because of its rarity here in England, though it's not unusual in its native France. It really needs a total rebuild, and to that end I have accumulated most of the cosmetic parts that will be needed; just as well, because most of the parts are no longer available. So one day, maybe, work will begin. It stands next to a restored MF130 so visitors can use their imagination.

A tired looking MF130 Vineyard.

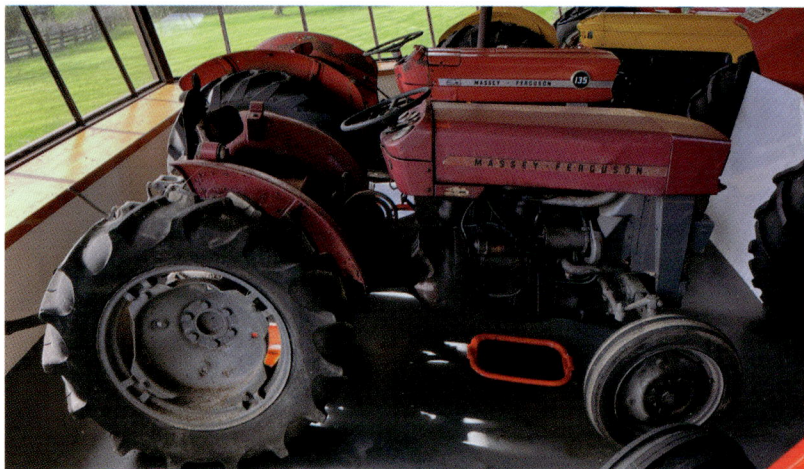

Just to highlight some of the special modifications made to the normal-width MF130 for the Vineyard version, apart from the reduced track width they are fitted with smaller wheels. The fenders are made smaller to suit the profile of the tyres, and finally the hydraulic control quadrant is placed centrally on top of the gearbox housing, with a pair of Bowden cables to connect it to the hydraulic lift unit. MF130 tractors were the smallest in the Red Giant line-up, manufactured only in France and produced in the following ranges: Standard Width in both agricultural and industrial versions, Narrow Width, Vineyard, and High Clearance.

Brief specifications:
• Engine: Perkins indirect injection; diesel; A4-107; capacity 107.4 cu in (1753 cc); power output at flywheel 30 hp at 2250rpm engine speed
• Gearbox: 8 forward and 2 reverse
• Hydraulic system: Cat 1; three-point linkage with draft and position   control
• Tyre sizes: front 4.00 x 15; rear 10 x 24
• Wheel base: 72 in (1830 mm)
• Weight: 2700 lbs (1230 kg)

No. 81, Massey Ferguson MF35X with Multi Power
Serial No. SNM 174897, Registration No. WCT 176

I purchased this tractor from the late John Popplewell, Ferguson enthusiast and dealer, in 1999. Although it was in a rather worn state, it was a pretty complete example of a well-regarded early MF tractor and it was equipped with Multi-Power.

In the course of its restoration, Ernie rebuilt the engine and overhauled the Multi-Power, brakes and steering. After having the wheels and sheet metal shotblasted, they were all primed and repainted by Peter in the correct MF colours. The body of the tractor was cleaned manually, followed by being painted in Stoneleigh Grey. Ernie then fitted new Goodyear tyres, front and rear, prior to reassembling the sheet metal panels and installing a new wiring loom.

Just for a bit of fun I should mention that on its

The MF35X Multi-Power outside Lower Park house. (Andrew Morland) first outing to a rally in South Molton the tractor ground to a halt in the parade ring, whereupon some comedian watching, knowing full well that Ernie was there, shouted out, 'Sack the bastard!' A quick bleed of the fuel system soon had it running again.

Brief specifications:
• Engine: Perkins A3-152, output 41.5 bhp at an engine speed of 2230rpm, measured at the PTO
• Dual clutch
• Gearbox: 6 forward and 2 reverse compounded by the Multi-Power to double that range
• Hydraulics: Cat 1; three-point linkage; draft and position control
• Tyres: from 6.00 x 16, rear 11 x 28
• Wheel base: 72 in (1830 mm)
• Weight: approx. 3185 lbs (1445 kg)

A rear view of the same tractor by the linhay at Lower Park. (Andrew Morland).

No. 82, Ferguson TE.D20 4WD
1952, Serial No. TE-D20 243575, Registration No. NTT 921

I first became aware of this unusual conversion at a local tractor rally held in the late 1980s. It was then owned by John and Andrew Caunter, who lived near Ashburton in Devon. John was an agricultural engineer and came across this tractor tangled in brambles, with a cracked cylinder block, near Kingsbridge in Devon. It was owned by a vet. John was able to buy it on the death of the vet, and with his engineering skill he brought it back to working order and fitted a second-hand cylinder block.

I took quite an interest in this tractor when I first saw it on the rally field, and thought then that it would sit nicely in the Coldridge Collection. It was fitted with a genuine Ferguson Tractormeter A-TE-93. So with that and the rarity of the 4WD conversion by Selene of Turin, Italy, I mentioned to John that if he ever wanted to sell it perhaps he would offer it to me first. For several of our early Open Days at Coldridge John kindly took the trouble to bring it up from Ashburton and put it on display for visitors to enjoy. Then he phoned me one day to say that the family had decided to sell the tractor as his son was off to Australia. I did not question his asking price as I knew full well that at least two other people had been pestering him to sell it to them. As for the rarity of these conversions, I know of only one other in England, one in Scotland,

A TE.D20 converted to four-wheel drive with the Selene conversion kit. (Andrew Morland)

The front axle was sourced from wartime Jeeps. (Andrew Morland)

one in Belgium, and have seen a photograph of one in France. So I felt that John's asking price was very fair, and he had kept to his word.

Oh, I've just remembered that when I was at Agricultural College in 1955/56 we had a speaker one evening from Harry Ferguson Ltd to give us a talk about their products. At the end of his talk there was time for questions, and I can remember one little Clever Dick (me) asking, 'Why does Harry Ferguson Ltd not make Four Wheel Drive tractors?' His answer was, 'Our tractors have such good traction they don't need Four Wheel Drive.' Well, today most Massey Ferguson tractors include 4WD, but Massey Ferguson still offers two-wheel-drive options on some models.

And now back to the story. On getting the newly-acquired tractor back to Coldridge in the late 1990s, Ernie and I did an evaluation of what was needed to return it to full working order: it needed a full engine

rebuild, a new clutch, brake linings, oil seals, new tyres all round, and a full overhaul of the front axle.

It seems appropriate at this point to outline the particular system Selene used for this application. It was known as System One, indicating that it used a sandwich transfer box mounted behind the main gearbox, thus extending the length of the tractor by 1.3in (34mm). The drive is taken from the output shaft of the main gearbox and transmitted by a train of spur gears incorporating a sliding gear selector controlled by an external lever. Drive was then taken by an open propeller shaft to the differential of the front axle, in this case a Willys or Second World War Ford Jeep axle modified to reduce the track width to the Standard Ferguson width of 52 in (1320.8 mm). There were four other Systems in the Selene line-up.

The brake shoes were discarded, but the drums remained in place. Sadly, one of the drawbacks of the conversion was the loss of a very tight turning circle. During the rebuilding of the axle we were able to source all the bearings, oil seals and bushes we needed from a specialist supplier in London. I was surprised to find that proper ball-type constant velocity joints were in the swivel housing.

The engineers at Selene must have got the gearing spot on, as one can drive the tractor flat out in top gear along the road and it is possible to engage the drive to the front axle without creating any horrible noises!

After Ernie had completed all the mechanical work the machine was sent over to Peter Clarke to carry out the repainting, which he did to his usual high standard.

To end this piece it's worth noting that Selene often bought in second-hand TE20s from the UK, fitted them with his 4WD conversion and also very often installed a Perkins P3 diesel engine to replace the petrol or TVO unit – after all, he was the main Perkins agent in Italy. I have been told that quite a few were exported to South America. Of course, 4WD not only gives better traction when operating in wet conditions, but when negotiating downhill slopes it gives engine braking on the front wheels, so there is quite a safety benefit.

Brief specification:
• Engine: Standard Motor company; petrol/TVO; 12 volt electrics; capacity 127.4 cu in (2088 cc); power output at PTO 25.4 hp at 2000rpm engine speed
• Gearbox: 4 forward and 1 reverse
• Hydraulic system: Cat 1; three-point linkage with draft control only
• Tyre sizes: front 7.50 x 16; rear 11 x 28
• Wheel base: 71.4 inches (1813 mm)

The close up shows the now-redundant brake drums still in place. (Andrew Morland)

No. 83, Massey Ferguson MF135 with petrol engine
1965, Engine No. SF 5210 EHD, Serial No. D8820, First registration J17537, now EDV150C

Petrol-engined MF135s are very rare in the UK. (Andrew Morland)

I first became aware of this tractor's existence when speaking to Greg Rowlands at the Ferguson Club AGM in April 2005 at Usk in South Wales. A few years prior to this Greg had bought the tractor in Jersey, Channel Islands. It was first registered on 25 November 1965 and had spent most of its working life on a mushroom farm there. My guess is that mushrooms, having such a large exposed surface area, would be very efficient at capturing diesel exhaust fumes! Petrol exhaust fumes would probably not be so noticeable.

Greg gave me a very fair account of its condition, making it clear that it was in a pretty sorry state because of exposure to salt air. I drove to Wales to collect it with my Land Rover 110 and Ifor Williams trailer. I remember having to detach the trailer from the Land Rover so that we could use it to tow the tractor on to the trailer using a long lifting strop.

Before going on to describe the work that Ernie had to put in to bring this unusual tractor back into good order, readers might want to know why a petrol-engined MF135? I don't know how many of these models were produced at Banner Lane Coventry, but I have been told by friends in both Denmark and New Zealand that quite a few were imported into these countries because they had a system of rebated petrol tax for vehicles used in agriculture. In my archive I have a copy of the instruction book for a MF135 (Petrol Engine), publication number 819 262 M3, which seems to indicate that a good number of petrol models were made.

I was told by the late Richard Dowdeswell (Dick was a respected tractor demonstrator who first worked for Harry Ferguson and then moved on to work in a similar role for Massey Ferguson until his retirement) that Massey Ferguson would loan petrol-engined tractors to horse riding events as their quieter engines were less likely to spook the horses.

Once we had the tractor in Devon we were able to do an evaluation of the restoration work – a lot

Looking at it now, it's hard to believe the state it was in when bought.
(Andrew Morland)

sent to Richfield Speedograph for refurbishment, but factored parts had to be used for the replacement lights and seat fittings. The repainted wheels were shod with Goodyear tyres, and finally Peter Clarke produced a first-class finish to the paintwork. Unlike the diesel MF135, petrol models were not fitted with a fuel gauge, and I wonder why.

The only work this tractor has ever done since I bought it was some disc harrowing for the *Early Massey Ferguson Tractors* DVD produced by Old Pond Publishing in 2005.

Brief specification:
• Engine: Standard Motor Company; petrol, bore 3.42 in (87mm); capacity 133.4 cu in (2186cc); power output at flywheel 3.86 hp at 2250rpm
• Carburettor: Zenith 28G-2 updraught
• Electrics: 12 volt negative earth
• Gearbox: 6 forward and 2 reverse
• Hydraulic system: Cat 1; three-point linkage with draft and position control
• Tyre sizes: front 6.00 x 16; rear 11 x 28
• Wheel base: 72 in (1830 mm)
• Weight: 3,200lbs (1,451.5kg)

In all other respects it had the same specification as the early MF135 diesels

– which, of course, was carried out diligently over time by Ernie. An engine rebuild was needed, new clutch and brake linings, new oil seals all around, an overhaul to the starter and dynamo, and new regulator and battery.

Most of the original sheet metal work was perforated with rust from the sea air so I had to source good second-hand parts where possible; even some of the forged front axle parts were so deeply pitted that body filler had to be used. The instruments were

No. 84, Pre-production TEF20, Diesel
Commission No. EXP11

Pre-production diesel-engined TE.F20 EXP11 remains unrestored in the top tractor shed.

I bought this tractor in February 2001 from an agricultural engineer, Nick Clarke, based near Hertford. He told me he had been servicing it for a good many years while it was being used for grass cutting on the sports fields of University College London. Eventually, the College had asked him to find them a more modern replacement, which he did, taking back EXP11 as part of the deal. Nick told me that Harry Ferguson had personally given this pre-production tractor to the College. Knowing Harry Ferguson's dislike of diesel engines, one can only assume that he did not want to have it on his Abbotswood estate! Nick had intended to keep the EXP11 for himself but as he was in the throes of restoring an Austin Healey 100 he needed the cash to complete the project.

Sadly, this tractor is not fitted with its original diesel engine, which would not have had a fuel lift pump. The replacement engine now installed is a later type, with a lift pump that has been plumbed into the system. I have endeavoured to find any differences from production models but so far I have only spotted one – the dash panel is made of aluminium, not steel.

No restoration work has been done on this tractor and for some reason the bonnet and mudguards are painted red.

Brief specification:
• Engine: Standard Motor Company; 20C indirect injection; diesel; capacity 127.68 cu in (2092 cc); power at PTO 25 hp at 2000rpm engine speed
• Gearbox: 4 forward and 1 reverse
• Hydraulic system: Cat 1; three-point linkage with draft control only
• Tyre sizes: (on this example) front 5.00 x 19; rear 10 x 28 grassland type
• Wheel base: 70 in (1778 mm)
• Weight: approx. 2700 lbs (1225 kg)

No. 85, Massey Ferguson MF135 4WD
1971, Serial No. 172880, Registration No. VOD 199J

The MF135 4WD was found in Austria (Andrew Morland)

My German friend, Norman Tietz, has a varied selection of early MF tractors in his collection and told me this tractor was up for sale in Austria. He asked if I would be interested in buying it. Yes, I would be, but I went on to explain that I was a bit scared about the payment arrangements and the shipping. He kindly offered to take care of all that, telling me that the tractor would not be delivered to Coldridge, but the transport firm would deliver it to a dealer based near Dorchester, Dorset along with some farm machinery. That eased my fears! I posted a cheque to Norman to cover the costs of the tractor and shipping, and in due course was informed that it was standing in the dealer's yard. All I had to do was to collect it with my Mercedes 814 Beavertail lorry. My friend Paul Delahoy came with me on this trip and when we arrived at the yard there was a surprise awaiting me. Not only was the MF135 tidy but it was also fitted with a 6 ft (1828.8 mm) mid-mounted mower driven by a mid-mounted PTO, an unusual feature on a Coventry-built example. After loading and strapping down we stopped off at West Bay for fish and chips as a treat. We had a good drive back to Coldridge and off-loaded the tractor and parked the lorry. A good day's 'work'!

This tractor had clocked up 8,900 hours so it was not surprising that the Perkins engine was showing signs of wear, but its general condition was fine. In fact, I wrote to the farmer in Austria who had used it to congratulate him on his good maintenance and careful use – he never replied, but I expect he couldn't read my English. The only sad point was that the German-made cab was an after-purchase fitment, but it was tidy and offered rollover protection.

It is fitted with the German-type adjustable height draw bar hitch. (Andrew Morland)

The German MF dealer's brochure given to me by Norman featured a MF135 4WD operating in a snowy landscape. This tractor, produced for the Continental market, is fitted with the German-type adjustable height draw bar hitch, which provides a choice of six different height settings.

The 4WD conversion is very neatly engineered by substituting the normal PTO control lever mounting plate with a special assembly with two levers: one of flat steel bar cranked to control the PTO selection with all the usual facilities, and the other with a ball end to the lever to select drive to the front axle. To protect the front axle from excessive loads a spring-loaded slip clutch is installed at the axle end of the propeller shaft. Apart from offering better traction when 4WD is engaged, it also provides a braking effect on downhill slopes – and there are plenty of them in some parts of Austria.

The mid-mounted PTOs were incorporated into some Coventry-built tractors that were exported to Germany and Austria. These were provided to power the mid-mounted mowers that were common in these countries at the time. This particular mower is raised and lowered by its own dedicated hydraulic ram and control valve. One other odd feature is the lugs welded to the outer rim of each rear wheel, evidence that cage wheels would have been used at times to aid stability when working across slopes.

Brief specification:
- Engine: Perkins A3-152 direct injection; diesel. Capacity 152.7 cu in (2500 cc); power output at flywheel 45.5 hp at engine speed of 2250rpm
- Gearbox: 6 forward and 2 reverse
- Hydraulic system: Cat 1; three-point linkage with draft position and response control
- Tyre sizes: front 8.00 x 20; rear 11 x 28
- Wheel base: 72 in (1828 mm)
- Weight: not known

Front hub of the 4WD-converted 135. (Andrew Morland)

No. 86, The Last Prototype Standard Motor Company Dumper Truck
1961, Commission No. X670, Registration No. WAC 942H

The Standard dumper truck waiting for some action at Lower Park.

I bought this dumper following a tip-off from my friend John Farnworth, who told me it was being offered for sale in the *Heritage Tractor* Magazine by a Mr Robert Thompson who lived near Alcester in Warwickshire. We made a deal over the phone and I collected it later. My reason for buying this odd-ball bit of Standard history was that I felt it would sit well with my Standard Prototype Tractor No. 70 which, by the way, would have carried commission number X671 or X672 but sadly that was missing.

I was eager to find out more about the background to this dumper, and Robert was able to give me the name and phone number of the person he bought it from in 1968: a Mr Bill Davies, who was most helpful, adding that he had used it in connection with his ready-mix concrete business for making small local deliveries; that is why it was registered. He also put me in touch with an ex-Standard employee, Mr Ron Easterbrook, and it was he who told me that a batch of twelve dumpers had been made by Standard for export to Israel but the order was cancelled at the last minute. I was told by either Bill or Ron that Standard sold the twelve dumpers to a Coventry building contractor. As an aside, I have a copy of the Standard Motor Company prototype listing from 1948 through to 1974, kindly given to me by Paul Homer, webmaster of the Standard Car Club. Only seven dumper trucks are listed there; perhaps the other five were considered as production models!

Just to extend this aside, readers may be interested to know that on this listing is prototype number X502, designation 20 SJ, 4 x 4 Jeep.

I have no story to tell of the restoration of this dumper, because it is stored as found in the reserve collection, to use posh phraseology!

Brief specification:
• Engine: Single-cylinder Petter Diesel No. PHTT 3930 PHI developing 8.2hp at 2000 rpm
• Clutch: Borg & Beck 9 in
• Gearbox, 4 speeds Triumph Herald
• One-piece propeller shaft by Hardy Spicer
• Front axle, Triumph Herald differential unit with the output fed into two reduction drop boxes at each front hub
• Brakes: front only, internal expanding hydraulic type by Girling, mechanical parking brake.
• Front tyres traction type 7.50 x 16; rears ribbed 6.00 x 15
• Rear axle and steering fabricated beam with centre pivot point; the hub swivels taken from the Herald parts bin and carry the road wheels
• Steering box (by Bishop Cam Steering) with the steering wheel taken from a Ferguson TE.A20
• The skip holds approximately 1 cu yd (0.765 cu m) and is mechanically tipped and counterbalance returned with a pair of coil springs to absorb shock loads when tipping

No. 87, The Turner Ranger Four
1976, Serial No. 57, Registration No. 92 RN 69

My Turner Ranger Four with nearside door removed.

In his early years, Peter Warr worked for Harry Ferguson as a general factotum at his Abbotswood Estate, and later moved on to work for Tony Sheldon, Harry Ferguson's son-in-law. After Harry Ferguson's death on 25 October 1960, Tony took over the running of Harry Ferguson Research and its offshoot, Tractor Research. Much later, Peter moved to the Isle of Wight to work alongside Jamie Sheldon, Tony's son, who has a farm there. It was Jamie, with a huge amount of input from Peter, who developed the Ferguson Family Museum there.

When writing my book *Ferguson TE20 In Detail*, published by Herridge and Sons, Peter was a great source of information and stories he was always happy to share. He, having witnessed the development of Harry Ferguson's 4WD vehicles, told me that it was Tractor Research Ltd who were commissioned by Calor Gas Ltd in the early 1970s to design and develop a prototype 4WD utility vehicle that would be suitable for ground care duties as well as being fit for use as a factory tug to be powered, of course, by Calor propane! The resultant prototype became the basis of a production vehicle. As an aside, it was a

visitor to the Coldridge Collection, Roger Whittle, who told me that he had designed the safety frame and cab while working as a design engineer for Tractor Research. Production eventually began, with Calor Gas awarding the contract to Tower Engineering, but they only produced about twelve examples. Then the manufacturing was taken on by Turner Engineering Ltd of Alcester in Warwickshire. According to Tony Turner, Director, they produced about 250 machines.

So being aware of the 'Ferguson' connection with these Rangers. I jumped at the offer that my friend Michael Hall, a private Land Rover dealer based near Swindon in Wiltshire, made to sell me the example he had bought for his son as a toy to play around with. This decision was fostered by the fact that I have always been keen on good design and appreciative of the work done by the Design Council to encourage the manufacture of well-designed British products. Artefacts submitted that met the required parameters were awarded recognition by the Council in the form of a certificate and a logo that could be affixed to the product. To further the appreciation of good design, the Design Council established a showroom, known as the Design Centre, in Haymarket in central London: here, approved products were put on display and could be viewed by the general public. A Turner Ranger Four was displayed there.

Now for more details and the specification of No. 87 in the Coldridge Collection. This Ranger is a fully equipped ex-naval machine, put into service on 22 June 1976 with the Registration No. 92 RN 69, Serial No. 57. When sold to Michael Hall it had covered 5,789 miles and clocked up 1,411 hours, it was painted yellow, had a petrol engine (some had propane) and the two front tyres were almost down to the canvas. Today it is fully restored with its correct livery, and carries an age-related plate. UOD 845R. The odometer now reads 5,918 miles and the hour meter 1,615.

Optional equipment could be added to the basic specification to meet a customer's exact requirements. To that end the following were made available: independent PTO, front and/or rear. Likewise, Category I three-point linkage but with no draft control. These lift assemblies were as fitted to the BMC Mini tractor. Lift capacity, front 336lbs (152kg), rear 672lbs (305kg); the hydraulic pump was belt driven from the engine. Capacity at 2500rpm of 2½ gal/min (11.37 litres/min). A safety frame could be specified and converted to an all-weather cab with a large, opening rear glazed panel if required.

A full lighting set and direction indicators could be fitted. Turner Engineering claimed a sustained drawbar pull in first gear on 5.50 x 12 tyres of 2,000lbs (907kg), wheel slip being the limiting factor. Of course, the option of Calor propane carburettor and cylinder was always on offer as a cheaper fuel with no duty. In fact, there is a person in North Devon who replaced the petrol engine/gearbox with a diesel power unit taken from a Volkswagen Golf.

I must say that over the years of ownership I have collected the names of about twenty people who own or have owned a Turner Ranger; it would be nice to update that list!

Brief specification:
• Engine/gearbox integral and taken directly from Austin Morris 1100 (a design by Alec Issigonis) of the period, so four cylinder inline OHV of 67.00 cu in (1098 cc) developing 28 bhp at 3000rpm
• Bore of 2.56 in (64.95mm), stroke 3 in (76.20mm), and compression ratio 7.5:1
• Clutch: Borg & Beck 7⅛ inch (180.8 mm)

The mid-mounted British Leyland 1098 cc A-series engine.

diameter
• Gearbox: 4 speed and 1 reverse with synchromesh on all forward ratios. With integral differential. Final drives BL (British Leyland) differential assemblies front and rear taken from Triumph Herald
• Reduction ratio 3.89:1 with drive shafts to each hub via constant velocity joints (I have a feeling that the centre differential may have been welded up because I can remember getting my Ranger bogged down and noticing that one front and one rear wheel were spinning.)
• Hydraulic brakes on all four wheels: 7 in (178 mm) by 1½ in (38 mm) with a 6 in (152 mm) disc parking brake
• All tyres: 23 x 8.50 x 12 (optional sizes were available)
• Independent suspension all round by rubber cone springs, i.e. Molton type
• Steering is mechanical (could do with power assistance!) to all four wheels, steering box by Cam Gears, worm and peg type; two and a half turns lock to lock
• Belt driven mechanical governor
• Electric fuel pump and carburettor by S.U.
• Electrical 12 volt negative earth, horn, double dipping headlights and flashing direction indicators
• Hydraulic system: Cat 1; position control only; front and rear three-point linkage
• Front and rear PTO
• Wheel base: 55 in (1392 mm)
• Weight: not known

No. 88, Massey Ferguson MF50 Shunting Tractor
Registration No. PDN 787P, Sold December 2010

This is the photo the vendor sent me. Having worked at Dungeness Power Station, I wasn't sure whether to test it with a Geiger counter!

I bought this unusual MF conversion in September 2003 from Mr Stuart Morrison who lived near Dungeness in Kent. He had acquired it from EWS (English, Welsh and Scottish Railway Ltd) in August 2002. It was he who told me it had been used at Dungeness Power Station. It came complete with shunting pole and two British Rail portable tail lamps: one is a 1950s vintage that burns paraffin,

and the other an early 1970s lamp, which is battery powered.

The machines were built by Sturdiluxe and designed for pushing or towing 'dead' railway wagons in sidings. The MF50 skid unit on which this unit is based incorporates a Perkins A4-212 engine mated to a MF Instant Reverse Shuttle with torque converter system, giving four speeds in each direction. The claimed drawbar pull was 9,000lbs with a total weight of 10,800lbs. During its time at Coldridge no improvement work was carried out on this tractor, but it was demonstrated on Old Pond's DVD, *Early Massey Ferguson Tractors*. It was eventually sold.

Brief specification:
• Engine: Perkins direct injection; diesel; capacity 212 cu in (3470 cc); power output at flywheel 60 hp at 2000rpm
• Gearbox: Massey Ferguson Instant Reverse Shuttle; 4 forward and 4 reverse
• No hydraulic system
• Tyre sizes: front 9.00 x 6; rear 14 x 28
• Weight: approx. 10,800 lbs (4899 kg)

No. 89, Lister Tug
1969 Registration No. RAD 919G

You may well ask, Reader, why a Ferguson enthusiast has a Lister Tug. When I bought this machine in 2004 I still had a prototype Lister Tractor (No. 59), which was known as a Gold Star, so maybe I thought the Tug would sit well alongside it, but I sold the Gold Star in early 2008.

The real reason for buying and retaining the Lister Tug was because it was offered to me restored to a very high standard and at a very, very fair price: I thought that this machine represents a bit of old England! It had in fact been used all of its working life by Lister at their Dursley works in Gloucestershire, but with the demise of that operation in 1986 it was scheduled for the scrap yard. John Jeffries, an Agricultural Engineer from Axminster, had a tip-off from a friend about its intended fate. By strange coincidence, John had followed his engineering apprenticeship with Lister at Dursley, offered to buy the Tug, and carried out the comprehensive restoration on it in his spare time.

The three-cylinder air-cooled engine, type SR3, was totally rebuilt with a re-ground crankshaft and

bearing shells. The three individual injector pumps and injectors were all overhauled. New clutch and brake linings were fitted, along with new pipe work for the hydraulic brakes which operate on all four wheels, with two leading shoes on the front. New handbrake cables were also fitted. New oil seals were installed for the hypoid rear axle, which is connected to the chassis by a pair of semi-elliptical leaf springs. The front axle, which is a steel forging, had new roller bearings fitted to the kingpins; the front leaf spring is semi-elliptical, mounted transversely. The rack and pinion steering box just needed new gaiters; and, of course, new track rod ends all around. New tyres and tubes were called for, being 18 x 4.5 fronts and 18 x 7 rears. The starter motor was overhauled, but John decided to replace the dynamo with an alternator.

The single front headlight, along with new side and rear lights, indicators and a new seat completed a first-class piece of restoration work – a credit to John. A point omitted: the chassis frame is fabricated in one piece using mostly ½ in (12 mm) plate steel!

It is worth mentioning that tugs made by Lister, Mercury and others were used extensively by British Railways, pre-Second World War and into the early 1970s, to tow trailers carrying luggage and parcels between platforms at large terminals, often having up to eight trailers in tow, snaking their way along a platform and attempting to avoid colliding with pedestrians! Tugs could also be found carrying out similar duties at airports, taking baggage from the terminal buildings to be loaded into the holds of waiting aircraft. Sometimes they were used to tow small aircraft from hanger to tarmac. Large engineering factories often used tugs and trailers to bring components from the stores to the assembly line.

Brief specification:
• Engine: Lister Diesel; develops 16.5 bhp at 2500rpm
• Clutch: Borg & Beck
• Gearbox: 3 forward and 1 reverse, with sliding spur gears
• Transfer case oil filled, drive by duplex roller chain, reduction ratio 2.26:1
• Electrics: 12 volt
• Drawbar pull in first gear, 2200 lbs (998 kg) – break-away
• Weight with cab: 3,136 lbs (1,425 kg)
• Ground clearance: 3.5 in (89 mm)!!
• Wheel base: 41 in (1040 mm)

The Lister Tug was bought fully restored by previous owner John Jeffries.

No. 90, Massey Ferguson MF35 petrol
1963, Serial No. SHM 33255, Registration No. ANU 729A

The petrol-engined MF35 is one of only four known examples in the UK. (Andrew Morland)

This was, for me, a rare find, believed to be one of only four known examples in the UK. It was offered to me along with a petrol MF35 Industrial model by a visitor to the Coldridge Collection, Cliff Yeomans, a Derbyshire collector, in July 2004. The prefix letters SHM mean: S = Standard Width Agricultural; H = Petrol High Altitude; M = Dual Clutch.

I don't know anything about its background: it was Cliff who had it fully restored, so it is displayed just as I purchased it. Just one point: the decals on either side of the bonnet should not be 35X. The 'X' relates to the slightly more powerful Perkins A3-152 engine. The petrol engine is the Standard 87 mm (3.43 in) equipped with a Zenith 28G-2 up-draught carburettor and a Lucas coil and distributor.

I have never used this tractor for any work as it would have been far too costly!

There are no differences from the diesel-engined MF35 at the back. (Andrew Morland)

Brief specification:
• Engine: Standard Motor company; petrol; 87 mm (3.43 in); capacity 133.4 cu in (2186 cc); power output at PTO 35 hp at 2000rpm engine speed
• Gearbox: 6 forward and 2 reverse
• Hydraulic system: Cat 1; three-point linkage with draft and position control
• Tyre sizes: front 4.00 x 19; rear 11 x 28
• Wheel base: 72 in (1828 mm)
• Weight: 3022 lbs (1371 kg)

The nearside view of the Standard petrol engine. Note the raised distributor and the drive take-off for the Tractormeter.
(Andrew Morland)

No. 91, Massey Ferguson MF35 Industrial Petrol
1964, Serial No. JGM 150451, Registration No. HSL 766

This is the other tractor I bought in the summer of 2004 from Cliff Yeomans: it is ex-army and still has its military commission plate in place.

I bought this tractor for its rarity and it is displayed as purchased. Sadly, the master cylinder for the hydraulic rear brakes is not the correct type: the one now fitted is taken from a BMC Mini. It is, however, fitted with the wide industrial rear mudguards and grassland tyres on the rear. An interesting and sensible feature is the fitment of a heat deflector just under the petrol tank and above the exhaust manifold, which seems exactly right to me!

The other petrol MF35 does not have the deflector. I have never used this tractor but it is a nice one for visitors to view.

Brief specification:
• Engine: Standard Motor company; petrol; 87 mm (3.43 in); capacity 133.4 cu in (2186 cc); power output at PTO 35 hp at 2000 rpm engine speed
• Gearbox: 6 forward and 2 reverse
• Hydraulic system: Cat 1; three-point linkage with draft and position control
• Tyre sizes: front 4.00 x 19; rear 10 x 28 grassland type tread
• Wheel base: 72 inches (1828 mm)
• Weight: 3022 lbs (1371 kg)

The ex-Army Industrial MF35. In the background are some of the Coldridge Collection's London Underground exhibits.

No. 91a, Prototype Ferguson TE.D20 with Meadows Diesel Engine
1950, Commission No. TE.D20 124639, Registration No. KDU 559

A prototype Meadows-engined Ferguson TE.D20.

I was first made aware of this tractor's existence when I was researching details of the LTX tractor in the Midlands in 1999. I was helped by three ex-Ferguson field test drivers – Colin Stevenson, Jack Bibby and the late Nigel Liney, as well as the late Erik Fredrikson, an ex-Massey Ferguson development engineer. This work was to lead me to commissioning a limited run of fifty 1/18th scale models of the LTX followed by a second run of sixty but with a different style of bonnet. It was Nigel who asked me one afternoon whether I would like to view a rare Ferguson prototype diesel TE20 he had been involved with in the early 1950s. The team had been using it in evaluation trials set up by Harry Ferguson. As we drove to the site at Priors Hardwick, Warwickshire, where the tractor was standing, or rather lying, Nigel explained a bit of the background to the evaluation field tests he had been involved with. It was a well-known fact that Harry Ferguson did not like diesel engines, or for that matter TVO, but farmers had a liking for the Perkins P3 conversion kits they were marketing for retro-fitment. These engines produced 32bhp compared with 24bhp of the Standard petrol engine

so there was a very useful increase in power. The diesel engine was more efficient, i.e. economical, but could be run on red diesel (rebated fuel) so it was a winner all around. Harry Ferguson realised he had to concede to customers' needs or lose out on sales: the result was that three manufacturers were asked to submit a diesel-engined TE20 for evaluation trials. This was duly done; Perkins supplied a tractor fitted with their P3. The Standard Motor Company, with help from Arthur Freeman-Sanders (a diesel engine designer), produced a prototype 20C engine, and Meadows submitted at least two tractors (no one is sure exactly how many), with an engine specially built up for these trials.

The details of this engine are as follows. It has exactly the same length as the Standard petrol unit, in fact the sump is taken directly from that engine, as are the oil filter (early T20 vertical type by Tecalemit), the water pump, the starter motor, the oil filler cap and the fuel filler cap (early bayonet type). The original pistons of this prototype engine were marked Petter. It should be noted that at this time, 1950, the Brush-ABOE Group owned both Petter and Meadows; it also embraced Nation, McClaren and Mirrlees. Later Brush-ABOE went on to purchase Glennifer Engines and Ruston & Hornsby, and in 1968 merged with English Electric, forming a group that included Dorman and Paxton.

Needless to say, I was very keen to buy it, but Nigel sensibly suggested that I put a written offer in the post to the owner, which I did on my return to Devon. I think the reply that I received was that it was not for sale. So that was laid to rest! On receiving my June/July 2004 copy of Vintage Tractor there was an extensive article on this tractor's recovery and the start made on its rebuild by a most competent engineer, David White, who had been told of its whereabouts while he was taking charge of John Moffitt's Ivel on its epic road run from Biggleswade (Bedfordshire) to the Royal Show Ground at Stoneleigh to celebrate its 100th anniversary. The second part of David's story was in the subsequent edition of Vintage Tractor – August/September 2004. I felt moved to write to him, telling him of my time with Nigel back in 1999 when I first saw the tractor, and to congratulate him on his monumental achievement. I did add as a corollary that if he ever wished to sell the tractor perhaps he would be good enough to offer it to me first. His response to my letter was appreciative, and sure enough, on a Wednesday late in October 2005, he phoned me to say that he was selling the tractor and was I still interested? Well, the answer was 'Yes' and his asking price was very fair. He delivered it to Coldridge the following Saturday afternoon and had thoughtfully included most of the 'scrap' bits and pieces as well as the wooden template he had made to fit the hole in the crankcase and oil gallery. He also included the original Meadow nameplates fixed to the sides of the bonnet, and the original front radiator grille badge. Other parts now fitted to the tractor are reproductions. He also included the four pistons marked Petter, the original fuel pump elements, and the remains of the bottom section of the radiator grille. David's reason for painting it the colour he did was because he found traces of it under the grey.

David's first job on getting the tractor back to his workshop was to strip the engine, to evaluate why number three connecting rod had made this hole. Well, it seemed that through lack of oil the journal had seized and bent the connecting rod as it hit the crankcase. The crankshaft journals had to be turned down prior to being built up by metal spraying then re-machined. The bores had to be machined and then sleeved back to standard size 80 mm (3.15 in): the replacement pistons cost David £60 each! The CAV series A injector pump had to be totally rebuilt with new pump elements fitted. David also had to source a second-hand bonnet and new rear mudguard skins and wheels.

By the spring of 2006 I was keen to do some stubble ploughing. Fitted with a 12 volt battery powering the original-type 6 volt starter, this engine only needed the excess fuel button to be pressed in, the gear stick moved to S, and it fired up instantly The only downside was that the draft control on the hydraulics didn't work. Ernie Luxton soon found the cause of this problem and sorted it out; the small rod that passes through the large coil spring to the control valve had seized. The engine pulled extremely well, validating Nigel's experience that it was the best of the three engine variants in the evaluation trials.

On another occasion, in the autumn of that year, the late Harold Beer and I took the tractor with a three-furrow MF793 12 in (304.8 mm) plough, to a ploughing day held at Landsend Farm near Crediton, on fairly hard, dry red Devon soil. The tractor took this all in its stride, purring along in second gear with virtually no smoke. I offered Harold a drive, which he was keen to accept, while I spent a bit of time talking to friends on the headland. Then at one point I looked across the field and noticed the tractor belching black smoke. I half walked, half ran to investigate the situation, 'Oh,' Harold said, 'I was just trying it out in third gear.' Not that one would abuse an engine to that extent – but to pull three furrows in third gear!!

When the NIAE (National Institute of Agricultural Engineering) at Silsoe was closed down in 2006, Stuart Gibbard was involved in cataloguing their extensive collection of archive photographs. He came across some photos of another Meadow engine

The battery carrier, fuel tank and oil filler were all specially made and the routing of the exhaust system is unique.

The neat installation of the Meadows engine in the the TE.D20. Note the Donaldson air cleaner, as fitted to the Ferguson Brown.

TE20 which he kindly copied for me; this one carries the registration letters FUT which is a Leicestershire designation, I also have a photograph of the same tractor that was given to me by an engineer who worked on this project. The photograph was taken at Brush Electrical, Loughborough, dated 1950. I'm sorry that I don't remember the engineer's name, but he was living in Bedfordshire at the time.

The tractor in this photograph has an early type TE20 oil bath, air cleaner and the induction and exhaust manifolds are in opposite relative positions to the one here at Coldridge. This direct injection engine starts instantly in cold weather, one just has to push the excess fuel device first.

Brief specification:
- Engine: Meadows engine No. BXA 105 Type 4DC 1/35; direct injection; capacity 2212 cc (129.5 cu in); ratio and power output not known
- Bore 80 mm (3.149 in); stroke 110 mm (4.33 in)
- Direct injection compression; ratio and power output not known
- Gearbox: 4 forward and 1 reverse
- Hydraulic system: Cat 1; three-point linkage draft control only
- Tyre sizes: front 4.00 x 19; rear 11 x 28
- Wheel base: 70 in (1778 mm)
- Weight: approx. 2700 lbs (1225 kg)

No. 92, BMC Mini Tractor Prototype
1962, Model TR MKI, Chassis No. TR503/1, Registration No. 495 EUE

Ray Fardon driving the BMC Mini Tractor prototype at the cricket club in Bourton-on-the-Water.

This Mini Tractor was designed and produced by Tractor Research and first registered with the Warwickshire County Council on 30 November 1962 as 495 EUE. It is recorded as blue and the engine number is SPL 931-A-D.

In April 1997, the Ferguson Club held its AGM at the White Hart Hotel in Moreton-in-Marsh, Gloucestershire. After the formalities of the AGM the assembled guests were given a most interesting talk by the late Ray Fardon about his experiences working as Head Gardener at Abbotswood, Harry Ferguson's home and estate near Stow-on-the-Wold. This was followed, in the afternoon, by delegates having the opportunity to visit the gardens – in the pouring rain. Not an ideal way to view a garden, but Ray was on hand to answer questions. I remember being with him and a few Club members sheltering in a garden building and saying to him, 'You know what these chaps are hoping to find here – an odd-ball Ferguson tractor.' Ray replied, 'The only odd-ball is in my care; I use it at the cricket pitch at Bourton-on-the-Water.' I quietly arranged with Ray to let me take some photographs of the tractor, which I duly did at a later date and as a bonus Ray let me have a drive of it.

Ray pointed out that there were a couple of spare engines and a pair of rear wheels with traction tyres in the shed where it was kept. I immediately recognised this as a prototype BMC Mini so was keen to buy it if possible. Eventually, the Cricket Club decided to sell it, but they first insisted that it be advertised in a couple of tractor magazines.

*The prototype outside
the Ferguson Shed at
Lower Park.*

Luckily for me, the advertisement described it as a Ferguson TE20, no doubt because by then it was painted grey! That was a tense time for me. Anyway, it was eventually agreed that I could buy it, including the registration documents, the two spare engines and the pair of rear wheels – but with the proviso that I find them a suitable replacement. This I did in the form of a BMC 4-25. Needless to say, I asked Ernie to service and check it over before I delivered it to the Cricket Club. I delivered the BMC and brought the prototype and spares back to Devon.

About ten days later I had a phone call from Ray to say that that a serious fault had occurred with the 4-25, and could I fix it? Not what I wanted to hear! I had to bring the tractor back to Devon, but luckily Ernie was able to sort out the problem promptly and I was able to return the machine to them. At one point I asked Ray how he found working for Harry Ferguson, and his reply was, 'He was my friend and I was his friend' – what a lovely comment.

Once the tractor was in Ernie's workshop we were able to evaluate its condition. One of the first points we noticed was that it was not fitted with its original engine, BUT one of the spare engines was SPL 931-A-D. What a bit of luck! So it was

that engine I had rebuilt by Kar Engine Services of Barnstaple.

Before we go on to compare this prototype with the production BMC Mini tractor introduced to the public in December 1965, I feel it would be prudent to try to unravel its development process, which is far from clear! So I will set out what I have been able to glean from various sources. It appears that in the mid-1950s, Nuffield (Morris Motors) was toying with the idea of producing a small tractor to market alongside their larger one. It is noted by Anthony Clare in his book The Nuffield Tractor Story: Nuffield & Leyland 1963–1982, Volume 2 that an Italian Nuffield tractor dealer, Vittorio Cantatore of Moncalieri, near Turin, sent one of his home-built tractors, the Field Boy, to the UK. It was powered by a 2.2 litre BMC diesel engine. Another point to note is that Morris Motors had been supplying Brockhouse Engineering of Southport, Lancashire, with 10hp side-valve petrol engines for installation in their light tractor, the President, which was sometimes displayed on Nuffield dealers' show stands alongside the bigger tractor. BMC was also in the habit of using some of the services of Tractor Research Ltd, a subsidiary of Harry Ferguson Research Ltd, based at Toll Bar End near Coventry, for some of their development work.

Harry Ferguson suffered from bouts of depression towards the end of his life, interspersed with periods of energy and enthusiasm, seemingly back to his old spirit. He was fired up on one of these occasions with his pet dream of designing a small tractor of 15hp incorporating several of his patents. So was it that 'dream' of Harry Ferguson's that became a reality in December 1965 when the production BMC Mini Tractor was launched?

The net result was that BMC and Tractor Research worked together to design and build four prototypes as a starting point, and according to records they went on to produce a total of fifteen. The design team at Tractor Research on this project was led by Alex Senkowski, a former Harry Ferguson employee of LTX fame, Charles Black was their agricultural adviser, and the six engineers on the project were Gordon Edwards, Dennis Langton, Frank Inns (in charge of hydraulics), Bruce Cosh, Ray Tyre and Geoff Burton, plus several draughtsmen. The basic concept was to produce a tractor with an underbody clearance similar to a TE20, which is 13 in. (330 m). The BMC Mini 14 in (355.6 mm) was to be made in two versions: a basic model with no PTO or hydraulics; and a deluxe version with PTO, hydraulic linkage and lights. The earliest known drawing as far as I am aware is dated 19 May 1961 (the day after my 23rd birthday!). In the early stages of development 5.50 x 15 and 10.00 x 24 front and rear tyres were decided on, as were spur gear reduction final drives, set at the outer ends of the rear axle. Dry disc brakes were incorporated on the high speed axle shafts, and differential lock was to be a standard fitment. For the hydraulic linkage, the normal Ferguson System Draught Control was dropped in favour of an earlier Ferguson design that consisted of height adjustable mounting points for the forward ends of the lower links. This proved to work fairly well in reasonably consistent soil conditions pulling a two-furrow Ferguson plough to which a depth wheel had been fitted. (I wonder what Harry Ferguson would have thought of that!) This was done in case maintaining a fairly even depth became a problem. In practice, though, this seemed not to be needed. Ploughing enthusiasts who use BMC Mini Tractors confirm this.

The engine chosen to power the tractor was a diesel version of the BMC 948 A series petrol

The 948cc BMC indirect injection diesel engine developed 15bhp.

engine. This engine had been developed at BMC under the control of Alex Issigonis (Head of Engineering at the time). I have read/heard it suggested that the idea behind this project was that such an engine might eventually be installed in the Morris 1000 vans used by the Post Office at the time: with an output of 15bhp at 2500rpm! Tractor Research claimed that it only developed 12bhp! This engine was indirect injection incorporating Ricardo designs. The first batch of four prototypes was registered consecutively as EUE 495, EUE 496, EUE 497 and EUE 498.

Now let us compare the prototype at Coldridge to a production BMC Mini (No. 63 in the Coldridge Collection). The most noticeable difference is, of course, the hand-fabricated bonnet and rear mudguards followed by the more crudely made radius arms, particularly the yoke ends. Next, the observant viewer would notice that the rear wheels have eight stud fixings, while the production models have six: the front wheels of the prototype have five, while the productions models have four – cost-cutting measures, no doubt. The gearbox arrangement is different in that the prototype has a three-speed gearbox compounded with a high and low range, while the production tractors have a three-speed gearbox incorporating a start position all on the same lever. The auxiliary gearbox has three ratios: High, Medium and Low, as well as a Reverse position. Using this lever with a gear selected one can shuttle between Medium and Reverse; ideal for loader work. There are, of course, many other minor differences but I should mention that the early prototype had heater plugs in each combustion chamber plus one on the induction manifold – this was not carried into production models. So, from all this development work BMC was able to launch the BMC Mini at the 1965 Smithfield Show in London. More about the production models can be found in the earlier section of this book dealing with No. 63.

Brief specification:
• Engine: BMC; indirect injection; diesel; capacity 57.85 cu in (948 cc); power output 15 hp at the flywheel
• Gearbox: 6 forward and 2 reverse
• Hydraulic system: Cat 1; three-point linkage position control only
• Tyre sizes: front 5.50 x 15; rear 9 x 28
• Wheel base: 44 in (1117 mm)
• Weight: approx. 2098 lbs (951.7 kg)

No. 93, Ferguson TE.F20 with a Reekie Conversion
1956, Serial No. TE-F20481047, Registration No. OSR 834

I bought this tractor from my friend John French in January 2005. For a time, John had lived in the North East of Scotland and while there had bought a number of Ferguson Vineyard tractors. These were popular in the raspberry fields around Arbroath and Blairgowrie, and the Scots referred to them as berry tractors.

Reekie was a well-established Ferguson distributor in that part of Scotland, and they had developed the process of modifying a standard TE-20 tractor to have a narrower track width. This was to enable the versatile little Ferguson to negotiate the narrow rows of raspberry canes. At first, his method was to shorten the rear axle trumpet housings and half shafts by cutting and welding.

It is said that Harry Ferguson became aware of this practice and instructed Reekie to stop using this crude method, warning that if he did not he would lose his Ferguson dealership. In the meantime, Harry Ferguson instructed his development department to design a well-engineered narrow TE20: this was duly done, and the tractors were

Reekie offered narrow-track conversions before you could buy one from Ferguson. This is a later diesel-engined version. (Andrew Morland)

built at Banner Lane, Coventry. This took place early on, when the TE20s were being powered by the Continental petrol engine Z120. These particular tractors were designated TEB20; later, with the introduction of the Standard petrol engine the designation became TEC20, for a TVO model it became TEE20, and the lamp oil model was TEJ20. No diesel-engined narrow Ferguson was ever made in the UK, but they were produced in France. Later on an even narrower model was produced, known as a Vineyard.

This late example was produced by Reekie way after the time of Harry Ferguson's original threats but, in my opinion and to be expected, this one is not a cut and weld job: he was able to use genuine Ferguson trumpet housings and half shafts that would have been used on the Ferguson Vineyard models. The front axle, track rods and radius arms were all modified by Reekie, as were the linkage lift arms. The first owners of this tractor were Angus Fruit Farms.

Brief specification:
• Engine: Standard Motor Company; indirect injection; diesel; capacity 127.68 cu in (2029 cc); power output at PTO 25 hp at 2000rpm engine speed
• Gearbox: 4 forward and 1 reverse; compounded by the fitment of a Howard reduction gear behind the main gearbox output, mounted internally
• Hydraulic system: Cat 1; three-point linkage with draft control only
• Tyre sizes: on this example, front 4.00 x 19; rear 4.00 x 36
• Wheel base: 70 in (1778 mm)
• Weight: approx. 2700 lbs (1224 kg)

No. 94, Ferguson FE35, Pre-Production model
Serial No. FE003, Engine No. SJ3E, Registration No. LJ0 507W

I acquired this tractor in 2001. According to Massey Ferguson records, production of FE35 tractors started on Wednesday, 22 August 1956, with six being assembled that day. The first had serial number SDM 1001 (Standard Agricultural Diesel 23C, Dual Clutch) and this now forms part of the collection on display at the MF Beauvais plant in France. The pre-production model at Coldridge has, over time, sadly lost its original bonnet and mudguards. These items were replaced by the previous owner, and the bonnet is a genuine MF part, but the rear mudguards are Ford Dexta.

One feature it bears is a crankcase breather on the left-hand side of the Standard 23C engine, which was only carried over on early production models. This tractor is displayed 'as found'.

Brief specification:
• Engine: Standard Motor Company; indirect injection; diesel; capacity 137.8 cu in (2259 cc); power output at PTO 34 hp at 2000rpm engine speed
• Gearbox: 6 forward and 2 reverse
• Hydraulic system: Cat 1; three-point linkage with draft and position control
• Tyre sizes: on this tractor, front 4.00 x 19; rear 10 x 28
• Wheel base: 72 in (1830 mm)
• Weight: approx. 3150 lbs (1429 kg)

The pre-produtcion FE35 in the Coldridge Collection is displayed in "as-found" condition.

The Crawley 75 Tractor
Not numbered in the Collection

Ernie Luxton ploughing on the Crawley 75.

I bought this tractor in August 1984 from a man living on the Kent/Sussex border. As with some other machines, I guess that it was its unusual, quirky design that attracted me. As with a good many other tractors that found their way to Coldridge it stayed around for a few years until I decided to move it on. This was not difficult, as the late Ernie Luxton was very keen to buy it, bearing in mind that it was in working order. Ernie made some minor repairs to it plus an oily rag restoration, and showed it off many times at tractor rallies and field working days, including several visits to the Royal Cornwall Show and the Dorset Steam Fair. On one occasion it won a prize for best exhibit in the show.

When they were introduced in the mid-1950s, the manufacturers, Crawley Metal Products of Ifield Road, Crawley (Crawley was developed as a New Town following the end of the Second World War), priced them at £280.

Brief specification:
• Engine: J.A.P. air-cooled petrol or petrol/TVO Type 5B 8 bhp, or as an alternative a Petter air-cooled diesel type PCI 7.5 hp
• Clutch: fully automatic centrifugal type
• Gearbox: 3 forward and 1 reverse
• Brake: drum type on rear wheels only operated independently by levers and together by pedal
• Width: 30½ in (774.7 mm) min, 48in (1219 mm) max
• Overall length: 83 in (2110 mm); wheelbase: 52 in (1320 mm)
• Tyres: front 4.00 x 12, rear 7.50 x 20
• Mid-mounted belt pulley was standard
• Bonnet of GRP (fibreglass)
• Weight: 1,300 lbs (589 kg)
Accessories listed were:
• Steel wheels
• Grass tyres
• Jack
• Rear PTO adaptor
• Front wheel weights
• Universal drawbar
• Foot throttle
This little tractor could be used for all sorts of light work, ideal for smallholders and vegetable growers.

Tractors on loan from AGCO

AGCO's 1955 Ferguson TE.F20.

When Banner Lane closed down in early 2003, AGCO then had to find new locations for their collection of display tractors. On 24 August 2006 Massey Ferguson published a press release setting out three chosen locations for the housing of their collection. This document was worked out by a small team of senior staff including Paul Lay (Manager Public Relations and Communication) and Jeremy Burgess (Director Licensees).

The locations in the document were as follows:-
To Beauvais Visitor Centre, Picardy, France:
• Ferguson Model A No. 1
• Ford Ferguson 9NAN
• Ferguson TE20, 'Sue' from the South Pole Expedition

AGCO's 1957 Massey Harris Pony.

• Ferguson FE35 No. 1
• Massey Ferguson 168
• Massey Ferguson 590 4WD.
To the Coventry Transport Museum:
• Ferguson TE20 No. 500,000
• Massey Ferguson 65 MKI
• MF4345: the last tractor ever built at Banner Lane and signed by all the people who had assembled it.

It was at this time that I had a phone call from Jeremy Burgess asking if I would be happy to have the final six standing at Coldridge, plus a couple of implements. I quickly agreed on a renewable five-year contract. The only condition I had to abide by was that they would be kept in a locked and alarmed building wired to a control centre: as this was already in place there were no further issues. AGCO would insure them.

I will describe each of these six tractors in chronological order. The first is a 1955 Ferguson TE.F20, serial number 487,570, and judging from the state of the tyres and the oil leaks it has seen a lot of service. An unusual addition is that it has ¼ in (6 mm) wide red lines painted on the major components. The descriptive plate that relates to this tractor example states 'This is a Standard Tractor and was used as a reference unit when monitoring production quality at Banner Lane.' My guess is that it was just a bit of nonsense designed to impress visitors being given a tour of the factory! Anyway, I have used it to display my Ferguson Potato Planter (type R-DE-20, Serial No. 808) with the Ferguson Fertilizer Attachment (model 720, Serial No. 3170) to good advantage.

Brief specification:
• Engine: Standard Motor Company; 20C; indirect injection; diesel; 127.6 cu in (2092 cc); power output at belt 25 hp
• Gearbox: 4 forward and 1 reverse (the descriptive plate states 3 forward!!)
• Hydraulic system: Cat 1; three-point linkage with draft control only
• Tyre sizes: front 4.00 x 19; rear 10 x 28
• Wheel base: 70 in (1778 mm)
• Weight: approx. 2700 lbs (1225 kg)

The next tractor in the line-up is a 1957 Massey Harris Pony. Why it was at Banner Lane is a bit of a mystery. The story is that it arrived on a lorry that had come over from Sweden to load up with a consignment of new tractors from Banner Lane, the driver having been told that it was to be unloaded on site. This was duly done and it was simply put into their collection. Since being at Coldridge it has been off site once, to be used as a prop in a film set, and was safely returned to Coldridge after six weeks.

Brief specification:
• Engine: Simca; petrol; capacity 1.2 Litre; Power Outlet 15.8 HP
• Gearbox: 5 forward and 1 reverse
• Mechanical rear lift (manual)
• PTO and belt pulley fitted
• 6 volt electrics
• Tyre sizes: front 4.00 x 15; rear 8.3 x 24
• Wheel base: 66.9 in (1690 mm)
• Weight: 1653 lbs (749 kg)

The third tractor is an MF35X, with Multi-Power and PAVT rear wheels. The Tractormeter is showing 278 hours, but I am sure it has clocked up a lot more by the wear of the tyres. As a point of interest, it was used by Universal Hobbies to produce their one-sixteenth scale model complete with the PAVT wheels!

Brief specification:
• Engine: Perkins A3-152; capacity 152.7 cu in (2500 cc); power output at flywheel 44.5 hp at 2250rpm or 41.5 hp at PTO at same engine speed
• Gearbox: 6 forward and 2 reverse, with Multi-Power giving overdrive effect in all these ratios
• Hydraulic system: Cat 1; three-point linkage with draft and position control
• Tyre sizes: on this example, front 6.00 x 16; rear 11 x 28, on PAVT rims
• Wheel base: 72 in (1830 mm)
• Weight: approx. 3185 lbs (1445 kg)

The next of the AGCO tractors is a late MF135, Reg. No. TRW 306R, fitted with a sound insulated Quick Detach Cab that enables the top part of the cab to lift off easily by using the built in lifting lugs. The tractormeter is showing 250.7 hours, but judging by the tyres it has done more. It is in a very well preserved state, and the door closes with a nice solid clunk.

Brief specification:
• Engine: Perkins; direct injection A3-152; diesel; capacity 152.7 cu in (2500 cc); power output at the flywheel 45.5 hp at 2250 rpm engine speed
• Gearbox: 6 forward and 2 reverse
• Hydraulic system: Cat 1; three-point linkage with draft, position and pressure control
• Tyre sizes: front 6.00 x 16; rear 11 x 28
• Wheel base: 72 in (1829 mm)

MF35X with Multi-Power and PAVT wheels.

AGCO's late Massey Ferguson MF135 with a sound insulated Quick Detach Cab sits next to the doors and clock from Banner Lane.

The Famous Nipper Pulling Tractor
Owned by AGCO

The Nipper was European Champion in the Super Stock Class in 1980 and 1981, and British Super Stock Champion in 1979, 1980 and 1981.

Some of the AGCO team with The Nipper.

This project was started by several Massey Ferguson engineering employees in the late 1970s as an after-work challenge; it was never supported by Massey Ferguson, but several other engineering firms contributed some of the special parts needed. The team was headed by David Parnell, who at the time was a Test Engineer with Massey Ferguson. The base tractor, a MF265, was sponsored by Ron Gibbons, a farmer contractor located at North Wheatley, Nottinghamshire, while some of the special components were supplied by the following firms:

• The cerametalic clutch by GKN Laycock
• Three turbo chargers supplied by Garrett AiResearch
• Special head gaskets by Coopers Payen
• A special aluminium front axle support bracket by DuPont Harper Castings Ltd
• Newbow Engineering supplied a special gauge for accurately shaping the treads of the rear tyres
• Gates Hydraulics, stainless steel hydraulic hoses and spun aluminium rear wheels (alas, the latter are no longer fitted to the tractor on display).

Alongside David were Tim Turner, driver, Bill Randle, Paul Herbert, John Mills, Steve Iveson, Dick Humphries and the late Rod Shirley.

From a technical point of view, I feel it is necessary first to summarise briefly the specification of a standard Massey Ferguson agricultural MF265 tractor. It has a Perkins A4-

236 direct injection unit that develops 69 bhp (BS) at 2000rpm. Compression ratio is 16:1. Clutch 12 in (304 mm) main, 10 in (254 mm) PTO split torque type. Main gearbox is three forward speeds and one reverse, compounded by a secondary epicyclic unit giving high and low range plus Multi-Power, so that in total there are twelve forward and four reverse speeds. The standard tractors were generally fitted with 7.50 x 16 front tyres and 12 x 36 rear tyres, giving a top speed of about 20 mph/30 kph.

Now for the details of the heavily modified Nipper:
• The engine was the same model of Perkins, but highly tuned. For a start, the compression ratio has been reduced to 11.5:1 by the expedient of cutting bowls in the piston heads; one of the (normally three) compression rings was removed; and the internal expander of the oil control ring was removed. This was done to reduce friction and create heavy oiling.
• The engine breather pipe was enlarged and leads to an oil catchment tank,
• The crankshaft was balanced; the connection rods were shot peened to relieve internal stresses and then matched for equal weight.
• The main and big end bearing shells, normally of white metal, were replaced by lead bronze, but with slightly more clearance than standard, again

to foster good lubrication.
• Twin CAV rotary fuel injection pumps were installed; originally, the intention was to provide sequential fuel injection. David told me they reverted to synchronising the injection of both pumps.
• Three Garret AiResearch turbo chargers have been fitted, giving a total boost pressure of 120psi; no waste gates are fitted. The first and smallest in diameter, but highest pressure, is driven directly off the exhaust manifold; its exhaust is fed into the second and slightly larger diameter turbo; in turn, its exhaust feeds the third and largest diameter turbo, with the lowest pressure. All three feature oil pressure lubrication from the engine's main higher capacity oil pump.
• A system of water injection under pressure was installed, feeding into the induction manifold at four points as well as to the first and second turbo chargers.
• Starter motor and alternator are standard units.
• Special single plate cerametalic clutch (the PTO drive is deleted).
As no official dynamometer engine performance figures are available, I can only quote from the *Autocar* Road Test Report, which gives estimated values of 450/500 bhp at 4500rpm, though the descriptive plate relating to the Nipper loaned to me by Massey Ferguson claims 1000 bhp at

Autocar *magazine achieved over 65mph with The Nipper.*

The Nipper leads a rather smokey parade.

5000rpm. With a standard MF265 in top gear and Multi-Power in high, the ratio is 13.9 mph (22.4 kph) per 1000rpm, which equates to 59.35 mph (63 kph), or is it Massey Ferguson's claim of an engine speed of 5000rpm = 65.95 mph (106 kph? *Autocar* achieved 65 mph (104.6 kph) with their observer sitting on the rear transmission towing a fifth-wheel speedometer!

A few other modifications:
• The power steering was deleted.
• A second stop control for the engine was installed that was connected to the towing sledge by a light break-away cable: this was to ensure that, should the connection between tractor and sledge break, the engine of the Nipper would shut down.
• The bonnet panels were hand fabricated in aluminium, as were a few other parts.
• An electric fan was fitted to a relatively small radiator.
• The fuel tank has a capacity of only 4 gallons (18 litres). The fuel was diesel plus 5% lanolin (to provide extra lubrication for the highly modified fuel injection pumps). *Autocar* reported a fuel consumption of 2 mpg at 30 mph and 1 mpg at 60 mph.

In its day, The Nipper was European Champion in the Super Stock Class in 1980 and 1981, and British Super Stock Champion in 1979, 1980 and 1981.

When The Nipper arrived at Coldridge, the original rear wheels, 30.5 in (775 mm) wide on 32 in (812.8 mm) diameter aluminium rims, had been replaced with 'slave' wheels and 12.4/11 x 32 tyres, thereby reducing its overall width from 107 in (2718 mm) to just under 96 in (2438 mm), thus making it more manageable. A bit of luck! Wheel base 91 in (2311 mm) and weight approximately 6126 lbs (2779 kg).

On one occasion, we – David Parnell, Bill Randle, Jeremy Burgess and Neil Murray from Massey Ferguson, plus my friend Robin Haughton and myself – fired The Nipper up. I have a photograph of one man with a can of Easy Start (ether) in each hand spraying it into the air intake. After a bit of hesitation it did fire up, but the black smoke from its 5in (125mm) stainless steel exhaust pipe was disgusting: one of the chaps said 'I hope you have friendly neighbours.' I said, 'No, you'd better shut it down.' David wouldn't allow them to bring it up to full revs because he'd noticed a broken rear cylinder head bolt, so we shut it down and manhandled it back into the Heptagonal Tractor Shed, where it is displayed for visitors.

The Last Prototype Tractor Built at Banner Lane, Coventry
Field Test Tractor No. 1175, Registration No. Y267 TOD, Owned by AGCO

This was the last of the six tractors that were placed on loan by AGCO to the Coldridge Collection following the closure of Banner Lane. I seem to remember Jeremy Burgess telling me that there had been some debate about this one's future, but I was given to understand that it was David Parnell who felt strongly that it should come to Coldridge. As an aside, the lorry driver who delivered it drove it down off his lorry and parked it up. He had a quick look around the Collection before heading back to Coventry. Looking at this 'tractor' I thought what a 'monster' it was, as I hadn't driven a large, modern tractor before, but once in the seat I found it surprisingly easy to handle.

Though it's badged MF4270 it is in fact the development model of what became the MF4370. David (at one time a hydraulics and electronics engineer with MF) pointed out that this particular tractor was also used for official testing for market 'homologation' requirements for the OECD (Organisation for Economic Co-operation and Development) as well as for EMC (electromagnetic compatibility). To that end it was usual for tractors submitted for 'homologation' to be loaded with every possible feature that might perhaps make its way into production at a later date. For example, this tractor is FieldStar Precision Farming ready. The inclusion of radar allows true ground speed to be measured and compared with wheel revolutions, thus calculating the percentage of wheel slip. HID (high-intensity discharge) work lights are fitted to the front and rear, high up on the cab: these give a pure white light. Another feature was the fitment of a hand-fabricated auxiliary hydraulic oil tank (production tractors had plastic); this was incorporated for the fitment of a power shuttle, thus giving 24 speeds in both forward and reverse.

Both front and rear differential locks operate simultaneously, controlled by a three-position switch: diff lock engaged; central position diff lock disengaged; and diff lock in automatic mode, i.e. only operates when the hydraulic linkage lowers an implement into work. Finally, the cab incorporates a high vis roof to improve visibility for the driver when operating a front loader.

On reading my draft description for this tractor, Jeremy thought he would be able to add some features I'd missed, and this is what he wrote:

The 4300 series was the last tractor range to be introduced into production at Banner Lane and represented the ultimate development of a driveline that could trace its history directly back to the FE35 of 1956. The 4300 series was a lightly upgraded version of the MF4200 series, which replaced the 300 series in 1997 and incorporated a new cab, new sheet metal styling and upgraded chassis castings to allow for increased 3-point linkage lift capacity. The 4200 series was known internally as the DXE project, shorthand for DX–Extended and was conceived after a much more ambitious project, the DXR (DX Replacement), was cancelled because of cost concerns.

When the FE35 was introduced to replace the TE20, the Banner Lane plant had a significant overhaul and very significant investment was made

Badged as MF4270, it is in fact a prototype of what was to become the MF4370.

in machine tools, particularly in several state-of-the-art transfer lines. These huge combination machining lines were designed as bespoke systems to machine large numbers of the same casting. There were therefore separate transfer lines for the main gearbox casting, axle centre housing, trumpet housings and so on. While the transfer lines were very good at repeat machining of the same casting, they were not flexible when it came to coping with design changes. The transfer lines remained in use until the end of tractor production at Banner Lane, and their lack of flexibility created a significant challenge during the DXE tractor range development.

The required specification for the new range included gearboxes of up to 24 forward and 24 reverse speeds, along with a clutchless 'power shuttle' to facilitate change from forward to reverse. All this had to be shoe-horned into a space designed for the 6 x 2 sliding mesh gearbox used on the FE35

To get the extended lift capacity required (up to 5 tonnes when used in conjunction with external tie bars) the gearbox and axle centre housings needed to be strengthened; this was achieved by adding more metal, carefully using computer aided design [CAD] and finite element analysis. But at the end of the day the new castings had to be machined by the existing transfer lines, which were also required to continue machining the old designs of castings for the ongoing production of MF 200 series tractors, together with supplying CKD kits for the numerous Massey Ferguson licensees around the world.

To assess how much scope there was to increase the wall thicknesses and flanges on the gearbox and axle centre housings, trial castings were prepared based on the old design and with the new profile mocked up with Plasticine. The castings were then run through the machine lines and if the Plasticine remained intact then the engineers knew there was enough clearance in the machine lines to accommodate it!

When the last tractor (a MF 4345) came off the production line on the afternoon of Christmas Eve 2002, it was the 3,306,997th tractor or tractor kit to be made at Banner Lane, and apart from just over 500,000 TE20s made before 1956, all of those tractors had castings machined on the same machine tools installed in that year. Sadly, though, the transfer lines were offered for sale along with all the other Banner Lane plant, but the age and specialist nature of this equipment rendered it obsolete and the whole lot was subsequently cut up for scrap.

Thank you for that information, Jeremy.

When this prototype was delivered I was handed two folders of information relating to it.

First there was a log of most of its field test work, repairs and modifications that were carried out. An amusing entry reads 'broken circlip on gear linkage temporarily held in place with string'. The second folder contained material relating to the production models that stemmed from this prototype, i.e. the MF4300 range tractors from 67hp to 116hp. This also included a 31-page sales brochure. Next was a MF4300 Series Product Information Guide, which had been produced for dealer use; this runs to 118 pages. Finally, an Operator Instruction Book that covered the following models in the range: 4315, 4320, 4325, 4335, 4355, 4360, 4365 and 4370. This document has 198 pages! All good stuff to have and share with interested visitors.

Brief specification:
• Engine: Perkins six-cylinder turbo producing 106hp (DIN) at 2200rpm. A very conservative rating.
• Clutch: Cerametalic 12.99 in (330 mm) diameter.
• Gearbox: 24 forward and 24 reverse speeds achieved by four main speeds, three ranges (high, medium, low) and a high and low splitter range, all selected on a single gear lever.
• The Power Shuttle Control lever (coloured orange), located to the left of the dash and incorporates a neutral safety start position. This allows the operator to change direction without the use of the main transmission clutch and also prevents starting the engine with direction selected.
• An operator's selectable variable 'comfort' control which adjusts the rate of engagement between forward and reverse direction changes
• PTO: 540rpm or 1000rpm by interchangeable shafts, speed selected by lever in the cab.
• Rear hydraulics three-point lift system, maximum lift at the ends of the arms, 11,023 lbs (5000 kg) achieved by the addition of two external assister rams.
• Steering: hydrostatic with fully adjustable tilt and telescopic steering column.
• Front axle centre drive – maximum turning angle 55°
• Automatic 4WD engagement with the application of the brakes effectively giving 4-wheel braking when both brake pedals are latched together.
• Brakes – oil cooled and hydraulically operated. Brake fluid is Castrol LHM mineral, the same as Citroen and Rolls Royce!
• Parking brake, which when applied automatically engages 4WD.
• Standard tyres; front 13.6R x 28; rear 16.9R x 38.
• Maximum speed 25 mph/40 kmh
• Overall weight approx. 9050 lbs (4105 kg).
What a change from a Ferguson TE20!

Old Implements on loan from AGCO

Now for the old implements on loan from AGCO. The oldest of these is a Massey Harris Binder No 3. The descriptive plate dates it as 1925, but knowledgeable visitors have told me that it is more likely to be from the early 1900s. These binders were very successful in their day, because Massey Harris designed them to deal with the long straw cereal crops typically grown throughout the UK and Europe. This success is validated by the fact that our local thatching straw grower, Roger Hill, uses a fleet of the Massey Harris Binders when harvesting his crops.

The other implement on loan is an eleven-row corn seed drill with wooden wheels. This example, I guess, dates from about 1920 and was arranged to be drawn by a pair of horses; typically, it has been converted at some point to be drawn by a tractor.

The seed drill and Massey Harris Binder on loan from AGCO.

Morris 1000 Pickup
1968, Registration No. LOD 802F

Perhaps not exactly part of the Coldridge Collection, but readers may be interested to find out why I have this vehicle.

It was the result of a dream, and I made it come true! Let me explain. I bought a new Morris 1000 Pickup in October 1959 from Henlys of North London to replace my Jowett Bradford ½ ton truck, which had a two-cylinder horizontally opposed engine.

I seem to remember that it cost me £378 plus £7.10s for the passenger seat. It was as basic as they came: no heater, and no form of direction indicators, so all down to hand signals; but I did pay extra to have it 'undersealed', a rubbery protective coating against rust. It was finished in Frilford Grey. I drove it home to Nicholls Farm, Redbourn, the day my father left home and soon set about fitting flashing directional indicators, front and rear. I found a second-hand Smiths re-circulatory heater unit and fitted that to the cab. I had a firm of coach trimmers from Edgware make a tonneau cover for the load area. I clocked up 187,000 miles with this vehicle, but that did ultimately include two Gold Seal exchange engines, together with two replacement gearboxes, and the replacement of the whole chassis.

Anyway, back in February 1992 I dreamt one night that I had bought a second-hand Morris 1000 Pickup, restored it and painted it in my firm's colour – BMC Limeflower Green. So on waking I thought it was a good idea and decided that this was what I would do! Asking around, I discovered that the late John Hocking of Winkleigh, North Devon, had one abandoned in his barn that he had previously used in his forestry work. He had put it to one side when it failed its MOT. It had initially been owned, from new, by motor cycle dealers Irelands of Barnstaple. John seemed very keen to sell it to me, knowing that it would be properly restored.

On getting it back to Lower Park, Robin Haughton and I set about dismantling it. We removed all the mechanical components, stripped out the electrics, took off the doors and unbolted the other body panels from the chassis. We were just left with the frame on the concrete floor. Taking an end each, Robin and I went to pick it up, with the intention of putting it in the scrap metal skip, and to our surprise it just folded up in the middle!

The next stage was to make a long list of all the major parts that would be needed for its restoration. The great majority came from a firm in Nottingham by the name of Henric, including a new chassis, a pair of front wings, radiator grille, rear springs, four shock absorbers, second-hand stainless steel window frames for the doors, various rubber seals and trims, hub caps and front bumper trim, and many other parts.

I had the engine rebuilt to run on unleaded petrol by Chris at Kar Engine Services of Barnstaple, while Gordon Rogers of Mid Devon Motors, Winkleigh, rebuilt the gearbox using genuine BMC parts. Probably the fiddliest bit of work was done by Robin, that of remaking the external rear wheel arches, as at the time these were not available as factored parts.

With the body panels repaired it was over to Peter Clarke of Lapford, Devon, to prime and repaint in Two Pack BMC Limeflower Green, which he did to a very high standard. Gradually, Robin and

I built the Morris back up and it was eventually sent for its MOT at Mid Devon Motors. It passed without a hitch! For the next phase of work it was taken to Exeter Auto Trimmers to have new door cards, a new brown carpet fitted, both the seats re-upholstered and a new tonneau cover made – all completed to a good professional standard.

There were a few 'modern' upgrades built into the project, i.e. a vacuum servo, a rear fog light and a reversing light, as well as hazard warning lights.

The final piece of work was done by the signwriter Ken Back of Exeter, traditional hand lettering using the Consul Light typeface with a few of the serifs joined together. I called to collect the Pickup just as Ken was finishing his work – what a privilege to watch the skill of a real craftsman.

Since then, the Morris 1000 Pickup has been used quite regularly in the summer months and clocked up about 27,000 miles since the restoration so was beginning to look a bit tatty in a number of places. Towards the end of 2019 I commissioned Alan at A&T Motors of High Bickington to give the body work some attention in the places where it was looking tired. Alan completed this work to his usual high standard and without interfering with Ken Buck's sign-writing – a real bonus. I now feel proud to be driving it again – weather permitting!

The pick up parked outside Winkleigh Post Office.

Land Rover IIB Forward Control
Registration No. EOJ 163

I bought this vehicle in 2001 from Dunsfold Land Rovers of Surrey, the business of the Bashall family; the founder of the business was the late Brian and it is now run by his son Phillip, a guru of all things Land Rover, and they have an impressive collection of rare and prototype vehicles.

When this Land Rover was first registered it was operated by the Post Office and equipped with a coachbuilt office-type body, very possibly a Mobile Communications Vehicle, and painted yellow. Dunsfold had taken this body off and replaced it with the normal drop-sided type, all finished in the correct Land Rover Mid Grey and showing 4,700 miles on the odometer.

These models were powered by a 2.6-litre capacity six-cylinder petrol engine, with overhead inlet and side exhaust valves. The gearbox fitted was known as the One Ton; this I changed to a gearbox from a Series III which had synchromesh on all four forward ratios; also the gearing to the transfer box was of a slightly higher ratio.

Before we put this Forward Control into use, Robin and I lined the load area with black-stained plywood, fitted it up with front and rear bolsters (the rear being removable) as well as strong strapping-down facilities for the load bed area.

We also made a side mounted storage box with a roller shutter door, and a rack to carry two jerry cans – yes, it was a thirsty Land Rover.

It had a good driving position, set high up on its 900 x 16 radial tyres but it would have benefited from having power steering!

I sold it in 2007 to generate some cash to go towards the development of the third tractor shed/building at Lower Park.

The ex-Post Office Forward Control Land Rover was convereted from an office-type body into a drop-side pick up.

A Ferguson TE-H20 Lamp Oil Engine
(as a box of bits)

As I understand it, two TE-H20 tractors were kept at Fletchampstead Highway, Coventry, as field test tractors. One is still complete and owned by George Willan, while the engine of the other is at Coldridge. This came about in the following way. It was bought from Massey Ferguson by David Treen, who sold it on to Peter Lewis in 2002. Peter restored the tractor to working order but fitted it up with a second-hand TVO engine: it carried the serial number TE-H20 143816, engine number SB251. It can be dated to being made on Friday, 18 August 1950.

Lamp oil or paraffin has a zero octane rating, so a very low compression ratio of 4.5:1 is necessary. The bore of this engine is 85 mm, with a stroke of 92 mm, giving a capacity of 2088 cc. Its quoted output is 22.9 belt hp at 2000rpm engine speed: just to compare it with a TE-D20 of the same capacity, the quoted output is 25.4 belt hp at 2000rpm.

At present this engine head is not on display, which is a pity because the combustion chambers are noticeably larger than those of a TVO engine.

The Ferguson R5 Prototype Car Engine

In 2015 I had a phone call from a man offering me two prototype Ferguson car engines. The earlier was an overhead valve engine that was developed to power the R4 road car. The other was the later overhead cam engine as fitted to the R5 estate car.

The asking price for these was beyond my budget, so I had to decline the offer, even though I was keen to have them and he seemed keen for me to have them! About ten days later he phoned again and asked if I might have a tractor I was willing to swap for the two engines. My reply right away was positive: yes, I have a MF165 with a Four-Wheel Traction Ltd conversion (No. 76 in The Collection). The deal was done and he delivered the engines within a week and took away the MF165.

This engine was designed by Claude Hill, Harry Ferguson's Chief Engineer and an ex-Aston Martin designer. It was a very much developed design from the OHV engine installed in the earlier Ferguson R4 prototype road car.

The main benefits of a horizontal layout are as follows:
• a lower centre of gravity
• a shorter but wider engine
• a larger bore to stroke ratio is possible, i.e. over square that enables higher crankshaft speeds
• because of the larger bore it is possible to install slightly larger diameter inlet and exhaust valves, which gives better gas flow
• the horizontal arrangement gives a better dynamic balance to an engine.

It is believed that these overhead camshaft engines were the first to employ a toothed belt drive to each single overhead cam. My example, stamped P94/4, is fitted with two SU HD6 carburettors, but Harry Ferguson Research experimented with a single twin choke Webber carburettor, as well as an engine of this type fitted with a single Solex type 34P A1A, and even the installation of a Paxton Supercharger and Bendix Stromberg 36 WW carburettor.

The specifications of this engine, the fourth of a batch of seven built, are as follows:
• Bore 95 mm, stroke 78 mm, swept volume 2212 cc, compression ratio 9:1
• Sump capacity 10 pints SAE 10/40
• Lucas alternator driven by a Micro-V belt.

The performance figures set out here are taken from the *Automotive Engineer* dated March 1965:
• Maximum power net 125 bhp at 5400rpm
• Maximum torque 131 lb/ft at 2500rpm.

Another set of performance figures taken from *Motor* dated 20 August 1966 states the following for the same engine, i.e. one fitted with two SU HD6 carburettors:
• Maximum power 111bhp at 5300rpm
• Maximum torque 128 lb/ft at 3500rpm.

The engine was sent off for a rebuild and in February 2019 I had a phone call to say that Peter Smith and Robert McCall had completed the rebuild and had made a framework to take both the engine and necessary ancillaries, i.e. radiator, fuel tank, battery and exhaust system.

It so happened that a Land Rover event was being held at the British Motor Museum at Gaydon in Warwickshire on 12 May 2019. I had heard that Bill Munro was to launch his latest book, *Traction for Sale, the Story of Ferguson Formula Four Wheel Drive* at this event. I also learnt that he was planning to have several cars on display that featured the Ferguson Formula conversions. I phoned him and asked if he would like to have on display my recently refurbished Ferguson Flat Four car engine. He accepted the offer with relish. So it was planned that Julie, Peter and Robert would bring the engine down from Cheshire ready for display on 12 May. The engine was run from time to time to draw attention to its presence. They delivered the engine to the Coldridge Collection the following day. Being cheeky, I suggested that they might like to take the earlier prototype Flat Four engine back with them. To my surprise they agreed enthusiastically to my suggestion and they set off on their long journey back to Cheshire. I must put a big thank you to Peter and Robert for all their work.

The rebuilt Ferguson flat-four engine is ready to run on its custom-made frame.

Some Other Stuff in the Coldridge Collection

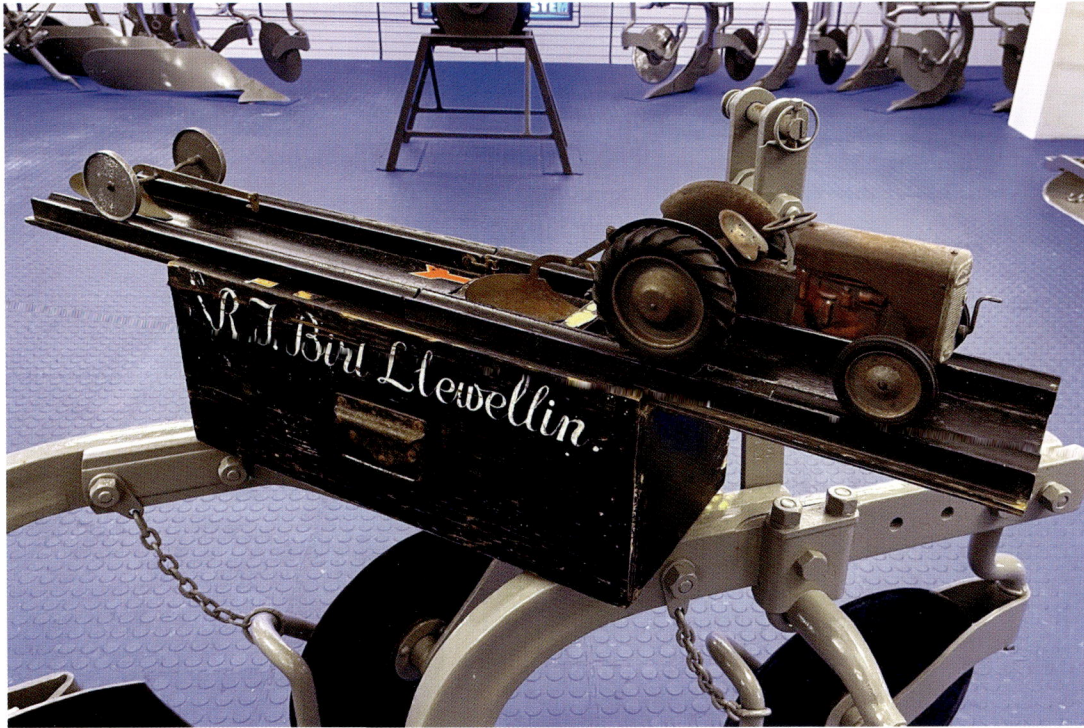

The Demonstration Model was used by Ferguson salesmen to show potential customers some of the benefits of the Ferguson System.

Having described the various tractors displayed at Coldridge, I think it would be useful to look at some of the other items that might be of interest to readers. So I will discuss the full-sized cutaway models that are here, followed by descriptions of a few implements that were not covered in my earlier books.

But first, possibly the most useful object is a small, wind-up Demonstration Model about one-sixteenth scale, used by Ferguson salesmen to show potential customers some of the benefits of the Ferguson System. In fact, Harry Ferguson took a prototype version of this model when he visited Henry Ford in America in September 1938 to show off his Ferguson Model A tractor. My model dates from the late 1940s.

As can be seen from the photograph, the tractor and the two ploughs can be packed neatly into their wooden carrying case. I bought this from the Llewellyn family, who were Ferguson dealers in Haverford West, South West Wales. Alas, the original instruction book was missing, but about a year after I had bought it I was kindly given a replacement by the late Keith Base, an ex-WWII Spitfire pilot and later an instructor at Stoneleigh Abbey Ferguson Training School. The model is 'powered' by winding up a light coil spring that extends the length of the 'starting handle', which turns the rear wheels via bevel gearing. The demonstration is done by hitching the simple trailing plough to the tractor, winding the 'starter handle' fully and being sure to hold the rear wheels, setting it on the track and when the plough reaches the obstruction set in its path the front of the tractor rears up. Then there follows a second demonstration run, but this time hitched to the Ferguson three-point linkage plough. The tractor is again wound up and set on the track towards the obstruction but this time it stays on all four wheels with just the rears spinning: all completely safe. The reason for this is that, when the plough hits the obstruction, the headstock of the plough tends to move slightly forward and that force is transferred via the top link, which tends to push the front wheels down.

The first full-sized cutaway to come to Coldridge was a motorised sectioned rear end of a TE20 designed to show off the operation of the draft control system. This cutaway was originally displayed at Hadlow Agricultural College in Kent. I have since noticed an identical one in the Science Museum Group Collection at Wroughton, near Swindon. When I bought this model it was just about working, but the Perspex windows were broken and most of the chromed parts were badly

This motorised sectioned rear end of a TE20 was designed to show the operation of the draft control system.

rusted; however, it was complete with its original stand. Again, it was Ernie who refurbished this unit, and I had the chromed parts properly replated, i.e. stripped and copper plated, followed by nickel plating and finally plating with chromium. The Perspex windows were re-manufactured by Richlite in Crediton, sadly no longer trading. To improve this unit's portability I made up a frame for it to stand on fitted with swivel castors and three-point linkage attachment Category 1!

From the same vendor I bought a cutaway

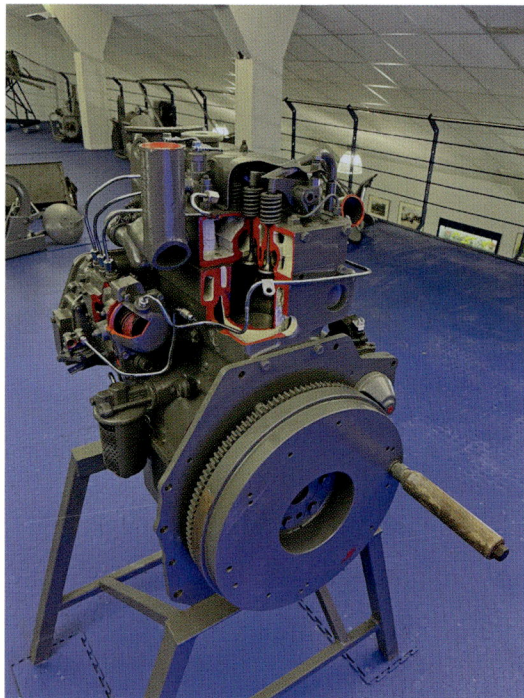

Cutaway of a Ford Dexta diesel engine, painted in Stoneleigh Grey.

gearbox from a MF35 but this is not yet on display.

Another motorised cutaway is of a MF165 gearbox equipped with Multi-Power. This had been at Seal-Hayne Agricultural College but I bought it from a South Devon tractor breaker, Ron Greet, along with a few other cutaways. Visitors are able to select different gear ratios as well as being able to operate the epicyclic unit that give High/Low. There is no provision to demonstrate the operation of Multi-Power, but the hydraulic clutch pack and power differential clutch coupler are slightly sectioned so it is possible to view the 'innards'.

Another cutaway that came from Ron Greet at the same time was a Ford Dexta diesel engine F3 fitted with Sims fuel injection equipment. This engine can be turned by a handle fitted to the flywheel, thus showing the movement of the component parts: even the starter, dynamo, pump and an injector are all cut away to some degree. Some may say that this Ford engine is out of place at Coldridge, which, of course, it is, but it is quite similar to the Perkins A3-152 engine and when it was refurbished it was painted in Stoneleigh Grey to disguise its true origin. Included in the deal with Ron were several other Ford cutaway gearboxes which I sold on to my friend Andrew Green, who has a good collection of early Ford tractors within the parish of Coldridge. He has now refurbished these and has them on display with his tractors.

From Luckham Agricultural College in Wiltshire I have two cutaway models. One is a hand-turned sectioned rear end of a MF65: this shows the working of the differential and its locking mechanism, the dry disc brakes and the planetary reduction hub at the far end of the half shaft. The other from Luckham is a motorised cutaway of a later MF135 with Pressure Control built into the hydraulic system: unfortunately, I have never quite worked out how to demonstrate it, but it was very well restored by Ernie.

Finally, I have a motorised sectioned Perkins A4-207 direct injection engine. This is actually an automotive unit with a cast aluminium sump, but in general terms it is more-or-less the same as the engine installed in the MF65 MKII. This engine was given to me by Bicton Agricultural College, Devon. I am ashamed to say that it has not yet been restored to working order but it is on view. It is motorised with a three-phase motor.

As most of the implements in the Coldridge Collection are described in my other books published by Herridge and Sons, I shall not be covering them here, but I feel that three American/

Canadian designed and built implements, all kindly sourced for me by the late John Moffitt, the well-respected Holstein cattle breeder and founder of the famous Hunday Collection of Ferguson tractors, should be noted. First, there is the Canadian-built Ferguson PTO driven baler (model F12, serial number 3891); these balers were not marketed in the UK. The American publicity material of the time lists seven special features, as follows:
• Only one nipple to grease once a year
• Able to drive through an 8-foot gateway
• Hay changes direction only twice
• Six different safety features
• Choice of PTO or engine driven. The petrol engine was an air-cooled two-cylinder unit made by Wisconsin that developed 14hp with a flat belt drive to the flywheel of the baler.
Specification of the PTO model:
• Overall length 15 ft 8 in
• Width 7 ft 10¾ in; pickup width 4 ft
• Height 4 ft 6 in; weight 2,600 lbs
• Bale chamber size 14 in x 18 in; length of bales 30 in or 38 in
• Plunger stroke 26 in; plunger speed 70–72 strokes per minute
• Maximum capacity 10 tons per hour.

Next is an American implement, the Rotary Hoe Type RKO-20, serial number 1136. This two-gang implement is in reality a rotary spike-toothed harrow designed for working down a seedbed: the instruction book recommends that it be driven as fast as possible.

Finally, there is the two-furrow slatted plough Type 14-AO-40, serial number 3175, of 1952. It is set at 14 in. Also an American Ferguson accessory, the PTO adaptor designed to bring the 1⅛ in PTO up to the SAE Standard of 1⅜ in and at 14 in to the centre of the draw bar pin.

There are some other items that may be of interest to readers. I was able to acquire the pair of doors and the glazed panel above from the main entrance to the Massey Ferguson offices at Banner Lane, just prior to their demolition. I did not just nick them! I first approached the developers of the site, Persimmon, who told me I would have to deal with the demolition contractors, which I did. They were quite happy for me to have the doors but I first had to provide them with a Method Statement setting out how the work would be conducted. Luckily, at that time I had in my employ a full-time Health and Safety supervisor, who kindly wrote me an acceptable procedure, which two of my staff were able to carry out. We had hoped to remove

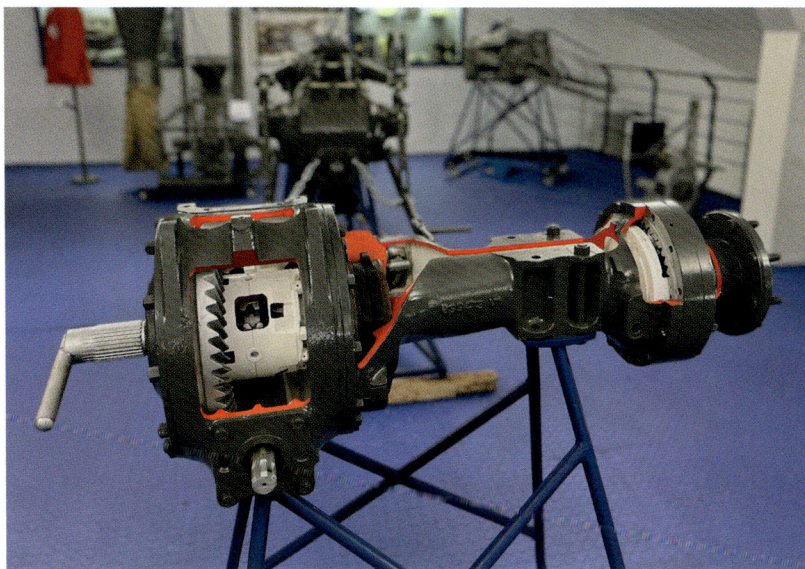

A cutaway of a MF65 rear axle.

A motorised utaway of a later MF135 with pressure control built into the hydraulic system.

the main frame from the original stonework of the 1937 architect-designed building but that was just not practical, so I commissioned a joiner to make a replica and I made the free-standing steel framework to support this exhibit. This work was done in 2009 but the steel work has still not been painted! The original glazing in the doors has been replaced with laminated glass to be on the safe side. I was also given two clocks from the site, and these are now fitted on either side of the door, at the top of the frame. It should be explained that most of the clocks on the Banner Lane site were of the electrically driven impulse type, controlled

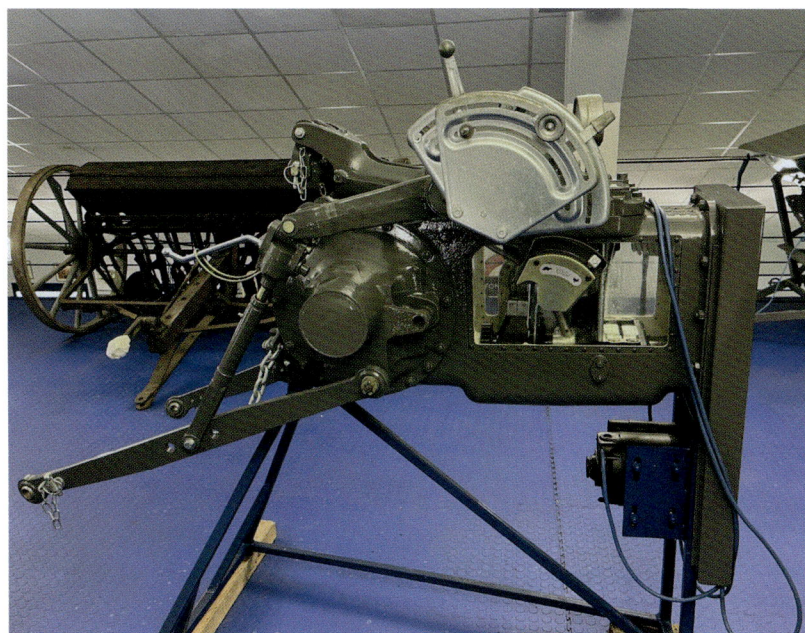

One of the 65 reproduction Ferguson clocks I made.

The Gilbert Gilkes Type B Hydraulic Governer I saved from the scrap man.

from a master unit with a pendulum, which I seem to remember was sited in the main reception area with its beautiful linen fold oak panelling – a bit of that here would have been nice! I was also given, by a former Massey Ferguson employee, a set of carpet tiles featuring the Massey Ferguson Triple Triangle.

When the Exeter depot of Medland Sanders & Twose closed down I was able to rescue three Massey Ferguson signs. The first was a large, 165 in (4190 mm) x 27½ in (700 mm), non-illuminated outdoor sign; this is now displayed in the heptagonal tractor

shed adjacent to the doors described above. The second, also outdoor, Massey Ferguson sign is illuminated and measures 48 in (1220 mm) x 32 in (812 mm) but this has not yet been properly displayed. The third is a hanging illuminated sign that would have been set over the store's parts counter. While dealing with the signs, I should say that in the Coldridge Collection we have a Ferguson illuminated double-sided hung dealer's sign that is one of seven replicas I made several years ago. Mine is displayed on a bent buck rake tine attached to my Ferguson Hammer Mill. Another replica item, one of about 65 that I made several years ago, is a hanging Ferguson Dealer's clock bearing the slogan 'Farm Better – Farm Faster with Ferguson System'. I have this displayed in the Ferguson Shed in full view of my desk: time of writing is 12:41, date: Tuesday 13 November 2018. All a bit of good fun!

Traffic lights: these are displayed here for two reasons. Our national traffic lights were the result of the Department of Transport commissioning the well-known silversmith and industrial designer, David Mellor, to produce a standard design, though he is better known for his cutlery designs and manufacturing at Hathersage, Derbyshire. The other reason is that I happened to stop at temporary traffic lights at Thornfalcon near Taunton one Sunday as the permanent ones were being cut down prior to replacement. I pulled in at the next lay-by and phoned my friend Steve at Thornfalcon Classic Cars and asked if he could get me a pair. A fortnight later he rang to say that he had been able to get two for me and two for himself. I asked another friend, Andrew Watson, to build me a unit so that we could have the lights going through a sequence. This worked well for about five years but sadly it has now failed and as yet Andrew has not been able to get it sorted – and he lives in Aberdeenshire.

Finally, one of the larger items on display is a Gilbert Gilkes Type B Hydraulic Governor, serial number 475. I saved this from being scrapped when a small hydroelectric generation set-up was being decommissioned from a mill near South Molton, Devon. Gilbert Gilkes & Gordon Ltd of Kendal, Cumbria, has a long history of turbine manufacture going back to 1856, and they are still very active today. Basically, this unit, which I guess dates from the early 1950s, would regulate the amount of water flowing through the turbine in proportion to the electrical load put on to the driven generator. To maintain a steady voltage and a frequency of 50 cycles per second the governor has to be capable of accurate operation.

Why Is This Railway Stuff in a Ferguson Collection?

I have always been interested in engineering, design, infrastructure, architecture and, above all, pioneering concepts such as Harry Ferguson's Draft Control System.

On the mezzanine in the Ferguson Shed I have my office area, bookshelves, telephone and an Espresso coffee machine that is only used once a day. There is no computer – that technology has never appealed to me, perhaps because I was too lazy to master it! Yes, it is very clever stuff and I know it appeals to many, but not to me.

I became aware of the famous British artist, Terence Cuneo (November 1907–January 1996) when I was thirteen, while on a visit to the Smithfield Show, and, as most youngsters did in those days, endeavoured to collect as many brochures as possible before being chased off a trade stand by an irate salesman. I managed to grasp, from the Massey Harris stand, a copy of their beautifully produced 35-page landscape format publication. The front cover has a reproduction of Terence Cuneo's painting of a MH744 ploughing, and on page 8 there is another of two MH726 Combines at work. I was reasonably proficient in art and maths (in that order) at school but otherwise quite disruptive. Terence Cuneo became a kind of a hero of mine as I tried to emulate his style of painting –

what a ridiculous challenge to set myself! Cuneo, by the way, was appointed as official artist for the Coronation of Elizabeth II in June 1953. The finished canvas ,which measures 11 ft x 8 ft (3.35 m x 2.44 m), was built up in his studio from dozens of detailed sketches he made, not only in Westminster Abbey but from sittings with the various dignitaries. It was at this point that the mouse became part of his signature.

Around me in my office area, as a gesture of homage to him and his work, I have five of his signed prints, a small reproduction of a British Railways poster, and an early reproduction print of him and his garden railway, plus two completed jigsaws: one of a 31p postage stamp featuring the Royal Scot locomotive and the other of a 22p postage stamp of the Southern Region Golden Arrow 34086. There are others to be found.

I also have a reproduction of a Terence Cuneo name plate as fitted to a Class 91 electric locomotive. There are two other reproduction locomotive name plates: the first is the Sir John Betjeman (whose writing appeals to me) plate, which was given to a Class 90 electric locomotive; and the second is the Sir Nigel Gresley plate. Gresley was the Chief Mechanical Engineer to the LNER (London and North Eastern Railway) and designed the

My 5-in gauge model of British Rail Class 7 Britannia 'Oliver Cromwell'. In the background is a reproduction locomotive name plate for Class 90 electric locomotive, 'Sir John Betjamin'.

streamlined A4 Pacifics, one of which, the Mallard, achieved the world record for steam traction of 126mph (203kph) on 3 July 1938, and that record still stands!

In 1959, the first 53 miles (85 km) of the M1 motorway were being built by Laing, its route cut through Nicholls Farm, Redbourn, Hertfordshire, where I was living at the time with my parents and sister; my father rented the house from the owner of the farm, and prior to us living there Nicholls Farm had been the base for the Ferguson dealership of L. F. Dave (Tractors) Ltd.

This massive motorway project was completed in 19 months! Laing commissioned the famous industrial writer L. C. T. Rolt to write the story of its construction, which runs to 65 pages. Terence Cuneo's painting of a section of the motorway under construction was produced on the front cover. The books were given to the sub-contractors who had worked on the project, as an appreciation by Laing for their efforts. The reproduction copy of this book that I have was kindly put together for me by Paul Rackham of Norfolk, who in his early years worked as a sub-contractor on the M1. The book combines the work of two of my heroes: Rolt and Cuneo. One other coincidence – when I lived in Totteridge Lane, Hertfordshire, Mr Laing lived three properties away.

The BBC broadcast a radio documentary telling the story of the men who planned and built the M1. It was produced by Charles Parker, with Ewan MacColl and Peggy Seeger making a recording in the field and later in the studio, enhancing the programme by using traditional folk tunes to weave the finished piece together. By coincidence, the manager of Nicholls Farm, Ian MacCloud, made a short contribution to the documentary.

Now for the descriptions of some of the railway models and the history of the originals that are on display in my office area. There is a 5 in (127 mm) gauge coal-fired model of BR (British Rail) Class 7 Britannia 'Oliver Cromwell' 70013. The actual locomotive is still in service, running on both main and preserved lines. At the Festival of Britain in 1951, 'William Shakespeare' 7004 was put on display from April to September. I remember seeing this on display when I visited the Festival of Britain as a 13-year-old with a school friend. This model was scratch-built by a retired naval engineer over a period of seven years: his wife then told him that it had to go! It is a very fine piece of miniature engineering; even the gauges in the cab are accurately reproduced to scale. I have a photograph

alongside it of a full-scale cab so that visitors can validate the details for themselves. So what was my motive for buying that? A moment of serendipity! I had an insurance policy maturing which coincided with this model being offered to me. The other influencing factor was that the BR Class 7s were the first of the Robert Riddles-designed Standard Classes, each suited to a particular duty but using as many interchangeable parts as possible, as well as incorporating facilities to simplify maintenance. I like the plain aesthetic of these locomotives, and to display the model here I asked Paul Dimmock, a model maker from Somerset, to produce a length of scale track to set it on, complete with a ground signal. I made the stand and had a Perspex cover made to keep fingers off.

The other models in the display cases on the mezzanine are:
- '0' gauge fine scale model of the A4 Class 'Sir Nigel Gresley'.
- '0' gauge GWR (Great Western Railways) Saddle Tank 0-6-0 .
- Two Class 100 DMU (diesel multiple units) built by Gloucester Railway Carriage and Wagon Company and each powered by 150hp horizontal AEC diesel engines.
- '0' gauge model of a 50-ton railway breakdown crane and matching trucks marked 'Crowland Sheldon' and scratch-built about fifteen years ago by a school friend, Roger Wilkes. It is a super model by an amateur – it really captures the massiveness of the real thing.
- '0' gauge model of a GWR diesel railcar No. 19, with streamline styling. This model is of a 1938 upgraded design. Same vintage as me! These GWR railcars appeal to me for several reasons. There is the nostalgia, having as a child travelled occasionally on one. I like the styling and, of course, they were a pioneering concept for branch line operation in their day. The railcars were powered by two six-cylinder AEC diesel engines mounted under the floor; maximum power output was 130bhp. The engines were mated to a five-speed Wilson preselector gearbox via a fluid flywheel. The units could achieve a top speed of 75 mph. On occasion, a trailer coach or a few goods wagons could be attached.
- '0' gauge three-car Southern Railway EMU and a similar LNER set; both tin plate models made in China.
- Just for fun, I had two '0' gauge kits made up: one a petrol tanker in grey and lettered 'Pool' (name of Second World War grade petrol), the name the farm

where I live; and the other is an open coal wagon operated by a firm of coal merchants by the name of Thorne.

• There is an '00' gauge example of the Blue Pullman rolling stock introduced by British Rail on 4 July 1960 – another pioneering concept in that they had a power car at each end of a six- or eight-car set. These units were designed for inter-city travel and, in my view, were the precursors to the InterCity trains introduced into service on 5 May 1975. Many of these sets are still running after being re-engined and refurbished, but they are now gradually being withdrawn. Sadly, British Rail scrapped all the Blue Pullmans; in my opinion a power car and a couple of trailers should have been preserved at the National Railway Museum in York. Sacrilege on the part of the powers that be!

• '0' gauge model of a British Rail 9F Class heavy freight locomotive 2-10-0 built to a Riddles design.

• '0' gauge model of a Class 47 Diesel locomotive – these were powered by a Sulzer engine. Adjacent to this is a full-size half main journal bearing shell as fitted to these engines.

• '0' gauge model I had made is a three-car set of London Transport's Underground 1938 stock. There are two reasons for having this model: first, the design was pioneering in that it was the first underground rolling stock to have all the electrical control gear set under the floor, thus giving extra saloon space for fare-paying passengers. The 1938

stock was designed by London Transport to meet their special requirements, and built by Metro-Cammell. The second reason is pure nostalgia – these trains operated on the Northern Line and out to my local station of East Finchley, and I like their shape.

• Finally, an '0' tin plate model by Corgi of LMS 4-6-2 Princess Elizabeth 6201.

Following the innovative theme I commissioned an '0' gauge four-car set of the London Transport Underground 1992 stock. This set's claim to fame is that they were the first underground trains to have solid state control gear (thyristors), again set under the floor. This model is displayed in a wall-hung illuminated Perspex tube adjacent to my desk, complete with a length of four-rail track. Hanging above this is a photograph of two one-sixth scale models showing the front and rear of a 1967 stock train in a Tube tunnel. The actual model is displayed at the National Railway Museum in York and I wouldn't mind nicking it!

Now for a bit about some of the other London Transport exhibits I have at Coldridge. My most regarded exhibit is a station sign 'Chalfont and Latimer Buckinghamshire' (an above-ground station on the Metropolitan Line). This sign has a bronze surround to hold the steel vitreous enamelled panels and measures 5 ft x 3 ft 6in. This roundel, and all London Transport lettering, was designed by

A sign for above-ground Metropolitan station, Chalfont and Latimer in Buckinghamshire.

A display case full of London Transport models.

modern Scandinavian and German architecture of the time: a plain but finely detailed style executed with high quality materials and craftsmanship.

I also have several scale models of London Transport buses, particularly the famous Routemasters, designed by London Transport to meet its specific needs, and they were ingenious! They were constructed with an all-aluminium monocoque body with detachable steel sub-frames, front and rear, for easy servicing, interchange ability and longevity. The engineer who oversaw this development was A. A. M. Durrant. The external styling was by an outside consultant, Douglas Scott, who had been involved with London Transport slightly earlier in the shaping of the single-decker RF (Regal Four) series of single-deck buses and coaches. An innovation introduced in the Routemaster design was the adoption of independent front-wheel suspension using coil springs, giving both a better ride and a better turning circle. The rear axle was solid but coil-spring mounted. To aid weight distribution, the fully automatic Wilson gearbox was mounted midships. The brakes were conventional drums but operated by external hydraulic cylinders powered by a pressure hydraulic system, thus eliminating the freezing problems sometimes experienced with air-braking systems.

There are numerous excellent books available for those wishing to gain more insight into the ethos of the London Passenger Transport Board across the whole field of London Transport operations.

Needless to say, as well as these models and so on, there are more artefacts in my office area! As well as books on related subjects that I won't elaborate on here, there is one little gem – a children's book by R. A. E. Linney entitled *Hollyhock Farm*, which was published in 1951 by Harry Ferguson Ltd. I was lucky enough to buy an original copy back in 2008. It tells the story of how nine-year-old twins, Peter and Pauline, visit their uncle's farm for two weeks. As the story unfolds, the Ferguson System takes centre stage. The twins are even allowed to drive one of the TE20s doing mowing! All the attributes of the Ferguson tractors are explained to the twins, helped by lovely hand-drawn illustrations. When I first read this book that is now long out of print, I felt it ought to be reproduced so that it would be available to a wider audience, and with that in mind I phoned Roger Smith, the owner and founder of Old Pond Publishing in Ipswich, Suffolk, suggesting he might like to take this idea on, which he did. That delightful little book is now available to budding Ferguson enthusiasts.

the famous typeface designer Edward Johnston to meet the requirements of Frank Pick, vice chairman of the London Passenger Transport Board (LPTB). Pick had a very strong sense of design allied to the need to create a substantial corporate identity for London Transport. To that end he employed Charles Holden as the main architect for what was known as the New Works Programme of Development just before the start of the Second World War. Holden, a Quaker, was trained in the Arts and Crafts style and his work for London Transport was modernist, perhaps somewhat influenced by examples of

Building the Tractor Shed

Late in the 1980s it dawned on me that it was all very well getting some of the tractors refurbished, covering the finished articles with dust sheets and then storing them in a dark but dryish ex-cattle shed, but what was needed was a proper display building so that visitors could view the tractors in a bright and clean environment. Well, being involved with the construction of steel-framed buildings for customers operating in both agriculture and industry I found, almost without exception, that they wanted a good quality job at an attractive price, which, of course, is right for a working building. I had hardly ever had a customer requesting his building to be a bit special, and who was happy to pay that bit extra for the wow factor apart from Yeovil Land Rover.

I have always been interested in design and architecture as well as making things, so here was my opportunity to build something a bit different – quirky, if you like! It did not take me long to come up with an idea and to sketch it out on the back of the proverbial envelope!

It would be set into the slope of the site; this I felt would help tie it into the landscape. It would have seven sides – heptagonal – some say a magic number. The angle between each side would be 360° ÷ 7 = 51.42857°. The orientation is such that most of the glazing would allow the arc of the sun's transit from east to west to be appreciated from within the building – that is, when it's not clouded over! I liked the idea of a design that is used on airport control buildings, where the tinted glazing is sloped inwards towards the base to reduce glare and heat gain. The building would rise vertically from the ground level by about 2 ft 6 in (762 mm). The main frame members would be 6 in x 4 in (150 mm x 100 mm) rectangular hollow section (RHS) turned through 20° outwards for about 6 ft 6 in (1.981 m); five of these faces would be glazed, with the other two boarded over. The main members would then turn through 90° to form the roof support. These seven frames converge towards a central ring beam to support a glazed finial about 5 ft (1.52 m) high. The infilling walls at the base would be of local stone and the roof insulated and slated.

One of the challenges I had set myself was not to have any fixing bolts used on the finished framework. To that end I fabricated the shot-blasted, zinc-sprayed RHS main frames on level concrete using full strength butt welds at the angle changes.

Once the basic steel frame was up, Robin Haughton did his bit with the rafters.

Craning the glazed finial into place. Note my Coles crane and Climax fork lift.

The top ring beam, where these seven main frames intersected, was again fabricated on level concrete with stub projections welded at each change of angle: these were made to be a snug fit on the inside of the main members. Both of these elements had a ½ in (12 mm) hole drill in them that aligned when assembled.

Prior to the first stage of erecting the steelwork we had set out and concreted in seven pairs of holding-down bolts that would connect with the base plates on each of the seven frames. The upper centre ring beam was set on a scaffold tower at the calculated height, so that as we craned each frame on to its holding bolts we could slot the top end into the corresponding projection on the ring beam and secure it temporarily with a long bolt. When all the frames were standing and bolted down we made a start of cutting to length the seven eaves beams, also made of RHS, with each end having a compound mitre – quite a fiddle! These were craned into place one by one and heavily tack welded. The same process was followed to place the other twenty-one purlins; these, by the way, are of diminishing-size sections of RHS going upwards towards the ring beam. This reduces the weight and looks more aesthetically pleasing.

Then I started all the position stick welding – it took ages, all carried out on an access tower. The final welding from the tower was to fill in the holes after the seven temporary bolts had been withdrawn. Then all the welds were painted with zinc-rich paint. Back to working on the floor, we positioned the RHS window sills and the steel work for the porch and doorway. The floor area was concreted, with a tamped finish. That was the end of phase one!

The recession of the early 1990s arrived and spare money became non-existent! I seem to remember having a couple of open days when we displayed a number of tractors in a circle within the skeleton of the building – needless to say this gave rise to a number of cheeky comments. Work on phase two started after the recession with the fixing of the timber rafters, which we stained red prior to fixing in place. My friend Robin Haughton, who had served his apprenticeship as a boat builder, did an excellent job of cutting the rafters to exact length, bearing in mind that these all had a compound mitre at one end: they extended beyond the eaves beam to give an oversail. My part in this was to do as I was told by Robin! Once the rafters were in place and red-stained board fitted at the oversail we could start laying and fixing the insulation board, with the textured surface showing between the rafters, and the felt and battens nailed for the slates on top of that.

I was hoping to use Delabole (Cornwall) slate for the roof but eight tons were needed and the cost became prohibitive so I had to compromise and use Spanish slate instead. The last thing I wanted was a lead roll capping at the intersection of each face of the roof: I felt that would detract from the beauty of having just slates. So it was for that reason that I chose to ask Geraint Vanstone and his son Graham, both fine craftsmen, who had the skill and experience to fit lead soakers at the changing point of the roof. This line needed to be dead straight, because any deviation would hit viewers approaching from the west right in the eye! Geraint and Graham did a spot-on job, but they did allow Robin and me to execute the more straightforward slate fixings. When the slating was finished, the glazed finial was craned into place and fixed down.

The stone wall infilling up to the sill height was set back from the framework by 1 in (25 mm). The infilling was carried out by a retired stonemason, the late Frank Conibere; he did a lovely job and it looks appropriate in its rural setting. The internal block cavity wall was built by Paul Bedford, who did a clean and tidy job. The cavity allowed us to install the first fix wiring for the ring main and lighting circuits, which were routed up inside the hollow steel sections. The next area to be dealt with was the

glazing. This was carried out by McKenzie Glass of Exeter using 0.24 in (6 mm) tinted and toughened glass. While this was going on, Robin and I fixed the heavy duty tongue-and-groove boarding on the diagonal to fill in the two unglazed sides: in one we incorporated a fire escape door, which has proved useful on hot days to create a bit of air flow. The next job was to make the main doors, which have concealed hinges, their metal frames being filled with the same heavy duty boarding to tie in with the other cladding, but these were stained red and finished off with a nice pair of home-made chromium plated door handles.

The floor screed had a power float finish. Then Robin, with my assistance, tackled the fitting of the 2 in (50 mm) thick pine window seats; the timber was milled nearby by the late Alfie Howard. Robin made a superb job of the mitres; two planks had to be glued together to obtain the required width. The last job was the second fix electrics. The fourteen spotlights are Italian-made units but the seven stainless steel uplighters at eaves level were of my design and inspired by some I had seen at the *Western Morning News* Building in Plymouth,

A recent photograph, taken just before the ash tree had to be taken down due to die-back.

designed by a hero of mine, Nicholas Grimshaw. These were beautifully made for me by Alco Engineering of Torrington, North Devon.

When the building was complete I had a plate made that names all those involved in the project and the build was signed off as complete on 18 May 1995, not exactly true, but that was my 57th birthday!

During the final stages of the work I had a consultation with an astrologer in Crediton, and during the session she said, several times 'I keep seeing a bleeding flying saucer!' Well, it does look a bit like that at night when the lights are on.

We have used the building for a few other purposes – after moving the tractors out and washing the floor! A midsummer yoga gathering, a funeral wake; and when the late Liz Abbott left my employment after being with the firm for many years we held a party in her honour. It was also used as the venue for the Ferguson's Club AGM held in April 2000.

Another interesting happening in the Tractor Shed was about fourteen years ago, when we had a serious leak on the water main. It was not clear where the exact spot was, so I called in Cyril Coles, a local water diviner of many years' experience, to find the leak, which he did. For a bit of fun I suggested that he try his enormous dowsing rods, at least 2 ft 6 in (782 mm) long, in the Tractor Shed. I knew beforehand what would happen as I had had a reaction with my small pair made of hydraulic brake pipe. When he visited, the pulling tractor on loan to the Coldridge Collection by Massey Ferguson was standing in the centre of the building. The reaction Cyril got was violent, both his heavy rods smashed against the stainless steel exhaust pipe of the tractor. His comment was 'Bloody hell – I've never had such a strong reaction in all my 37 years of divining! I'll try it again.' With the second try, the same thing happened. A lot of visitors to the Collection over the years have made positive comments which have been much appreciated. A couple stick in my mind. Twice I have had people mention that they felt that the building had a healing quality about it. Another said to me as he was leaving 'This must be a shrine to Harry Ferguson,' and my reply after a slight delay was, 'Well, I suppose that it is.'

This photo was taken several years ago, so you can see some of the tractors that have since been moved on.

The Building Conversion for the Ferguson Shed

Following the completion of the heptagonal Tractor Shed in 1995, it was not long before it became obvious that more display accommodation was needed. By about 1998 I'd saved up enough money to start work on it, and had realised that I could use, by clearing out the tractors and 'junk', an adjacent 60 ft x 30 ft (18 m x 9 m) general storage lean-to building with sliding doors along the long side that I'd erected in 1979. It was my vision to bring this basic agricultural building to a form that would relate to the Tractor Shed; and I also wanted to give it a bit of a 'high tech' look, which I felt would contrast nicely with the older tractors displayed in it – a bit of a visual dynamic if you like!

My friend Robin Haughton and I set about the steelwork side of this project. To start with, the sliding doors were taken out and the four main rakers were extended by about 5 ft (1.5 m) so that we had an oversail on the outside and a full-length run of tinted glazing leaning outwards by 20°, with the sills set on a stone plinth wall 2 ft (610 mm) high, thus tying in with the arrangement on the Tractor Shed. As part of the idea to give it a 'high tech' look we cut lots of 5 in (127 mm) diameter holes in the rakers and stanchions, burning out one electric drill motor in the process. On the inside, Geraint Vanstone and his son Graham built the internal walls with lightweight blocks, thus creating a cavity within which nine built-in and illuminated display cases were constructed, as well as one larger one dedicated to books. Part of the ground floor facilities were separate ladies' and gents' lavatories. In each of these I have installed a smallish engraved plate reading 'Please close WC cover after use. By order of Harry Ferguson', and it is usually respected!

The low internal wall below the glazing is capped off by a 15 in (381 mm) wide timber sill that can be used as a seat where space allows.

We decided to include a mezzanine, which hovers over about a quarter of the floor area, and is reached by an offset staircase with open aluminium chequered-plate treads and stainless steel handrails that are continued along the open edge.

This area provided me with an office space, where the bills are paid and the writing done! Also, to enhance the 'high tech' look we made the lighting fixtures on site. They are basically two runs of suspended, helically formed oval ventilating ducting, with home-made uplighters on the top surface and a mix of downlighters and spots on the underside. Outside lighting was provided by eight low-voltage downlighters on the undersides of the sills. A medium-blue paint finish was used on all the internal steel fittings to enhance the Ferguson connection –

Geraint Vanstone cleaning off the stonework while his son Graham appears to be checking the level of the steel sill member.

A view of the Ferguson Shed and entrance. The plough is a 1937 version.

i.e. the same shade of blue that is used on the bonnet badge. The main structural steelwork doors and glazing bars are finished in Massey Ferguson Brown.

In mid-1999 I was asked by the Ferguson Club General Committee to host the AGM in April 2000, which I agreed to do, so work on this project was forced along a bit; but we managed to get it finished, and with the tractors and display cases sorted out, about 24 hours before the deadline. I must own up to one mistake, though, which I like to put down to pressure! The handrails for the staircase should have been dropped by the height of one tread but I forgot, so they are rather high: sorry, folks.

We moved most of the tractors out of the heptagonal shed for the AGM and arranged seating for about a hundred people. I invited Jamie Sheldon along in his role as President of the Club. One of the speakers was Peter Warr, from the Isle of Wight, who had worked for Harry Ferguson at Abbotswood. He was slightly nervous initially in presenting his talk but after a few minutes he got into his stride by telling lots of stories relating to his time working for Mr Ferguson. If only I had thought to bring along my tape recorder – what marvellous personal recollections would have been stored. After the meeting ended we all moved across to the Ferguson Shed for its formal opening by Jamie, then it was lunch and refreshment time! Sadly, I did not have the visitor's book ready in time but that was remedied a fortnight later, and at the same time I had a plaque made to mark this event which also includes the names of those who worked on the project. Thank you all.

Inside the Ferguson Shed, looking towards the entrance. Note the holes on the steel work.

Extending the Ferguson Shed

As time went on I gave further thought to extending the display area for tractors, implements and models. The obvious building for this development was the adjoining 60 ft x 50 ft (18.3 m x 15.24 m) storage building, which can now be accessed by visitors from the mezzanine in the Ferguson Shed.

It may be worth relating that when I bought Lower Park Farm in 1977 part of this building was already there, in the form of an Atcost 45 ft x 30 ft (13.7 m x 9.14 m) shed, with an adjoining 45 ft x 20 ft (13.7 m x 6.09 m) lean-to on one side; the frames of these were pre-cast concrete sections. About a year later I decided to extend this building by adding 15 ft (4.57 m) to its overall length and providing a 30 ft (9.14 m) lean-to on the other side. Needless to say, this was made from steel sections. The side cladding was 5 ft (1.5 m) high concrete block walls with space boarding above and was used for over-wintering cattle, arranged with a straw bedded area in each lean-to and a central feed area. This was used by John Down, the farmer who rents the farmland at Lower Park. For several years cattle were kept in this building over the winter months, then a change in John's farming practice meant that this facility was no longer required. So, not surprisingly, it soon became a tractor and implement store!

By 2007 I decided that the space could be converted, so a start was made by moving all the stored 'junk' into another building. With the space clear, we could evaluate the possibilities it offered to make a clean and comfortable display area. The most obvious first requirement was to screed over the existing concrete floor with a power float finish. This was done so there was just a shallow step down to the mezzanine in the Ferguson Shed through an opening about 5 ft (1.5 m) wide that we made. The next stage was to board over, with marine plywood, the inside of the space boarding. This was followed by employing a specialist firm to spray a foam insulation material to the underside of the roof sheets, the plywood surfaces and the internal face of the concrete block walls. I was so impressed by the two chaps who did this filthy work (epoxy-resin based) that I gave them a well-deserved gratuity. The thinking behind installing this insulation was to seal the building against water leaks and draughts. This worked for a while, but over time a few small leaks have become apparent.

Robin and I did some careful measuring of heights available, thinking that it would be sensible, if possible, to install a mezzanine floor in the central part of this building and still have enough height to operate a small forklift. This was just possible by setting the mezzanine floor back by about 10 ft (3.05 m) where the height is most restricted. At this end we have installed an electrically operated

The Atcost barn when I bought Lower Park in 1977.

roller shutter door to enable machines to access the building. Before this floor space was installed I had a cavity wall of light-weight blocks built from floor level to the underside of the roof. As in the Ferguson Shed, numerous illuminated display cases were set in.

The next stage was for Robin and I to install the steel work I'd made up that connected with the concrete stanchions to support the floor deck and the weight of the exhibits that would be placed on it. Rather than finish the edge of this floor in line with the stanchions, I thought it would look more pleasing to extend the leading edge by about 2 ft (610 mm), and to have the ceiling below tapering upwards so that the edge steel was just 6 in (152 mm) high: this in turn would support the balustrade and give a lighter feel to the deck.

The design of the balustrade and the staircase followed closely what was used in the Ferguson Shed eight years earlier, but this time we got the relationship between the stair rails and the aluminium treads right! The fact that this upper floor area is not along the full length of the building allows us to bring machinery through the roller shutter door and placed on the ground floor prior to being lifted to the mezzanine.

Once the timber floor joists and the chipboard floor were nailed down, a start was made on the staircase and then the surrounding three sides of balustrade. A 5 ft (1.5 m) wide section adjacent to the roller shutter door is designed to be removable, to give better access when moving exhibits in and out. I should mention that several years prior to this work I had been given, by a German friend, Norman Tietz, a stainless steel laser-cut profile of a TE20 and plough (the Ferguson trade mark). I decided to have another made to the same dimensions by Lowman Engineering of Tiverton and to use the

two to make a double-sided illuminated sign with three blue fluorescent light tubes installed: I like to think that it forms a bit of a focal point. After some deliberation I eventually decided it was essential to install a central crane track to facilitate the moving of display items safely. This we did, and equipped the track with an electrically powered hoist and trolley. I don't use this facility often but, like the electric roller shutter door, it always gives me a little thrill to use it – I'm glad I went that bit further!

With all the structural work completed, the next job was to call in an outside firm to install a suspended tile ceiling to follow the line of the sloping roof. They achieved a first-class finish with a perfect alignment of the lightweight metal framework. The final part of the fitting out was mostly down to me – for example, the laying of the interlocking plastic floor tiles; a lot of work and just before I had both hips replaced at different times later in the year 2008.

Just two more small features worth mentioning:
• By careful juggling we managed to 'conceal' two longish walk-in cupboards within the layout. They are now pretty jammed full with odds and ends – the flip side of Mike Thorne, I suspect!
• We installed a VHS/DVD player and a 45-inch screen so that visitors could view machinery-related films.

In the previous year, 2007, I had been asked by the Ferguson Club to host the 2008 AGM; I was helped enormously by my friend, John Upfold, who dealt with all the forward planning and administration. Jamie Sheldon was again invited along to do his bit as President of the Club. The overall result brought many positive remarks from those attending, which are recorded in the Visitor's Book. Please feel free to contact me if you fancy a visit.

Ed Herridge's panoramic view, taken with his back to the roller-shutter door.

Biographies

I felt that readers might like to know a bit about some of the people I have been privileged to meet, who either worked with Harry Ferguson or for Massey Ferguson. They have been happy to share some of their experiences with me over the years. I have not set this section out in any chronological order, some pieces are lengthy, while others are much less so.

Alan Starley

I first made contact with Alan and his wife, Elizabeth, in 2003, at the time of writing *Massey Ferguson 35 & 65 In Detail*. Although he left Massey Ferguson in 1975 he was always most helpful, passing on intelligent and knowledgeable gems of information which he referred to as 'grist for my mill'. Alan was kind enough to give me, over a period of time, numerous items of Ferguson and Massey Ferguson archive material from his own collection.

Alan is now sadly deceased, but Elizabeth has helped me with this section and recently gave me several documents and photographs relating to Alan and his background, some of which is outlined here. The Starley Family Tree begins with Walter Starley of Cockfield Sussex (b.1615, d.1662). The next Starley of note is James (b.1830, d.1881) who became the managing foreman of the Coventry Sewing Machine Company and was responsible for several design innovations incorporated into their machines. Later, James became interested in designing bicycles and in 1870 was granted a patent for his safety bicycle, a precursor of what we have today. By 1877 James Starley had patented his design for the bevel gear differential – this mechanism is ubiquitous worldwide to the present day. What a gift for mankind!

Alan was born at Albourne, Sussex, in August 1929. His father was a market gardener. According to the family tree there appears to be several generations of Starleys in that part of Sussex. Alan's secondary education was at Hove Grammar School, followed by a year at Plympton Agricultural College. On leaving Plympton in 1946 he worked for three years for a well respected vegetable grower at Milford in Surrey: then six months back home working for his father. Between 1951 and 1953 he worked for the NIAE at Silsoe, Bedfordshire in their Implement Testing Department. He then moved to the Engineering Department of Harry Ferguson Ltd until 1960, when he was transferred to the product planning department and by 1966 was appointed to the position of Product Specialist. Following his redundancy from Massey Ferguson in 1971 Alan took a job with the Department of Employment!! (the exclamation marks are Elizabeth's) and then decided to do a one-year teaching course. Once qualified, he taught for a year but that work did not suit Alan's strong engineering background, so in 1973 he returned to Massey Ferguson, this time working in their Engineering Design offices, ensuring that the Massey Ferguson designs did not violate other manufacturers' patents – a pretty demanding role. He left Massey Ferguson for the second time in 1975 and took up employment with BT as a draughtsman, mainly concerned with 'local line' records: that is recording in diagrammatical form the position and specification of the copper wires along the route from the exchange to the customer. In Alan's last year with BT he prepared and enhanced a massive amount of filed archive material, compiling an index of it so that it could be transferred to a computer system BT were introducing. He finally retired in 1989.

Both Alan and Elizabeth had a strong artistic bent for model making and belonged to the Guild of Model Wheelwrights (1990–2005). A fine example of their work was on display at the Coventry Transport Museum: I guess that it is about 1/6th scale, of a horse and gig with two figures in it. Elizabeth made the model horse and people while the gig was Alan's handiwork. Sadly, this display seems at present to be relegated to a store room! As mentioned earlier in this book, there are five exquisitely presented model farm trailers at Coldridge made by Alan.

Keith Base

I first met the late Keith when he came with his wife, Julia, to one of our early open days at Coldridge. They came with their friends, the late Ron and Joan Stanbook.

Keith had been a Spitfire pilot in the Second World War and was shot down near the Sussex coast by a German aircraft. He was just able to crash-land the Spitfire, whereupon it burst into flames. He was lucky to be pulled alive from the burning wreckage by two farm workers and another man, but he suffered severe burns, especially to the right side of his face, and he lost the sight in his right eye. After his rescue he was transferred to East Grinstead Hospital, where New Zealand surgeon, the now famous Archibald McIndoe, was pioneering skin grafting and plastic surgery. McIndoe also knew that it was of paramount importance to maintain positive morale in his patients. To that end he tried to ensure that there were plenty of attractive female nurses to look after these heroes, and did his best to foster relationships between nurses and patients. This happened for Keith, as he fell in love with one of his nurses, Julia. Eventually, as their relationship developed, Julia invited Keith to her home for tea and to meet her parents. Julia's father apparently said, 'I've met this man before, I recognise his voice' – he was one of the three men who had helped to rescue Keith!

On leaving East Grinstead, Keith worked on the farm of Harper Adams College at Newport in Shropshire for a time, prior to enrolling on a formal training course there. That completed, he obtained work with Harry Ferguson Ltd at their Stoneleigh Abbey Training School near Coventry in Warwickshire. After a brief spell of training (indoctrination?) in all things Ferguson he went on to become an instructor and was later promoted to a more senior position. During his time with Harry Ferguson he was posted to New Zealand, where he was responsible for setting up a training school, based with Norwoods, the main Ferguson agency in the country. It was while he was there, in that role, that Sir Edmund Hillary, of Everest fame, and his small team were preparing their Ferguson TE.A20s for their trip to the South Pole. One of the many modifications that were made to the tractors, to equip them for this tough environment, was the fitment of skis in place of the front wheels, and half tracks to the rear wheels. However, this arrangement did not work at all well in deep snow. Keith told me several years ago that he, Hillary and his team were gathered in Norwoods' tractor yard one day, scratching their heads and trying to think of a way to overcome the problem. Hillary said 'Why not put the effing tracks around the front wheels as well and weld the steering up in the straight-ahead position?' Keith said everyone had looked amazed and a bit sheepish – why hadn't they thought of that! Then some bright spark in Keith's team asked, 'Well, how are you going to steer it then?' 'I'm going straight to the South Pole so I won't need to steer the effing thing!' So that was the system chosen to be used on all three tractors on the South Pole expedition.

Keith eventually returned to England, and moved to Exeter to work for a grain handling plant supplier. In retirement he was very keen on classical music, did a lot of scholarly reading, and often gave tours of Exeter Cathedral to visitors.

He was a great support to me in developing the Coldridge Collection, with his enthusiasm and wide-ranging knowledge; not to mention his command of Ferguson technical data, and he gave me many workshop manuals and instruction books. He passed on two precious items to me. The first was a Ferguson spanner, and he told me the story of how he came by this. Apparently, Harry Ferguson came into the training workshop on one occasion and caught Keith using an adjustable spanner; Harry grabbed it out of Keith's hand and threw it across the workshop. He then took a Ferguson spanner out of his pocket, telling Keith that was what he should be using! Keith gave me this spanner in 1996 and it is now proudly displayed in my Ferguson Shed with its own case and descriptive plate.

The second item relates to a Ferguson wind-up Demonstration Model I was able to buy from the Llewellin family of Haverfordwest – at one time a Ferguson dealership. The Demonstration Model had its original carry case but sadly it was missing its instruction book. Keith noticed this and on his next visit to Coldridge he gave me a copy and said, 'Michael, I think you should have this to go with the model. I got it from Stoneleigh.' What a kind deed, and it is something else I treasure. On the inside of the front cover Keith had written his name and the words NOT TO BE REMOVED FROM FIELD OFFICE but it has ended up in Coldridge. When I give visitors a demonstration of this model I always make a point of showing them the instruction book and what is written inside the cover.

Keith always used to sign off his letters to me with a little sketch of the Ferguson tractor and plough logo. A lovely man – cheers to Keith.

Peter Warr

Early in Peter's working life, in the 1950s, he was employed by Harry Ferguson at the Abbotswood Estate at Stow-on-the-Wold, Glos. His duties there were wide-ranging, attending to estate matters as well as being involved with Harry Ferguson in demonstrations of their early 4WD vehicles. Following Harry's death in October 1960, Peter stayed on at Abbotswood working for Maureen, Harry's wife, until her death some five years later. Following that, Harry's son-in-law, Tony Sheldon, took over the chairmanship of Harry Ferguson Research, to continue with the development and application of the Ferguson Formula 4WD system for road vehicles, in which Peter was heavily involved. Later, Peter and his wife Ann moved on to work for Harry Ferguson's grandson, Jamie Sheldon, at Kings Manor Farm, Freshwater, on the Isle of Wight. Even in retirement he has been very active with Jamie in establishing the Ferguson Family Museum at Kings Manor.

I first met Peter when he came to Coldridge for the Ferguson Club's AGM in April 2000. He was to be one of our speakers, giving the audience of about a hundred people a most interesting talk about his life working for Harry Ferguson and the Sheldons. For the first couple of minutes Peter seemed rather shy about addressing so many people, but he soon found his voice and went on beyond his allotted time to everyone's joy. If only I had taken along my tape recorder I would have bagged beautiful reminiscences – I still kick myself for that failing.

I had cause to make contact with Peter many times while I was writing my first book for Herridge and Sons, TE20 In Detail; he was always most helpful, being able to supply me with 'missing bits of the jigsaw'. I have continued contact with Peter over the years and visited him on the Isle of Wight to view the Ferguson Family Museum several times. On one occasion my visit was to deliver a TEF20 Ferguson tractor that Jamie had bought from the mainland.

More recently, Peter was most helpful when I was digging around for details about the various 4WD vehicles Harry Ferguson Research and Ferguson Formula Developments had been involved with, and I am glad to say that this is still ongoing.

Thank you Peter for your enthusiasm and help over the years.

Michael Winter

I first met Michael at one of our open days in July 1995, and our 'loose' friendship lasted for several years, until his death. We occasionally met up in those intervening years for an evening meal at the pub in Sheepwash – about halfway between his home in Bude and mine, at that time, at Coldridge.

Michael, noticing an advertisement in a January 1947 copy of the London Times placed by Harry Ferguson Ltd for a Personal Assistant and Private Secretary, applied for the job. He was surprised to get through the screening process as there had been just over a thousand applicants. On 18 March of that year he was at the Harry Ferguson headquarters in Coventry for the interview, which lasted five minutes. Harry Ferguson questioned him about his ability to speak fluent French, his shorthand and typing and his personal hygiene!

On leaving this brief interview he was told to report to Freddie Nelms, Harry Ferguson's Personnel Manager to negotiate his salary. Michael told me he suspected Nelms had quite a bit of influence on his appointment. Nelms had a son who had served on the lower deck in the Royal Navy in the conflict known as the Eastern Mediterranean War, 1941–43, and Michael had also served in the Royal Navy.

Michael eventually resigned from Harry Ferguson Ltd in 1962.

Michael was aware that Harry Ferguson Research was working on 4WD car projects but he did not share Harry Ferguson's confidence in the project. Michael stated in his autobiography, 'I should have bitten my tongue but there is a limit to what flesh and blood can stand!' He went on to spend 20 years with the Pilkington Glass Group and eventually retired as Sales and Marketing Director of the Safety Glass Division. He was told at his shortlist interview with Pilkington, 'If you are good enough for Harry Ferguson, you are good enough for us!'

Readers would find his book, *Harry Ferguson and I*, compulsive reading.

Erik Fredrikson

The late Erik was born in Norway in 1928. Soon afterwards the family moved to Belgium, but returned to Norway at the end of the Second World War. His first encounter with a Ferguson was in 1947, when he drove a Ferguson Brown on steel wheels; this was followed by driving a brand new TE20. After completing a degree course in Agronomy, he came to England on a student exchange scheme for 12 months, working on farms in Lincolnshire, Kent and Shropshire. Next was a year back in Norway driving mainly Fordson E27Ns. Tiring of that, he returned to England and took a job with Jack Bean (Beans Industries and Midland Industries – MIL) on his farm near Stourbridge, driving, of course, TE20s and demonstrating them equipped with MIL loaders; as a result of the demonstration tours he met many Massey Ferguson dealers, in both the UK and Europe. He had an ambition to join Massey Harris Ferguson Ltd, and Jack Bean kindly arranged for him to have an interview at Stoneleigh Training School. This proved successful and he joined the firm in 1956, three years after the merger.

I first met Erik when a small group of Massey Ferguson employees visited the Coldridge Collection in the mid-1990s. I contacted him again in 1998 to ask what he knew about the LTX as I was about to begin my research into the LTX prior to having some $^1/_{18}$ scale models made. He happened to still be working for Massey Ferguson, albeit part-time, completing a history of the firm to be placed on their website. So he was there digging around in the Massey Ferguson archives.

Erik was very keen to help me with this project, and having worked for Massey Ferguson for about 37 years he knew a lot of the right people for me to meet. The original plan of approach was that I would stay with Erik and his wife Mary at their house near Leamington Spa for two or three nights. Unfortunately, Mary was ill at the time of my visit so Erik arranged for me to stay at a B&B nearby run by a retired farmer, John, and his Dutch wife, Rodi. When I arrived, I explained to John my reason for visiting – to meet men in this area who had worked with the LXT. 'Oh yes,' he said, 'we had one here on my farm for a while on loan, it was a super tractor. It even had diff lock operated by a long lever on the right-hand side', his arm moving in a gesture of engaging diff lock; what a coincidence to stay at a B&B whose owner had used just the tractor I had come to research!

The next day, Erik and I set out early on a whistle-stop tour he had planned with true Ferguson precision, ending at 10 o'clock at night! During those two hectic days I had the privilege of meeting several people who had worked with Harry Ferguson on the LTX project, including Irishman Alex Patterson, who had worked for many years as a senior engineer for Harry Ferguson. Some of the Field Test Team, all of whom had worked for Harry Ferguson, comprised Nigel Liney, Colin Stevenson, Jack Bibby, Dick Dowdeswell and Nibby Newbold – the latter had been a mechanic on this venture. I also met up with farmer Derrick Hiatt from Ufton. Derrick had been lucky enough to have been chosen to run an LTX for testing on his heavy clay land for a good many years, but it was eventually taken back by Massey Ferguson and cut up for scrap. Sacrilege!!

It was the LTX model project that brought me to meet these men who had worked alongside Harry Ferguson. They all, in their individual ways, had positive recollections of working for Harry Ferguson, despite his foibles

Dick Dowdeswell

I first met Dick and his wife Beryl in 1996, when The Ferguson Club held its AGM at Larne in Northern Ireland. It was while on the coach trip from Larne to the Ferguson linen mill on the afternoon following the AGM that I got into conversation with Dick. I tentatively asked him about his experiences of being a driver for Harry Ferguson in the days when the LTX prototypes were under field test. Dick was highly enthusiastic about their terrific pulling power, so much so that the lugs on the Dunlop rear tyres were torn off the casings. Dunlop had to develop a more substantial rear tyre. More conversations followed over that weekend but I had to be careful not to monopolise Dick, and by using my discretion I like to think that I handled it appropriately. We continued our dialogue later by telephone. It was wonderful to hear his stories as a field test driver and later as a demonstrator for Harry Ferguson and then for Massey Ferguson. According to one of his colleagues in the Field

Test Team he was known as the 'wrecker', always pushing a machine to its limits – and sometimes beyond. The stories he told me of life would fill a book – I wish I had recorded it all. Dick was a lovely man but sadly died in 2000. A few months after his death Beryl asked me if I would like to have his Red Coat – this was the 'uniform' of Massey Ferguson employees when moving tractors and machinery at the stands of the major agricultural shows. This coat is now on display within the Coldridge Collection.

Thank you for that gift, Beryl.

Dick Dowdeswell's red Massey Ferguson blazer, now on display at the Coldridge Collection.

Ray Fardon

I have told Ray's story in Coldridge Collection No. 92: BMC Mini Tractor Prototype.

Following my encounter with Ray, my partner Alison and I always made a point of calling on him and his wife Carole when we were in the Cotswolds. We were always made most welcome with cups of tea and cakes. This gave us the opportunity to view Ray's extensive and prolific vegetable garden as well as hearing stories about his time working for Harry Ferguson, who he described as his friend.

David Walker

David, to be pedantic, falls outside the exact remit that I set out at the start of these brief biographical sketches of people, but because of the help that he provided in connection with the writing of my previous book, Massey Ferguson 100 Series In Detail, I felt it appropriate to ask him to write a short piece in his own words about working for Massey Ferguson.

Coming to Massey-Ferguson, in 1966, from the machine tool industry was a big change of scene, for someone with absolutely no agricultural background. I started as a Technical Author, and writing the instruction Books and Workshop Manuals made for a rapid learning curve, but one that I will be forever grateful. The key to enjoying not only this initial task, but in later times, as a Service Engineer, UK Regional Service Manager and European Service Manager, was more than anything being part of a great team effort, which had been part of the credo originated within the company from long before my time. Harry Ferguson had, on many occasions, stated, 'Ferguson people are family' and it was always true that you could call for help and advice on a huge number of the workforce, whether they were engineers, factory manufacturing staff, quality control, training, or parts departments. This, maybe, was not unique, but was unusual in a company of that size. One fascinating aspect of joining Massey Ferguson at that time, was that even twenty years after tractor production had started at Banner Lane, there were still many of the original Ferguson team there, and their vast fund of experience was vital to new recruits such as myself. That the legacy of that vast organisation is being kept alive is also vital, making the Coldridge Collection the showpiece that it is.

Thank you for that, David. Readers wishing to learn more about David's time with Massey Ferguson, his book *Inside Massey Ferguson: A Story of Service* is an honest and accurate account of working with a huge organisation.

Jeremy Burgess

Jeremy never worked for Harry Ferguson, but joined Massey Ferguson in 1990 as a design engineer after completing an apprenticeship with David Brown, followed by an engineering degree at Silsoe in Bedfordshire. Jeremy rose through the ranks of Massey Ferguson, with roles in design, test, manufacturing and technical service before crossing over to sales, then marketing and eventually becoming a Licensee Director with responsibility for significant business carried out with various Massey Ferguson licensees around the world.

Throughout his time with the company, Jeremy maintained a keen interest in its heritage and history, and a strong appreciation of the achievements of Harry Ferguson. Sadly, the closure of the Massey Ferguson Banner Lane plant in Coventry was announced in June 2002, with the last-ever tractor rolling off the production line on Christmas Eve of that year. The company's offices remained at Banner Lane until the new facility at Abbey Park, Stoneleigh, Warks, was completed and the final move to vacate the Banner Lane site was made in September 2006.

Earlier in 2006, the future of the famous Banner lane heritage tractor collection was discussed, and Jeremy offered to work out a plan that would allow multiple things to be achieved. First, the new technology centre at the factory in Beauvais in France was conceived to celebrate milestones of technology and achievement from the first Ferguson Model A up to current production. Clearly, some of the machines at Banner Lane represented these milestones and should be retained as part of that rich heritage. Second, the connection with the city of Coventry should be maintained, and certain machines, in particular the last tractor ever built there, should remain in the city. And third, the company wanted to forge a link with a leading Ferguson collection and museum that could house and display any remaining machines.

It was in mid-July 2006 that Jeremy first contacted me with a request: 'Would I be happy to have six of the Banner Lane tractor collection machines on display at Coldridge?' My answer, of course, was yes!

So it was that on 24 August 2006, Paul Lay (Public Relations and Communication) and Jeremy Burgess (Licensee Director) issued a Massey Ferguson News Release stating which of their tractors from the collection would be displayed at their three chosen sites.

The lists are as follows:

Beauvais, France
- Ferguson Model A No. 1
- Ford Ferguson 9NAN
- Ferguson TE20 No 1
- Ferguson TE.A20 'Sue' from the South Pole Expedition
- Ferguson FE35 No. 1
- Massey Ferguson 590 4WD

Coventry Transport Museum
- Ferguson TE.F20 No. 500,000
- Massey Ferguson 65 MKI
- Massey Ferguson 4345, last-ever tractor built at Banner Lane

Coldridge Collection
- Ferguson TE.F20 'Standards' tractor No. 487570
- Massey Harris Pony 820
- Massey Ferguson 35X with Multi-Power and PAVT rear wheels No. SNMYW355101
- Massey Ferguson 135 with Quick Detachable cab No. 473009
- The Nipper, based on a Massey Ferguson 265, former European champion pulling tractor
- The last hand-built prototype tractor produced at Banner Lane, badged as an MF 4270 but actually a 4370
- Also included was a MH No. 3 Binder and a MH Corn Drill

Jeremy Burgess helped organise for the front doors to the main 'C' Block Ferguson Centre to be saved. They are now on display at Coldridge.

A press conference was arranged at Banner Lane to announce these moves and I attended. It was at this event that I asked Jeremy what was likely to happen to the famous front doors to the main 'C' Block Ferguson Centre. He said, 'I don't know, leave it with me', and after some negotiation with the new owners and the demolition contractors the doors were saved, transported to Devon and are now proudly displayed with the Coldridge Collection.

Following on from this arrangement, Jeremy

and I have forged a good friendship and I must say that he has been a guiding light with two of my books, *Massey Ferguson 35/65 In Detail* and *Massey Ferguson 100 Series In Detail*.

Along with the doors mentioned above, he was instrumental in my acquiring a number of other items and documents from Banner Lane, including a couple of impulse clocks and some brass door plaques from within the building – how I would have liked to acquire a bit of the beautiful linen fold oak panelling, but I made do with 15 bricks!

Bob Dickman

Bob first worked for Harry Ferguson Ltd and continued on into the Massey Ferguson era. He started his career as a trainee instructor at Stoneleigh and then progressed to become fully qualified in that role. In the early days, he was involved with students learning about the working of the TE20s, and their implements. After a short time he was moved to evaluate a training scheme enabling instructors to teach students about the workings of the FE35 tractors that were introduced to the UK market in October 1956. Particular reference was given to the CAV DPA (distributor type fuel injection pump). Attention was also focused on the two-lever hydraulic control system. Yet another area for special consideration was the function of the two-stage clutch fitted to the de luxe models: another Massey Ferguson first. Included in the study was a schedule for the six-speed gearbox, which had sliding spur gears as opposed to constant mesh helical cut gears as used on the TE20s.

After four and a half years in the role of senior trainer instructor, Bob was moved to the Export Servicing Department at Fletchamstead Highway, Coventry, then under the control of Charles Voss. In 1960, following another spell of successful training, he was given his first export assignment working alongside Jaap Vogelsang, and they both attended the Leipzig Fair in February 1965 with the introduction of the MF100 series of tractors.

Bob remained with the Export Service Department in a more senior role developing Distributor and Dealer After Sales Service Standards, which included premises, workshop layout, special service tools, signage etc. Bob told me 'A great deal of resources and effort were given to markets apart from pure product and technical support.' He added as a caveat, 'At this time I first encountered company

politics and the need to know the right people at the top end of the hierarchy in order to progress one's career.'

Bob also outlined for me a major Massey Ferguson initiative introduced in 1980, first in Mozambique and over the years spreading to other countries, including Somalia, Ethiopia, Tunisia, Sri Lanka and Bangladesh. This initiative was named 'Refurbishment of Original Components', or ROC, which was a registered Massey Ferguson trademark, chosen because it was like the roc, the legendary bird in Sinbad the Sailor, which was strong and lived to a great age. The programme came about through the realisation that there were thousands of MF100 series tractors in 'graveyards' in developing countries.

There is more of Bob's working life with Massey Ferguson in my book Massey Ferguson 100 Series In Detail. I remember him telling me that towards the end of his 43-year-long career with Massey Ferguson, he headed a team of 12 full-time Export Service Managers, as well as about 40 contracting part-time training instructors covering the Far East, Middle East, Africa and Europe, but he was in charge of the service side in Japan. I asked why this was necessary and his reply was, 'Because the Japanese are so pedantic about the quality of a product (no oil leaks and a first-class paint finish) and they have great respect for experienced, mature people with grey hair!'

It was mooted by the General Service Manager of Beauvais, Pascale Hedouin, and the President of Beauvais, Richard Markwell, that Bob, at the age of 84, would go to Japan for the launch of the 7000 Series MF tractors, thus personalising the link between the Ferguson TE20 era and the present day; sadly, though, this idea did not come to fruition.

Thank you for all your help, Bob.